PELICAN BOOKS

THE CHICANOS

Born in 1920, Ed Ludwig grew up in California. After graduation from the College of the Pacific in Stockton, he taught high-school English and journalism. During the war, he participated in the invasion of the Philippines. His postwar career has included work as a professional pianist, writer of science fiction and detective stories, and bookstore manager. He is married and has two daughters.

James Santibañez was born in Colorado in 1931, of parents who had worked their way north from Mexico. When he was still a child his family moved to California. During the Korean War, he was in the Navy's Construction Battalion. Mr. Santibañez is now a Master Tutor at San Jose State College. In addition to tutoring and completing work for a degree in the social sciences, he is active in various Chicano organizations.

THE CHICANOS

MEXICAN AMERICAN VOICES

Edited by Ed Ludwig and James Santibañez

PENGUIN BOOKS INC
Baltimore · Maryland

Penguin Books Inc, 7110 Ambassador Road,
Baltimore, Maryland 21207

First published 1971
Reprinted 1972

Made and printed in the United States of America by
Kingsport Press, Inc, Kingsport, Tennessee
Set in Monotype Bruce Oldstyle

Library of Congress Catalog Card Number 74–29454

ACKNOWLEDGEMENTS

TALE OF LA RAZA, THE ORGANIZER'S TALE, THE NUN'S TALE and EL
TEATRO CAMPESINO, ITS BEGINNINGS by Luis Valdez, reprinted from
Ramparts, July 1966, copyright 1966. THE PLUM PLUM PICKERS by
Raymond Barrio, copyright 1969, by Ventura Press, Box 2268,
Sunnyvale, California 94087. SATURDAY BELONGS TO THE PALOMIA
by Daniel Garza, copyright 1962 by *Harper's Magazine, Inc.*
Reprinted from the July 1962 issue of *Harper's Magazine* by per-
mission of the author. STRIPPER WHIRLWIND: THE PIZCADORES AND
THE MACHINES by Daniel Garza, copyright 1966 by Southern Meth-
odist University for *Southwest Review*, Autumn, 1966. SANCHEZ by
Richard Dokey, copyright 1967 by Southern Methodist Univer-
sity for *Southwest Review*, Autumn, 1967. MARIA TEPACHE and
MALA TORRES by Amado Muro, copyright 1964 and 1967 by the
University of Arizona for *Arizona Quarterly*. THEIR HERITAGE—
POVERTY by Manuel Aragon, and WE'RE SUPPOSED TO BELIEVE
WE'RE INFERIOR by Ronald Arias, reprinted from July 1966 issue
of IUD Agenda, published by Industrial Union Dept., AFL-CIO,
Washington, D. C. Reprinted by permission of the editor. BAR-
RIOLOGY EXAM #3 by Antonio Gomez, copyright 1970 by *Con Safos,
Inc.*, for *Con Safos Magazine* Vol. 2, #6. Reprinted by permission of
the author. THE LIVES OF LOS SIETE reprinted by permission of
Basta Ya! and Research Organizing Cooperative (ROC) of San
Francisco, California. A CHICANO VOTING RIGHTS ACT by Roberto
and José Aragon, reprinted from *Regeneración*, Issue No. 5, Vol. 1,
1970, by permission of the authors. CHICANO STUDIES: SENSITIVITY
FOR TWO CULTURES by Richard Vásquez, copyright 1970 by *The
Los Angeles Times* under the title CHICANO COURSE HOLDS MIRROR
TO OTHERS; reprinted by permission of the author. THE EDUCATION
OF MEXICAN AMERICANS by Philip D. Ortego, copyright 1969 by
The New Mexico Review for *The New Mexican Review*, October 1969.
SUMMER WATER AND SHIRLEY by Durango Mendoza, copyright 1966
by The University of Nebraska Press for *Prairie Schooner*, Fall,
1966. MY NAME IS JESUS by Jesús Ascension Arreola, copyright 1966
by *The Texas Observer* for *The Texas Observer*, December 9, 1966.
BACK TO BACHIMBA by Enrique Hank López, copyright 1967, American Heritage Publishing Co., Inc., for *Horizon*, Winter, 1967

There are a thousand ways to seek and to find justice. Thus, as the cricket in the fable defeated the lion, the king of beasts, by climbing into his ear and tickling him, we shall do the same . . .

—Reies López Tijerina

THE CHICANOS

Mexican American Voices

The Barrios, a Growing Awareness

Education, a Way In or Out

Facing Anglo Society

Between Two Worlds

INTRODUCTION

I remember a small town with hot summer evenings and sleepy Sundays, with quiet streets, and with cold winter nights when bed warmth, for us, would come from hot, towel-wrapped bricks heated in a woodstove oven.

The town was Tracy, where I was born, in the northern section of California's San Joaquin Valley.

It was a farming town, surrounded by bright fields of tomatoes and sugar beets and barley stretching interminably to the south, flanked on the distant west by the wrinkled brown mountains of the Coast Range.

And it was a railroad town, a hub for a converging and almost fantastic interlacing of tracks around roundhouse and depot. But except for the frequent screams of steam whistles and the grinding of wheels of switch engines, it was a gentle town, somewhat subdued during the Depression years. Its Main Street then was usually filled with travelers and vagrants from Oklahoma and Arkansas and Texas, many of whom had arrived on freight cars, huddling or clinging to them like swarms of dark, shaggy moths.

There was a sizeable Mexican American population in the town. Most of the men were section hands for the Southern Pacific Railroad, with steady jobs and orange-yellow houses supplied by the railroad.

I remember some old friends: Alfonso Gomez, Santos Gamino, Johnnie Rodriquez, Joe Diaz, and many others. Most of them were gentle, quiet people, although I think that I, perhaps conditioned in part by a Cherokee heritage, was the most quiet of all.

During sports we usually sat on the sidelines, and although Johnnie's fists could move—and still move—like brown bullets in a fight or in boxing, we were usually the last to be chosen on teams. There was always a very definite difference that set us apart.

Today the depot and roundhouse and most of the railroad tracks are gone, and also the orange-yellow houses. But three of my friends still live within a block of each other; Santos is working for the railroad, Johnnie is a labor contractor, Al has taken an early retirement from Civil Service.

"It was a lot better here," says Al, "than in most places. Of course, we lived 'across the tracks,' and we didn't go to any parties or things like that, but we could go to restaurants or any place we wanted. I don't think I really felt different until a 7th-grade teacher—with a drinking problem—said in class one day, 'I'm sick and tired of looking at Mexicans.' Then everybody in the class turned and looked at me."

Al thought for a moment. "The Army wasn't so bad at times, depending on what kind of buddies you had. But when we got leave in Texas we tried to eat in one of their restaurants. We were refused service, and they told us to get the hell out." He smiled his satisfaction. "We tore the place apart."

Santos, married and with a son about to enter college, said wistfully, "We always had enough to eat. One thing about being in a farming town like this—you might have no shoes, but at least you get enough to eat." Then he shook his head. "But it was hard for a Mex to get a job after high school. I'd apply for one, along with other fellows, and the bosses would say, 'Okay, you're hired, and you, and you,' whether the fellow was white, yellow, or black. But when it came to a Mex, then it was, 'Okay, you come back tomorrow.' "

Al and Santos and Johnnie were among the lucky ones.

During the depression the U. S. Government and public agencies, in what was called a "repatriation program," deported literally hundreds of thousands of Mexicans and Mexican Americans to cut down on welfare costs. Roundups extended through southern California, to most cities of the Southwest, and as far north as Chicago and Detroit.

In Los Angeles, official trucks would grind into the barrios —the Mexican American neighborhoods—and the occupants would be herded into them. There was little or no determination of national origin. Citizenship or noncitizenship was not considered. Families were divided; the bringing of possessions was not permitted.

The Mexicans and Mexican Americans were then trucked to Mexico or transferred to a special train which left Union Station each Thursday. Each trainload cost the County of Los Angeles over $75,000, but officials declared that each load would save the county over $350,000 in welfare payments.

"They pushed most of my family into one van," one of the victims, Jorge Acevedo, remembers bitterly. "We drove all day. The driver wouldn't stop for bathroom nor food nor water. Everyone knew by now we had been deported. Nobody knew why, but there was a lot of hatred and anger . . . We had always known that we were hated. Now we had proof."

A repeat performance of the program was held in the early 1950's under the name "Operation Wetback." Possibly conceived in good faith by Anglo politicians, the object of the program was supposedly to return all illegally entered Mexicans to their homeland. Again, as authority was delegated, there was little checking as to citizenship or the legality of the subject's entry into the U. S. Families were again divided without recourse to legal counsel. In a three-year period 2.9 million Mexicans and Mexican Americans were deported.

The significance of these events has been greatly minimized in the history books—if, indeed, they found their way into the books at all.

For many *Mexicanos* (the name had not yet been popularly shortened to "Chicano") the coming of World War II brought a new awareness, an interchange of information and experience, often a disillusionment, but at other moments a rebirth of pride.

Most Mexican American young men, financially unable to attend college and lacking the special skills required to enter defense industries, were drafted into or volunteered for the armed services. In his book *Among the Valiant* Raul Morin tells the story of the Mexican American in World War II and in Korea. "At least a quarter of the blood spilled at Bataan," says Morin, came from the 200th and the 515th

C. A. C., New Mexico National Guard. Seventeen Mexican Americans in World War II were awarded the Congressional Medal of Honor. Company E, 141st Regiment of the 36th (Texas) Division, an all-Mexican American Infantry Company, was one of the most highly decorated in the War.

Paradoxically, at that same time groups of younger Mexican Americans in the barrios of Los Angeles sought to express an identity and an individuality, however logically, by wearing what were called "zoot suits," with their long coat tails and padded shoulders. Police were alerted to the "zoot suit" menace. The wartime imprisonment of Japanese Americans in concentration camps had deprived local newspapers of a source of alarming, threatening news. The papers turned their attention to the Mexican community in a fresh campaign of hatemongering. Bands of Anglo soldiers and sailors would seek out the groups of zoot suiters, or *pachucos*, forcing them to undress and beating them up. Police usually ignored the attacks or else responded by arresting the victims.

Today, a generation later, the war record of the Chicano is still unequaled. In the five-state area of California, New Mexico, Colorado, Arizona, and Texas, Chicanos make up 10 percent of the population. Twenty percent of the war casualties in Viet Nam, Laos, and Cambodia are Chicano.

There comes a point in time when pride can turn to resentment and anger.

There are known to be over seven million Mexican Americans in the United States, and some estimates run as high as nine million. *La Raza*, the Race, is like an awakening giant with seven million faces, each different, ranging from those of Mexican Americans with five generations of residence in the United States behind them to those of former braceros, transported across the Rio Grande for work in American fields as late as 1964, the closing year of the bracero program.

As Charles and Patricia Bustamante point out in their very readable and concise little book, *The Mexican-American and the United States*, the bloodlines of the Chicanos are as varied

as those of the so-called Anglos. The European portion of
their ancestry goes back to the Phoenicians, who brought
their sailing vessels, along with an alphabet, to the Iberian
Peninsula, which is now Spain. Later came the Greeks, and
then the land became a part of the Roman Empire while, at
the same time, Africans were docking at Iberian ports.

The barbarians, or Goths, swept down from the North, followed by the Berbers from Africa, the Africans themselves,
and Arab followers of Islam.

Centuries later there emerged the "pure-blooded" Spaniard.

The bloodlines appear equally complex in the Mexico of
Montezuma. The dominant and ruling race, highly cultured
and civilized, was called the Aztecs by Cortés. Actually, the
tribe occupied only a small portion of Mexico with its capital
of Tenochtitlán at what is now called Mexico City.

But there were other tribes, each with their own dialect,
religion, and culture—the Zapotecs in southern Mexico, the
Totanacs about Vera Cruz, the Pipils on Mexico's West
Coast, the Otomis of Guanajuato and Querétaro, the Mixtecs
on the Gulf Coast.

Legend indicates that the original home of the Aztecs,
which has been translated to read "Crane People," was called
Aztlán, "The Place of Reeds."

Aztlán—a great and proud nation. Remember the name.

Who knows what groups, prior to Aztlán, might have ema-
nated from Polynesian Pacific tribes to be nourished by Asi-
atic nomads wandering down from the Bering Strait? The
world is round and bloodlines can travel like slow winds
through the centuries.

It was in 1519 that Hernán Cortés, with 400 men, 200 Indians, 16 horses, and 14 guns, conquered the Aztec city of
Tenochtitlán, capital of an empire of 20 million Indians.

How could it happen?

Aztec legends had prophesied the return of a great white
God, Quetzalcoatl, who had once stayed with the Aztecs and
been kind to them and who had then sailed away on the east-
ward ocean with a promise to return. Cortés, astride a huge
white horse, must be that god.

The Aztecs had never before seen a horse. One theory suggests that they thought the invaders in their clanking armor were supernatural godlike creatures, half men, half monster, horse and man as one. When the horse of Cortés died at Peten Itza, the Indians carved a statue of the animal and named it *Itzmin Chac* ("Thunder and Lightning"), venerating it as a god.

If Montezuma had seen a single horse before, the course of history in the Western hemisphere might have been radically changed.

However, also aiding the bloody conquest by Cortés was the fact that many of the tribes of central Mexico were dissatisfied with Aztec rule. Gifts were given, beautiful promises made, voices of opposition silenced by Spanish steel; and an alliance was promoted.

After the conquest appeared the *mestizos*, the Spanish Indians who soon comprised the major portion of Mexico's population, just as they do today. Also, there emerged the *mulattoes*, the Spanish Negroes. Other descendants of the conquerors continued to identify with the "pure" Spaniard.

The Spanish contributed their Roman Catholic religion, their art, literature, and culture.

Then the historians took over. They recorded many of the Spanish triumphs. Why not? They were glamorous and romantic. The sweep of stately galleons through the wild seas, the heroic stride of armored *conquistadores* through the steaming jungles of central Mexico, the evolution of the conquerors into wealthy *dons* clad in spangled trousers and wearing silver spurs, all of them astride fast black steeds and preparing for fiestas—all was immortalized by the historians in what Carey McWilliams in his book *North From Mexico* calls "The Fantasy Heritage," a Mexico that never was.

The real Mexicans—the mestizos and mulattoes—were virtually relegated to historical oblivion. The romantic exploits of the Spaniards remained to form what has been considered the cultural heritage of Mexico, even though the Spanish themselves, despite their remarkable talents at sexual reproduction, numbered no more than 300,000 during the colonial period. In fact, many of them, as if bored with it all, returned to their homelands in Spain.

Meanwhile, the mestizos and mulattoes began filtering northward. Although Los Angeles historically was settled by the "Spanish," a sampling of the first settlers includes two Negroes, two Spaniards, nine Indians, nine mulattoes, one mestizo, one coyote (three-quarters Indian and one-quarter Spanish), as well as a male Chinese and his daughter.

The historians didn't notice.

They were, no doubt, well intentioned, but most of them were English, Anglo-Saxon, or English American and writing usually, to make matters worse, from the eastern seaboard, which was then, as it is today, about as far from the Rio Grande, both geographically and culturally, as you can get and still be in *los Estados Unidos*.

As the earth turned into the nineteenth century, new legends grew about the Mexicans and Mexican Americans. Fiction writers, along with ignorance and prejudice, contributed to the development of the stereotyped images which grew and solidified in the minds of Anglos.

Let's take an old book, a juvenile, *Bushy*, published in the 1890's and as popular, relatively, with the grandparents of present-day Anglos as Snoopy and Charlie Brown are with Anglo children today. Our sweet little Western heroine discovers that her Daddy's mules and horses are stolen:

> . . . The scene that they witnessed was startling. There was a Mexican greaser, as the half-breeds are called, riding one of the mules and leading the other animals . . .

But Bushy, with her revolver and her trusty dog, Rover, traps the Mexican.

> . . . Slowly he advanced, and in cowardly fashion gazed back every few seconds into the muzzle of the revolver . . . Then the Mexican's eyes flashed wickedly and, with a sudden, lightning movement, he turned and made a dash at Bushy, with a bright dagger in hand . . .

A generation later, writers, appealing to the parents of today's Anglos, adopted the same stereotypes. In a popular and widely read magazine of 1913, *The Argosy*, we find a thrilling story of Western ranch life, *The Abduction at Del Rancho*. The characters are discussing a new farmhand:

> "What's he like?"
> "That's rather hard to say," she answered. "He—he's a Mexican."
> "A Mexican!" exclaimed Florence, her uncle, and Ted simultaneously . . .
> In a few minutes the Mexican made his appearance. He was attired in typical greaser fashion and his big sombrero was pulled well down over his face disguising his identity.
> "Isn't he picturesque?" asked Mrs. Garrett . . .
> "Nonsense," broke in Mr. Garrett. "I don't like the fellow's looks at all."

Our Anglo heroine is subsequently kidnapped, and our Mexican (who is not given the courtesy of a name) has evidently disappeared. Our Anglo hero cries: *"Have some handbills printed . . . Five thousand dollars for the Mexican, alive or dead!"*

These examples call to mind one of the main tenets of Hitler's *Mein Kampf*. Tell a lie often enough and it becomes the truth. They could be multiplied by ten thousand to show how the images of the Mexican have been twisted, dwarfed, swollen, distorted, erased, and re-created like ten thousand reflections in a sideshow's racist Hall of Mirrors. Favorite images born of prejudice and ignorance are those of the lazy, sleeping Mexican, sombrero pulled over his face; the hot-blooded Latin lover; the fat, good-natured but stupid Pancho; the insidious, black-mustachioed *bandido*; the fiery-eyed revolutionary with a pistol in each hand; the sensual *señorita* slyly lifting her skirts and whirling to the click of castanets.

In fact, the stereotyping is threatening to linger on into the twenty-first century. In a syndicated cartoon strip, *Flash Gordon*, as late as November, 1970, our old good-natured, fat, stupid, sleepy Pancho—as if perversely blessed with immortality—accompanies Flash on a spaceflight to the planet Pluto.

Flash asks, "How'd you enjoy the trip, Pancho?"

Pancho, complete with *mustachio*, sleepy eyes and with sombrero now perched on his space helmet, answers, "Ha! Too short! Pancho never even slept! You think maybe in the morning the sun shines here, *Amigo* Flash?"

Actually, in the nineteenth century Mexican Americans were busy in the United States teaching Navaho women to weave wool, creating a sheep-raising industry in the Southwest, mining gold in California (before John Sutter's discovery in 1849), working in the new western industries fostered by cotton, sugar beets, and the railroads.

At the dawn of the twentieth century—as Feliciano Rivera outlines in a *Mexican American Source Book*—the mines of the Southwest were worked by 60 percent Mexican labor, the railroads by 90 percent. More and more Mexicans and Mexican Americans found jobs in agriculture and industry, and because of the lack of an Anglo education and the inability to bargain, they were almost invariably underpaid.

But the Mexican Americans were not always the docile, accepting creatures of the stereotyped concept. One of the first strikes for higher wages and better working conditions was that of the sugar-beet workers at Ventura, California, in 1903. And there were others: the copper miners in Arizona in 1915 and 1917, the Los Angeles railway employees in 1910, the agricultural workers in the fields of Los Angeles County in 1933, and the Orange County citrus-crop workers in 1936. Usually the strikes were quelled by the National Guard and failed, or at best achieved a limited success. The Mexican American continued to suffer from exploitation and prejudice, as well as from stereotypy.

Little wonder today's cry is BASTA YA!—Enough!

If any one moment symbolized the birth of a new determination and fresh courage, it was just before dawn on the quiet morning of September 8, 1965, near the town of Delano, California. Headlights of many cars needled through the darkness to illumine the dusty roads and fields of vineyards. Now and then the lights would pick out black signs bearing the white letters: HUELGA.

This was a beginning.

On the surface, the strike was the result of the growers' refusal to recognize the AFL-CIO Agricultural Workers' Association as bargaining agent for the workers.

But in the hearts of the strikers, many of them migrant crop-followers, there was cold anger that, like water long contained in a capped jug, at last had burst forth in a silent, determined explosion. The time for *La Huelga*, the strike, was long past due.

There were not only anger and determination. There were doubt and uncertainty, too, and often fear. But the future, if there were no change, would see the average worker here continuing to live in primitive shacks usually supplied by the growers. He would spend most of his $1,500-a-year income for rent and for food, usually at the company store. He would have a life expectancy of 49 years. The mortality rate of his children would be 125 percent above the national average, the same rate applied to tuberculosis. His accident rate would be 300 percent above the national average. He would have no toilets or drinking water or hand-washing facilities in the fields. He would have no unemployment insurance or hospitalization. The increasing usage of poisonous pesticides would prove so deadly that the workers would soon coin a name for pesticide sickness: *La Muerte Andando*, the Walking Death.

The leader of *La Huelga* is a quiet man. Soft-spoken, gentle-eyed, a devotee of nonviolence, Cesar Chavez is also tough—of necessity. The son of migrants, a field worker since the age of ten, Chavez is a symbol of strength and hope for a reawakening people.

The DELANO PROCLAMATION was issued:

"This is the beginning of a social movement in fact and not in pronouncements. We seek our basic, God-given rights as human beings. Because we have suffered—and are not afraid to suffer—in order to survive, we are ready to give up everything, even our lives, in our fight for social justice. We shall do it without violence because that is our destiny . . . .

"We shall unite. We have learned the meaning of UNITY. We know why these United States are just that —united. The strength of the poor is also in union. We know that the poverty of the Mexican or Filipino worker in California is the same as that of all farm workers across the country, the Negroes and poor whites, the Puerto Ricans, Japanese, and Arabians . . . .

"That is why we must get together and bargain collectively. We must use the only strength that we have, the force of our numbers. The ranchers are few; we are many. UNITED WE SHALL STAND . . .

"We do not want the paternalism of the rancher; we do not want the contractor; we do not want charity at the price of our dignity. We want to be equal with all the working men in the nation; we want a just wage, better working conditions, a decent future for our children. To those who oppose us, be they ranchers, police, politicians, or speculators, we say that we are going to continue fighting until we die, or we win. WE SHALL OVERCOME."

Cesar Chavez emphasized: "We are not fighting farmers, but the banks and railroad companies and big corporations that run California's $4 billion-a-year agri-business."

Labor department statistics showed that of the money expended by growers only two to five percent was paid to the workers. Even if the salaries of the workers were doubled, the price of produce would increase by only a cent or two a pound.

Ralph Guzman, in the Industrial Union Department *Agenda*, wrote:

"From the hot, dusty fields of Delano, California, a new cry has torn into the hearts of *La Raza*. Like the historic *Noche del Grito* (Night of the Cry), which unleashed the Mexican Revolution, the Proclamation of Delano has helped to loose a modern social revolution, disciplined by nonviolence and inspired by the ideals of social justice.

"*La Raza* (The Race—the most evocative and unifying phrase used by Mexican Americans for self-identity) has responded.

"Mexican Americans are on the move largely because La Huelga of Delano has moved them."

La Huelga grew, and the cry spread from the fields to the cities, towns, schools, and colleges. Grocery stores selling non-union grapes throughout California and throughout many states were picketed or boycotted. Canada had its National Boycott Day.

Under the leadership of Chavez, the Farm Worker Press was established in Delano, and *Huelga, The First Hundred Days of the Great Grape Strike*, by Eugene Nelson, was published. Nelson, no stranger to the fields, was a picket line captain and later led the union drive for organization in the South Texas melon fields.

El Malcriado, the Voice of the Farm Worker, a monthly newspaper, made its appearance. The first true Chicano theater was born—El Teatro Campesino—under the directorship of Luis Valdez to present the story of *La Huelga* to the people.

California's agri-business fought back, sometimes violently. Subsidized by the U. S. Government, enough surplus grapes were sent to Vietnam to feed each serviceman there six pounds a day.

Finally, nearly five years later, the headlines of *El Malcriado* read:

HUELGA ENDS!
DELANO STRUGGLE CONCLUDES WITH DRAMATIC SIGNING

"The Delano Grape Strike came to a dramatic ending at 11:10 a.m. on Wednesday, July 29 [1970], at UFWOC's headquarters at Forty Acres, one mile west of Delano. Five hundred farmworkers and boycott supporters jammed the hall, sang Nosotros Venceremos, and shouted Viva la Huelga!, Viva la Causa! and Viva Cesar Chavez!

"When the twenty-six growers entered the hall, strikers

began to shout "HUELGA" in unison, and then into the verses of another popular song of the five-year-long struggle: De Colores. It was an emotional occasion. Farm workers had suffered many long years. They had fought patiently and non violently and had made many sacrifices. The signing of the Delano grape growers was always a distant hope. It was an event their bosses swore would never happen. But it happened and there was an electric sense of joy that ran through the crowd.

"The San Francisco *Chronicle* stated the next day that Chavez finally had his day. And no one expressed the meaning of the events at Forty Acres better than Chavez. 'Today,' he stated, 'when we see so much violence in our midst, this event justifies the belief of so many people that through nonviolent action across the world, that social justice can be gained. We are proving this here every day. Without the help of those millions of good people who believe as we do that nonviolence is the way to struggle, we would not be here today.' The 42-year-old union leader also thanked his supporters throughout the United States and abroad for their dedication and support of his movement. He also commented on the sacrifices of the Delano strikers. 'The strikers sacrificed all of their worldly possessions,' he stated solemnly. 'Ninety-five percent of the strikers lost their homes and cars. But I think that in losing their wordly possessions they found themselves, and they found that through serving the poor and through complete dedication they could find themselves.' "

The grape strike is over, and yet *La Huelga* is not, for this is a time when the whole is more than the sum of its parts. The battle for equality and justice for the farmworker will continue, as it will for *La Raza* and for humanity. There will be more battles, more victories, more defeats and imprisonments. This is not the end of a movement. It is still the beginning.

During those five years of the strike the voice of Cesar Chavez was not the only brown voice to be heard, *La Huelga* not the only cry.

Also in 1965, a kind of year of decision for the Chicano, *La Crusada para la Justicia*, the Crusade for Justice, was founded in downtown Denver, Colorado, and was soon to become one of the most prominent Mexican American civil rights organizations.

Its founder has written in his fine epic poem, I AM JOAQUIN:

> I am still here!
>
> I have endured in the rugged mountains
>   of our country
> I have survived the toils and slavery
>   of the fields.
>
> I have existed
> in the barrios of the city,
> in the suburbs of bigotry,
> in the mines of social snobbery,
> in the prisons of dejection,
> in the muck of exploitation
> and
> in the fierce heat of racial hatred.

The poet is Rodolfo "Corky" Gonzales. Born in Denver in 1928 and the son of a migrant worker, he worked in a slaughterhouse to put himself through high school. Usually, at school or at home, his shoes were stained with the deep brownish red of dried blood.

He graduated at sixteen.

He was fast with his thoughts, with his tongue, and with his fists. As a featherweight boxer in his teens, he won the National A. A. U. Boxing Championship as well as the International Championship. As a professional, he was rated the third ranking contender for the World Title.

Apart from his boxing career, he was a *campesino* in the fields, a lumberjack, soldier, insurance salesman, and, like many of the new breed of Chicano, he found time to enter politics.

He has been many things: Democratic party leader (until severely disillusioned), Colorado coordinator of the "Viva Kennedy" campaign in 1960, a leader in the Poor People's

March on Washington. He has worked with Reies Tijerina of New Mexico's Alianza and the Brown Berets of Los Angeles. During the darkest days of *Huelga*, Corky was there. At a Chicano Peace Moratorium, whether in Denver, San Francisco, or Los Angeles, Corky would be there.

Today his headquarters for the Crusade for Justice include a school, a gymnasium, the El Grito Art Gallery, shops, a library, and a bail bond service; and here the newspaper *El Gallo* is published. Often the place is one of happiness, of singing and dancing; at other times it is a symbol of hope and a refuge for those escaping from intolerance. One of Corky's greatest dreams is to establish a Chicano university, free from the educational prejudices and omissions of Anglo schools.

Lee Schroeder, Denver columnist, describes Corky as having "a craggy sort of face, with curly black hair never in any sort of apparent pattern. He is small, walks with an easy, springy step.

"He is quick—quick to sort what he likes from what he doesn't like, quick to grasp ideas and their significance to the Revolution, quick to chastise and criticize when the need arises. Yet he appears gentle, concerned with and loving people, especially youth. He seems patient with them, but specific and firm. In person he appears a much more winning and warm individual than he does during the heat of a speech.

"One receives the impression that he is wrapped up in details too numerous to grasp all at once. His desk is piled with papers, his office crammed with books, together with projects in progress or waiting to be acted upon. He resembles a kind of terribly busy minister with his flock, doing everything from personal counseling to repairing a doorknob."

On Palm Sunday, 1969, Corky sponsored a Chicano youth conclave, the Chicano Youth Liberation Conference, which 1,500 attended. Here came the almost unanimous vote to revive in spirit the ancient Aztec nation, a union of free pueblos, named Aztlán. Thus the Nation of Aztlán was reborn—not yet, to be sure, with clearly defined physical, territorial boundaries, but with all the spirit and pride of its ancient people. "Before the world, before all of North America, before all our brothers on the Bronze Continent, we are a union of free pueblos, we are Aztlán," it was declared in the "Spiritual Plan of Aztlán."

Under Corky's guidance, the new Chicano party, La Raza Unida, with its platform EL PLAN DE AZTLÁN, is flourishing. In explaining the need for a party of Third World citizens, Corky says, "The two-party system is one animal with two heads eating out of the same trough ... If four grains of arsenic will kill you, and eight grains of arsenic will kill, which is the lesser of two evils? You're dead either way."

Although many Chicano leaders have contributed to *la Causa* in specialized ways, such as Chavez in California, Rodolfo Gonzales has perhaps done more than any one man to unify *La Raza*, to bring the vision of a single cause to all Chicanos, Hispaños, Mejicanos, Mexican Americans, or whatever they might call themselves.

Also, in that year of 1965, far to the southeast, another voice was speaking, that of a fiery ex-preacher who had spent five years traveling through the villages of the upper Rio Grande:

> You see, for us the land is mother. But it is not just land—for us there must be truth and justice—which is the teaching of the Bible. When the land is returned to us we will make cities, churches, schools. The day will come ...

Reies López Tijerina was born in 1927 in—literally—a Texas cotton field. His mother, who had had the dubious blessings of old mattresses while giving birth to her other children, had erred in predicting the time of Reies' arrival. The pains came while she and her husband, a Texas sharecropper, were hoeing cotton. Cotton sacks became her bed.

The depression years were hard on the Tijerinas and their eight children. The father, Antonio, was once driven off his land, beaten, a leg tendon slashed, and thereafter was a partial cripple. Reies' mother died when he was six.

Antonio and his children followed the crops now as far as

the beet fields of Colorado. Reies spent only six sporadic months in school, but somehow he learned to read and write. Often he would rummage through garbage cans for his lunch. At other times he and his brothers would capture rats from the fields and eat them.

At fifteen, he was given a New Testament by a Baptist preacher, Samuel Galindo, and the course of his life was changed. He would be a minister; and after saving what money he could, he entered the Assembly of God Bible School at Ysleta, Texas, where he became known as a spirited, dynamic speaker. After graduation, he wandered for ten years over the Southwest, preaching in Spanish to, as he describes it, "the people . . . farm workers, in the towns, going from one church to another where I was invited. I would sleep under bridges, or in the open. Drunkards and poor people would give me a dollar to keep me going."

Tijerina loved the land and thought of it as a mother. And the time came when—perhaps even as he wished for the return of his flesh-mother—he believed that the land should be restored to its rightful owners, the Hispaños.

The problem of land ownership over much of New Mexico originated with the Treaty of Guadalupe Hildalgo, ratified by the Congress of the United States on March 10, 1848, and ending the two-year war with Mexico.

San Jose columnist Luis G. Juarez calls the Treaty "a cruel deception. The only article that was ever enforced was one insuring the validity of land grants made by the government of Mexico . . . Within two years, the Mexican had lost his plurality in the ceded land, and saw the first overt, discriminatory legislation by the new rulers."

There was an era of confusion, of corruption, of upheaval, that was to last many years as land titles changed hands and families were uprooted.

Tijerina's goal did not spring into his mind like a blazing comet; it evolved slowly and methodically. He spent several years in preparation, researching old land titles, studying in Mexico any history which might pertain to the Mexican American in the United States Southwest.

Finally the goal was defined: to recover the land lost or stolen throughout the years.

He first formed the Alianza Federal de Las Mercedes and incorporated it on October 7, 1963. It was later renamed the Alianza de Los Pueblos Libres, the Alliance of Free City States.

Membership grew to between 10,000 and 20,000. Under Tijerina's guidance, petitions were drawn and presented to the government of New Mexico and to the President of the United States. On July 4, 1966, a march was made from Albuquerque to Santa Fe to present the governor with an additional petition and, through resulting publicity, to place the cause of the Alianza before the people. That same year a group of the Alianza attempted to take over a portion of the national forest lands, and five of the membership were convicted on charges ranging from the killing of a deer to assault on the officers.

In June, 1967, Tijerina attempted to hold a mass meeting of the Alianza. The District Attorney of Rio Arriba County, Alfonso Sanchez, issued a statement on a radio broadcast:

> . . . I wish to give notice to all Alianza members who plan to be present and participate in the meeting at Coyote tomorrow. That meeting is versus the law since it is planned to take over private property. Criminal charges of unlawful assembly will be filed against all persons who attend.

The District Attorney did not stop with the warning. The night before the meeting, cars of the State Police traced swift paths through the night, through the small, darkened towns of Rio Arriba County and to the homes of those members of the Alianza who, they thought, might attend the meeting arranged by Tijerina. There were sudden poundings on wooden doors; house lights flicked on; startled faces appeared in the night.

"You're under arrest," were the often-repeated words.

Nine Alianza members were jailed.

Two days later the Alianza had procured a warrant for the arrest of District Attorney Alfonso Sanchez. Armed, their

group entered the courthouse at Tierra Amarilla in an attempt
to make a citizen's arrest.

There was opposition; guns were drawn and fired. A jailer,
Eulogio Salazar, was wounded. A state policeman, Nick Sais,
was shot through the chest. Miraculously, he survived.

During the scuffling, according to one witness, a voice cried
out, "Don't hurt anybody! Reies said not to hurt anybody!"

The Alianza group held the courthouse for two hours, then
escaped with two hostages. They were pursued by a small
army—men, cars, horses, tanks, and helicopters of the
National Guard as well as the Jicarilla Apache police. After
the greatest manhunt in the history of the state, Tijerina and
many of the Alianza were captured.

It was not until December, 1968, that Tijerina was tried on
charges of kidnapping, false imprisonment, and assault on a
jail. Always a powerful and fiery orator, he acted as his attorney and was acquitted by a jury of twelve. Two jurors after
the trial declared, under oath, "We think the man actually
was trying to keep the people from getting hurt."

Meanwhile, despite the uncertainties cast by impending
trials and conflicts with the law, the Alianza had broadened
its activities. Tijerina had traveled to California, visiting campuses and political meetings in Berkeley, Santa Barbara, and
San Bernardino. He attended the fast-breaking of Cesar
Chavez in Delano. He conferred with Dr. Martin Luther King
in March, 1968, in Atlanta, Georgia, and took part in the
Poor People's March on Washington. He was considered as a
nominee for Vice-President on the Peace and Freedom Party,
with Dick Gregory as candidate for the Presidency. Later, he
flew to Atlanta to attend Dr. King's funeral, and here he
talked with actor Marlon Brando, Panther leader Bobby
Seale, and Stokely Carmichael, author of *Black Power*.

Then new charges were prepared by persistent officials. A
fresh charge of false imprisonment was filed against Tijerina,
despite the previous acquittal, and also a charge for assault
with intent to commit a violent felony.

In June, 1970, Tijerina was at last convicted and sentenced

to serve two concurrent prison terms of from one to five years and from two to ten years.

Today, many of the Alianza and La Raza remember an old legend—perhaps of Aztec origin, perhaps Pueblo, perhaps imagined—telling of "laughing" people who would come from the East to steal homes and lands of the Hispaños; and that eventually, after years of oppression and suffering, a powerful leader would appear to drive the enemy back to his homeland. And they wonder if Tijerina is that messiah.

A petition recently published in the Denver paper *El Gallo* reads:

> We Petition the Nation of Aztlán to
> Act on the Following Resolutions:
>
> 1. That the new nation of Aztlán recognize Reies López Tijerina as an official hero of this nation.
>
> 2. That the new nation of Aztlán recognize Reies as a political prisoner and concentrate its power as a nation to free Reies by any means necessary.
>
> 3. That June 5 be recognized as a national holiday in the new nation of Aztlán.

The Courthouse Raid, like *La Huelga*, is now a part of history; and although Tijerina has not yet achieved the victories that Cesar Chavez is winning, the Alianza remains. More of the problems of La Raza, and more of the injustices endured by it, have been presented to the world.

Other brown voices have risen to prominence during the decade of the 1960's. Headquartered in East Los Angeles, predominantly Mexican American, are the Brown Berets, founded and led by David Sánchez, still in his early 20's. The Berets, according to Sánchez, have 26 chapters in California, Texas, and other states as far east as Michigan. Their goal is to "restore dignity in our people" and to achieve unity for those in the barrios. While not devotees to the cause of nonviolence, like Chavez, they do say they would resort to violence only in self-defense.

In San Antonio, Texas, there is the Mexican American Youth Organization (MAYO) symbolized by serape jackets and clenched fists raised in defiance of Anglo oppression. Like the Brown Berets, they declare they will resort to violence only when necessary and try to aid the cause of the Chicano through education, politics, and the establishment of Chicano-owned businesses.

The youth organization MECHA (Movimiento Estudiantil Chicano de la Raza), both active and vocal, is gaining more and more support throughout the colleges and universities of the West. At Stanford University its official publication, *Chicanismo*, is one of the most complete and caustic of any Chicano paper. Stanford's Mecha Casa (House) has hosted conferences, Chicano theatrical groups, art and photograph exhibits. The growing mood of the students was perhaps expressed by Elizabeth Montoya, from the Crusade for Justice, who told them in an address, "You can't wait four years before you do anything. By that time you will have left the movement behind. Don't just yell *Viva la Raza!* or Chicano power! Get off your asses and do something about it!"

Chicano voices are being heard in the fields of law, education, politics. Among our new Congressmen are Edward R. Roybal of California, Henry Gonzales of Texas, and Eligio De La Garza of Texas.

Chicanos are developing their own art, their own music, their own writing—as they must, if they are to be Chicano. *El Grito*, edited by Octavio Romano in Berkeley, is one of the finest literary magazines published anywhere. Also growing in both quality and impact are *Con Safos, Regeneración, La Raza, Inside Eastside, Inferno, Compass,* and *El Papel.* Chicano prison inmates have begun to publish their own papers: *Aztlán* at Ft. Leavenworth, Kansas; *El Chino* at the California Institute for Men, Chino, California; *La Voz del Chicano* at Soledad, California.

The Afro-American has succeeded, to a great extent, in

erasing many of the old false images. Al Jolson with his black-face is no longer with us. Little Black Sambo is exiled.

Now it's the Chicano's turn.

Maybe this book will help.

—Edward W. Ludwig

The Fields of the Past

SATURDAY BELONGS TO THE PALOMÍA

By Daniel Garza

Every year, in the month of September, the cotton pickers come up from the Valley, and the braceros come from Mexico itself. They come to the town in Texas where I live, all of them, the whole *palomía*. "Palomía" is what we say: it is slang among my people, and I do not know how to translate it exactly. It means . . . the cotton pickers when they come. You call the whole bunch of them the *palomía*, but one by one they are cotton pickers, *pizcadores*.

Not many of them have traveled so far north before, and for the ones who have not it is a great experience. And it is an opportunity to know other kinds of people, for the young ones. For the older ones it is only a chance to make some money picking cotton. Some years the cotton around my town is not so good, and then the *pizcadores* have to go farther north, and we see them less.

But when they come, they come in full force to my little town that is full of gringos. Only a few of us live there who speak Spanish among ourselves, and whose parents maybe came up like the *pizcadores* a long time ago. It is not like the border country where there are many of both kinds of people; it is gringo country mostly, and most of the time we and the gringos live there together without worrying much about such matters.

In September and October in my town, Saturdays belong to the *pizcadores*. During the week they are in the fields moving up and down the long cotton rows with big sacks and sweating frightfully, but making *centavitos* to spend on Saturday at the movie, or on clothes, or on food. The gringos come to town during the week to buy their merchandise and groceries, but finally Saturday arrives, and the *pizcadores* climb aboard their trucks on the cotton farms, and the trucks all come to town. It is the day of the *palomía*, and most of the gringos stay home.

"*Ay, qué gringos!*" the *pizcadores* say. "What a people to hide themselves like that. But such is life . . ."

For Saturday the *pizcadores* dress themselves in a special and classy style. The girls comb their black hair, put on new bright dresses and low-heeled shoes, and the color they wear on their lips is, the way we say it, enough. The boys dress up in black pants and shoes with taps on the heels and toes. They open their shirts two or three buttons to show their chests and their Saint Christophers; then at the last they put a great deal of grease on their long hair and comb it with care. The old men, the *viejos*, shave and put on clean plain clothes, and the old women put on a tunic and comb their hair and make sure the little ones are clean, and all of them come to town.

They come early, and they arrive with a frightful hunger. The town, being small, has only a few restaurants. The *pizcadores*—the young ones and the ones who have not been up from Mexico before—go into one of the restaurants, and the owner looks at them.

One who speaks a little English says they want some *desayuno*, some breakfast.

He looks at them still. He says: "Sorry. We don't serve Meskins."

Maybe then one of the *pachuco* types with the long hair and the Saint Christopher says something ugly to him in Spanish, maybe not. Anyhow, the others do not, but leave sadly, and outside the old men who did not go in nod among themselves, because they knew already. Then maybe, standing on the sidewalk, they see a gringo go into the restaurant. He needs a shave and is dirty and smells of sweat, and before the door closes they hear the owner say: "What say, Blacky? What'll it be this morning?"

The little ones who have understood nothing begin to holler about the way their stomachs feel, and the *papás* go to the market to buy some food there.

I am in the grocery store, me and a few gringos and many of the *palomía*. I have come to buy flour for my mother. I pass a *pizcador*, a father who is busy keeping his little ones from knocking cans down out of the big piles, and he smiles to me and says: "*¿Qué tal, amigo?*"

"*Pues, así no más,*" I answer.

He looks at me again. He asks in a quick voice, "You are a Chicano?"

"*Sí.*"

"How is it that you have missed the sun in your face, *muchacho?*" he says. "A big hat, maybe?"

"No, señor," I answer. "I live here."

"You have luck."

And I think to myself, yes, I have luck; it is good to live in one place. And all of a sudden the *pizcador* and I have less to say to each other, and he says adiós and gathers up his flow of little ones and goes out to the square where the boys and girls of the *palomía* are walking together.

On the square too there is usually a little lady selling hot tamales. She is dressed simply, and her white hair is in a bun, and she has a table with a big can of tamales on it which the *palomía* buy while they are still hot from the stove at the little lady's home.

"*Mamacita, mamacita,*" the little ones shout at their mothers. "Doña Petra is here. Will you buy me some tamalitos?"

Doña Petra lives there in the town, and the mothers in the *palomía* are her friends because of her delicious tamales and because they go to her house to talk of the cotton picking, of children, and maybe of the fact that in the north of Texas it takes somebody like Doña Petra to find good *masa* for tamales and tortillas. Away from home as the *pizcadores* are, it is good to find persons of the race in a gringo town.

On the street walk three *pachucos*, seventeen or eighteen years old. They talk *pachuco* talk. One says: "Listen, *chabos*, let's go to the good movie."

"O. K.," another one answers. "Let's go flutter the good eyelids."

They go inside a movie house. Inside, on a Saturday, there are no gringos, only the *palomía*. The *pachucos* find three girls, and sit down with them. The movie is in English, and they do not understand much of it, but they laugh with the girls and make the *viegos* angry, and anyhow the cartoon —the mono, they call it—is funny by itself, without the need for English.

Other *pachucos* walk in gangs through the streets of the town, looking for something to do. One of them looks into the window of Mr. Jones' barber shop and tells the others that he thinks he will get a haircut. They laugh, because haircuts are something that *pachucos* do not get, but one of them dares him. "It will be like the restaurant," he says. "Gringo scissors do not cut Chicano hair."

So he has to go in, and Mr. Jones looks at him as the restaurant man looked at the others in the morning. But he is a nicer man, and what he says is that he has to go to lunch when he has finished with the customers who are waiting. "There is a Mexican barber across the square," he says. "On Walnut Street. You go there."

The *pachuco* tells him a very ugly thing to do and then combs his long hair in the mirror and then goes outside again, and on the sidewalk he and his friends say bad things about Mr. Jones for a while until they get tired of it, and move on. The gringo customers in the barber shop rattle the magazines they are holding in their laps, and one of them says a thing about cotton pickers, and later in the day it is something that the town talks about, gringos and *pizcadores* and those of my people who live there, all of them. I hear about it, but forget, because September in my town is full of such things, and in the afternoon I go to the barber shop for a haircut the way I do on Saturdays all year long.

Mr. Jones is embarrassed when he sees me. "You hear about that?" he says. "That kid this morning?"

I remember then, and I say yes, I heard.

"I'm sorry, Johnny," he says. "Doggone it. You know I'm not . . ."

"I know," I say.

"The trouble is, if they start coming, they start bringing the whole damn family, and then your regular customers get mad," he says.

"I know," I say, and I do. There is no use in saying that I don't, because I live in the town for the other ten or eleven months of the year when the *palomía* is not here but in Mexico and the Valley. I know the gringos of the town and what they are like, and they are many different ways. So I tell Mr. Jones that I know what he means.

"Get in the chair," he says. "You want it short or medium this time?"

And I think about the *pizcador* in the grocery store and what he said about my having luck, and I think again it is good to live in one place and not to have to travel in trucks to where the cotton is.

At about six in the afternoon all the families begin to congregate at what they call the *campo*. *Campo* means camp or country, but this *campo* is an area with a big tin shed that the State Unemployment Commission puts up where the farmers who have cotton to be picked can come and find the *pizcadores* who have not yet found a place to work. But on Saturday nights in September the *campo* does not have anything to do with work. The familes come, bringing tacos to eat and maybe a little beer if they have it. After it is dark, two or three of the men bring out guitars, and some others have concertinas. They play the fast, twisty *mariachi* music of the places they come from, and someone always sings. The songs are about women and love and sometimes about a town that the song says is a fine town, even if there is no work there for *pizcadores*. All the young people begin to dance, and the old people sit around making certain that the *pachucos* do not get off into the dark with their daughters. They talk, and they eat, and they drink a little beer, and then at twelve o'clock it is all over.

The end of Saturday has come. The old men gather up their sons and daughters, and the mothers carry the sleeping little ones like small sacks of cotton to the trucks, and the whole *palomía* returns to the country to work for another week, and to earn more *centavitos* with which, the Saturday that comes after the week, to go to the movies, and buy groceries, and pay for tamalitos of Doña Petra and maybe a little beer for the dance at the *campo*. And the mothers will visit with Doña Petra, and the *pachucos* will walk the streets, and the other things will happen, all through September and October, each Saturday the same, until finally, early in November, the cotton harvest is over, and the *pizcadores* go back to their homes in the Valley or in Mexico.

The streets of my town are empty then, on Saturdays. It does not have many people, most of the year. On Saturday mornings you see a few gringo children waiting for the movie to open, and not much else. The streets are empty, and the gringos sit in the restaurant and the barber shop and talk about the money they made or lost on the cotton crop that fall.

STRIPPER WHIRLWIND:
THE PIZCADORES AND THE MACHINES

By Daniel Garza

The Farm Labor Services for the Department of Labor in Dallas says that in the last ten years mechanization has moved faster in agriculture than in industry. The whirlwind of mechanization has meant the displacement of thousands of field hands, and labor statistics reveal that in 1965 farm employment dropped by 60 percent, largely because of farm machinery.

In Texas, one of the biggest agricultural areas hit by automation is cotton harvesting; these days, 86 percent of the cotton in Texas is harvested mechanically. In the Rio Grande Valley, cotton machinery has literally evicted *pizcadores*, or cotton pickers, from their environment. For several years, these people have traveled north seeking their livelihood.

Each September, *pizcadores* gather their little ones, sign on with a trucker, and come to harvest the cotton crop, which now for the greater part is being handled by what is known to both the farmer and the field hand as the "stripper," the automatic cotton harvester. Every year, *pizcadores* become less enchanted with the cotton crop; sometimes because, as they say, the cotton is *muy malancones*, very bad, but more often because machinery has taken a firm hold on cotton harvesting. In consequence, they come in smaller numbers to the north of Texas these days.

Up until recent years, cotton in central Texas was labeled for *pizcadores*. Fall months would bring them to labor camps set up by the Texas Employment Commission, and wherever you went in small towns, you'd see the big trucks. In the camps themselves, large Chicano families would congregate on Saturdays and Sundays and talk about how good or bad the crop was that year. Bronzed children begged their *papás* for candy money; and the women, the *viejas*, would walk in groups to clothing stores to buy bright tunics to show their gringo neighbors back in the Valley.

Those days are nearly gone. Automation has taken over cotton harvesting in central Texas, but *pizcadores* continue to trickle to the northern part of the state hoping, always hoping, that they'll find their small pot of fortune. One place which still holds some promise is the small community of Princeton in North Collin County. You don't expect to see *pizcadores* in such a place, because the small town is located just thirty-five miles from the cultural and industrial metropolitan Dallas-Fort Worth area.

In the migrant camp in Princeton, generations of *pizcadores* have come to live and work in surrounding cotton fields. Once established, the crew chief, the *jefe*, seeks out farmers or ginners who want their crop harvested. But now, even in Princeton, those jobs are becoming scarce.

Pizcadores used to be a carefree group. They knew that each fall there would be enough money to buy frijoles and flour and *masa* to make tortillas. They knew they would earn enough money during the season to tide them over until the following year. And there was always enough money left to buy the little ones new jeans and maybe a new *morral*, a cotton-picking sack, for next year's harvest.

The migrant camps had a festive air about them. On Saturday nights there was gaiety and foolishness. The old men, the *viejos*, sat around in circles smoking their Bull-Durham and making sure the *pachucos* didn't get their daughters in dark places. There was dancing, with the younger men playing twisty music on their guitars and *concertainas*, and always someone threw his head back and let out with a yell, the way the *mariachis* do when they sing ballads. The *viejas* busied themselves making hot tamales and tangy tacos, filled with frijoles and *salsa picante*. They went well with a little beer.

You don't see those things any more. The romance of it all has disappeared, and in its place remains the cold, hard fact that machinery, not *pizcadores*, is here to help the farming economy. Labor camps throughout central and north

Texas are small ghost towns, where now, during spring and summer months, area farmers bring their fruits and vegetables to sell.

You don't see groups of brown children running about, or the big canvas-covered trucks lined up along the corrugated metal sheds, or a *mamá* and *papá* arguing about a dress seen in a gringo's shop. The sounds which were so associated with *pizcadores* at migrant camps no longer exist. The camps are now quiet as though a battle had been fought there and both the victors and the defeated had returned to their homes.

Small towns are also feeling the impact of the new age. During the cotton season, *pizcadores* crowded the streets on Saturdays, keeping shop owners busy replenishing their shelves. But now only memories remain while merchants talk among themselves about the money they made when *pizcadores* flocked to town.

Pizcadores and their leaders complain. They complain of many things, but mostly about machinery. In the fields, you hear them curse in Spanish about the new inventions. One man who is bothered about it is Juan Martínez, a rotund fifty-year-old *jefe* from Robstown, whose father used to pick cotton for a living.

"*Esas máquinas desgraciadas*," he says, "they take the bread from our mouths. The machines are like locusts; they leave very little cotton for us to pick."

But the machines do leave a little cotton for the *pizcadores*. Señor Martínez says farmers give them fields which are choked with Johnson grass.

He smiles proudly and adds, "Those damn machines don't separate the bolls from the weeds."

You hear other complaints, and they're all about the stripper. Back in the early fifties, *pizcadores* received two and a half dollars for each hundred pounds of handpicked cotton, and each individual tried to pick more cotton than his *compadre*. Now, Señor Martínez says that in most places in north Texas only a dollar-seventy-five is paid for a hundred pounds of handpicked cotton. Twenty-five cents of that goes to the trucker for travel expenses. In a place such as Princeton, each *pizcador* is required to pay three dollars a week for quarters and lavatory facilities, which amount to several privies and three outdoor water faucets. The hard-earned money goes fast, and *pizcadores* return to their homes in the Valley, a very disgruntled society.

While *pizcadores* argue, farmers and ginners alike, in Princeton and throughout the state, are happy with the results they're getting from the new machinery. One of Princeton's long-established ginners, J. L. Phillips, who has been in the business for over forty years, says, "A stripper can pull eight to ten bales of cotton a day, whereas it takes nearly twenty men picking an average of five hundred pounds of cotton each to make up that amount."

"What's really important," Mr. Phillips says, "is that you save between fifteen and twenty dollars a bale with the machinery."

Pizcadores are slowly realizing their plight, and most of them have no ready solution to the problem. Some say they'll return to the Valley and find construction work to supplement their cotton harvest earnings. Others nod slowly and say, "*¿Quien sabe?*"—"Who knows?" Still others say they'll return to work in the fields, optimistic that the *patrones*, the farm owners, will have cotton for them to pick.

While modern farm machinery is posing economic problems for the *pizcadores*, it is also opening new financial avenues and a new way of life for some of them. Within the last few years, vocational schools have opened with the financial assistance of the federal government's Manpower Development Training Act. Under the program, *pizcadores* learn to operate farm machinery, including the stripper. Labor experts say that even though the program got a late start, it is proving successful. Hundreds of farmhands have graduated from the sixteen-week schools, which are located in such south Texas towns as Laredo, Edinburg, and McAllen. In addition to the training, the students receive financial assistance comparable to unemployment compensation during their schooling period. Still, these schools are not enough to fulfil the educational needs of thousands of *pizcadores*.

Another agency concerned with what has been termed the "great human problem" is the Texas Council of Churches in Austin. Heading the Migrant Ministry Department is Leo Nieto, who stated, "*Pizcadores* are the poorest people in Texas. They have an annual income of between one thousand and eighteen hundred dollars, and sometimes, when the cotton crops are bad, the amount is much less."

The Migrant Ministry is involved in alleviating many problems confronting *pizcadores* who are far away from home. For instance, church women are united in providing needy families with clothing for all the family, especially the little ones. Doctors give of their time without monetary compensation in administering to the sick. But their big task is that of educating these people.

While some south Texas communities have thrown their support into fulfilling educational needs of *pizcadores*, other towns are reluctant to get into the assistance programs. An official of the Texas Council of Churches noted, "In a recent church meeting in a south Texas town, a rancher who made most of his money off cheap labor said the only solution to the migrant problem is to kill them all."

Others, who fail to see the socio-economic problem, or who are blinded with prejudice, say *pizcadores* cannot be educated. Surveys indicate that one quarter of all adults in the Latin American population, twenty-five years and older, are functional illiterates. For many of the adults, education means very little. What is important to them is to be able to work and have food on the table for their families. For these types, education is mere tomfoolery.

The Texas Education Agency is also involved with the educational problems, and the organization is sponsoring the Migrant Education Project, using antipoverty funds. Special schools for children have been established in south Texas, and to fit the needs of the wandering families there is a six-month curriculum, during which youngsters undergo a rigorous learning period. The unique schools have been lauded by state education leaders because the dropout and absenteeism rates have been very low. The important thing is that these children have been able to concentrate on their studies without interruption.

While *pizcadores'* children learn and try to better themselves through education, many of the adults follow their heritage by continuing to wrest a living from cotton harvesting; some, perhaps, are too proud to learn the ways of modern man and the machinery he has devised.

The day will come when *pizcadores'* children will grow to be adults, and possibly then they will tell their own children tales of the days when big trucks loaded with large families and their meager belongings lumbered across Texas to where cotton flourished. Then, maybe, they will tell their flow of little ones about camp life on Saturday nights, and how the children chased each other in circles and around the big trucks while *papás* sat and talked earnestly about the crop and about the problems they faced with the new machinery.

MALA TORRES

A Story

By Amado Muro

Now my old friend Memo Torres, once nicknamed La Malita, is different. He wears a black suit and a black hat and a Roman collar whenever he appears in El Paso. He comes to El Paso once a year and that is the only time Salvador Zavala and I ever get to see him. He still calls Chava and me by our first names and jokes with us when we are on our lunch hour at the ice plant. But now we are always polite to him and wait until he has gone before we finish our stories about Mexico.

"Good afternoon, *Padre* Guillermo," the other icemen say to him.

"Good afternoon, *Padre* Guillermo," I say to him.

Chava and I were in Our Lady of the Thunderbolt Church in Parral, Chihuahua, the day Memo said his first mass and became different. The church was crowded with people, relatives and friends, but Memo did not make a mistake. Chava knew because he was once an altar boy. Memo and Chava used to serve mass together when they went to Our Lady of the Thunderbolt School.

That was long ago—before Memo took the holy orders. He was like us then. He lived in our neighborhood, La Primavera, and his father worked in La Prieta mine like ours. We played *La Viborita* and the Burro and the *Rayeula* every day in the streets.

Memo Torres had big placid eyes and a round smooth face with freckles across the nose. He had a calm air which underlined his deep, slow voice, and his black hair was always combed flat with every strand in place. Broad-shouldered and compact with bulging biceps, he was stronger than any of us. When we went to the General Rodrigo Quevedo Gym, he bench-pressed more weight and punched the light bag faster than anyone. Skipping rope, shadow boxing, and working on

37

the body bag, he looked so much like Carlos Malacara, the
Chihuahua lightweight who once beat Champion Juan Zurita,
that countrymen called him La Malita or Little Mala.

"The boy moves like the great Mala himself," they en-
thused. "He's *muy Mexicanota*."

Memo was a year older, and we all tried to be like him.
The boys in our neighborhood always let him be the leader.
He had an air of importance which appealed to us in a way
that more reasonable people had never done. We did everything he said. When he told Chava and me to play hooky
with him, we carried out his order though our mothers
called us *vagos* for it. But Chava and I agreed a scolding was
a small price to pay for a footloose day with Memo Torres.

Memo could think of more reasons for playing hooky
than a country Mexican can for going to Chihuahua City.
Memo and Chava and I lived within tobacco-spitting distance
of school. But at least once a week we never got there.
Memo led us down to the Street of the Crazy Women instead.
Wandering up and down it was more fun than staying in a
classroom.

"It's more educational too," Memo always insisted, and
we couldn't help agreeing. What we saw and heard there we
never forgot. The classroom was different; what we heard
there we never remembered.

The street that enthralled Memo so wasn't much to look at.
It was just another broken-down street in a mining town that
had many like it. But to Memo and Chava and me it was an
exciting change from our own neighborhood with its poor
homes on crooked streets that wound up hillsides.

Then, too, in those days the Street of the Crazy Women
was a village in itself, northern as the *nopal*. One Viva Villa
was worth four Viva Zapatas there, and its *mariachis* sang of
Blondie Lopez instead of Gabino Barrera. *Chihuahuenses*
said this long, dusty street held more poor Mexicans than
jails do. Its sights and sounds made them all feel at home.
Mesquite wood smoke fogged it. Bawling vendors filled it.
Misty vapors from steaming cornmeal drifted down it. There,
women vendors scrubbed griddles with maguey fiber brushes,

and countrymen scrubbed their teeth with their fingers in primitive Mexican village style.

Toward sidehills matted with chaparral, mesquite, and *gobernadora* stood adobe homes with blessed palms hanging over their doors to keep evil spirits and lightning away. Stumpy cottonwoods, misted with gray veils woven by caterpillars, leaned before them. On clear days, the gossiping housewives, whose doings gave the street its name, sat on rush-plaited chairs under the heavy-leafed trees where, wrapped in thick *mantas* woven by High Sierra Indians, they patched *Tenancingo rebozos* and Santa Maria prayer shawls in the sunshine.

Their conversations were famous. They talked mostly about their husbands. Some said they wished they had gone into the convent instead of getting married. Others disagreed. "*Ay Madre*, it's better to undress one-horned drunkards than dress plaster saints," they insisted. Sometimes we listened until they drove us away.

We liked the street vendor's crowing cries too. They merged into a boisterous tympany. It was like Memo said. There was always something to see, something to listen to on the Street of the Crazy Women.

At one end of the street, near Jesús María Alley, was a rabbit warren cluster of rickety *puestos* that slumped and sagged like miniature Towers of Pisa. Robust women with nicknames like Maria la Bandida, La Tompitas, and La Chata Micaela operated these foodstands popularly called *agachados* because they are so lowslung.

When we got hungry, we went to the Pearls of Coyame *puesto* run by Petra Porras, a buxom, smiling woman nicknamed Petra la Pozolera. In this little hut, made of rough boards so badly painted the wood's natural color showed through, we were always welcome.

Petra the Pozole Vendor, gray-haired with a broad, pleasant face, greeted us with a wide smile that showed the glittering gold fillings of her teeth.

"*Mira no mas—pura raza*," she said when she saw us. "*Ay, Jesús me valga*. What vagabond's faces you have."

Sometimes we helped her scrub with shuck brooms and a

bucket of hot water and lye. Then, too, we carried water on shoulder yokes, emptied ash buckets, and brought ice cubes for *tepache*.

"Now we'll eat with the big spoon," Dona Petra promised after all the chores were done.

The Pozole Vendor worked à la Mexicana singing at the top of her lungs. While she cooked *pozole* in a big black *cauela*, we listened to her sing *corridos* that exuded blood and gunpowder and watched Jesús Maria Alley's milling crowds.

Many of the men going past us trudged as if they were exhausted or sick, their bodies stooped as if bent by pain. Where they'd been and where they'd yet to go, we couldn't tell. But many hungary men, broken by suffering, came to the Pozolera's *puesto*. Some, so weary they spoke in a whisper, told her they lived on mesquites, *quelites*, and even *sabandijas*. She never turned them away.

"Money is only a means of capping hunger," she said when she served them. "Eat, and may San Francisco give you his most sacred blessing."

The Pozolera's dark eyes were steady with hope and courage, and to us she was beautiful as an angel of Puebla. Many times this kindly woman told us about the destitute men who came to her *puesto*.

"They are men for whom a day without work is a tragedy— *Ay Madre*, the wind blows colder on them," she said. "Most don't have enough flesh on them for an *albondiga*, and all have a hunger from here to Balleza. May *Nuestro Señor* give them all a good place in the sky *con todo y zapatos*."

After lunch, we camped on a grassy bank near the Guanajuato Bridge where the Parral River was brown and swift and deep with quicksands making little whirlpools on the surface. The river bank was a nice place to be. The sound of the wind in the cottonwoods was like a gentle rain, and doves teetered nimbly on the branches and opened and closed their wings. Beyond the stone bridge, Parral looked like a mirage city with its low-built homes and broad, quiet squares colored by stone-bordered flower beds.

We built a chunk fire on a patch of beaten, grassless earth, and then sat down on the ground with our backs against a big limestone rock. We talked of far-off places and read dog-eared copies of *El Ruedo* and *Box y Lucha* until the first stars appeared and were reflected in the quiet river.

When Memo wasn't poring over boxing and bullfighting magazines, he read poems by Juan de Dios Peza and Manuel Plaza. Their poems inspired him to write poetry too. One poem, about the San José Bakery, I remember especially. This was probably because Jacinto Turrieta, a spindly Southerner with a dark, scowling face, owned the bakery.

Don Chinto Turrieta came from Michoacan and his high-pitched voice was pleasant with the slurred, lilting drawl of Mexico's big harp country. His way of speaking was like a song in our ears. But he was high-strung and when he got mad his breath came with heavy, rasping gasps.

I remember the day Memo printed his poem on the San José Bakery's front window. It was pale and windy with the chilled tang of approaching winter, but Memo was bareheaded and the sleeves of his home-sewn shirt were rolled high on his biceps. With the incontrovertible assurance that characterized him, he stepped up to the window and wrote boldly and legibly. When he finished printing with yellow chalk, he stood back and studied the poem which read:

El que puso este letrero	The man who named this place
No supo lo que ponia	Didn't know what he was doing.
San José fue carpintero	Saint Joseph was a carpenter.
No tuvo panaderia.	He didn't have a bakery.

Chava and I waited to see what would happen. We did not have to wait long. Soon grinning *paisanos* gathered to read the verses. Their laughter filled Noche Triste Street like fresh notes on a musical scale, bringing Don Chinto out to see what the trouble was.

"*¿Tengo monos?*" he snapped petulantly when countrymen smiled at him.

Don Chinto wrinkled his brows together, and read the

poem. Then anger made him double up his fists, and he glared darkly at Memo.

"Son of the bad sleep, I'll make tortillas out of your snout," he shouted. "By the barricades of Guerrero I swear I'll carve a *Viva Mexico* on your face."

But Memo, resolute and composed, remained adamant.

"What I wrote is the truth as God lives," he maintained.

When Don Chinto's tantrum subsided, he rubbed out the poem and then was quiet again. But not long after that he changed the bakery's name to El Suriano.

Now Memo is different. He has taken the holy orders. He wears a black suit, and we don't joke with him any more.

"Good morning, *Padre*," I say to him now.

SUMMER WATER AND SHIRLEY

By Durango Mendoza

It was in the summer that had burned every stalk of corn and every blade of grass and dried up the creek until it only flowed in trickles across the ford below the house where in the pools the boy could scoop up fish in a dishpan.

The boy lived with his mother and his sister, Shirley, and the three smaller children eleven miles from Weleetka, and near Lthwathlee Indian church where it was Eighth Sunday meeting and everyone was there. The boy and his family stayed at the camp house of his dead father's people.

Shirley and her brother, who was two years older and twelve, had just escaped the deacon and were lying on the brown, sun-scorched grass behind the last camp house. They were out of breath and giggled as they peeped above the slope and saw the figure of the deacon, Hardy Eagle, walking slowly toward the church house.

"Boy, we sure out-fooled him, huh?" Shirley laughed lightly and jabbed her elbow in her brother's shaking side. "Whew!" She ran her slim hand over her eyes and squinted at the sky. They both lay back and watched the cloudless sky until the heat in their blood went down and their breath slowed to normal. They lay there on the hot grass until the sun became too much for them.

"Hey, let's go down to the branch and find a pool to wade in, okay?" She had rolled over suddenly and spoke directly into the boy's ear.

"I don't think we better. Mama said to stay around the church grounds."

"Aw, you're just afraid."

"No, it's just that—"

" 'Mama said to stay around the church grounds!' Fraidy-cat, I'll go by myself then." She sat up and looked at him. He didn't move and she sighed. Then she nudged him. "Hey".

43

She nudged him again and assumed a stage whisper. "Looky there! See that old man coming out of the woods?"

The boy looked and saw the old man shuffling slowly through the high Johnson grass between the woods and the clearing for the church grounds. He was very old and still wore his hair in the old way.

"Who is he?" Shirley whispered. "Who is he?"

"I can't tell yet. The heat makes everything blurry." The boy was looking intently at the old man who was moving slowly in the weltering heat through the swaying grass that moved with the sound of light tinsel in the dry wind.

"Let's go sneak through the grass and scare him," Shirley suggested. "I bet that'd make him even run." She moved her arms as if she were galloping and broke down into giggles. "Come on," she said, getting to one knee.

"Wait!" He pulled her back.

"What do you mean, 'wait'? He'll be out of the grass pretty soon and we won't—" She broke off. "What's the matter? What're you doing?"

The boy had started to crawl away on his hands and knees and was motioning for her to follow. "Come on, Shirley," he whispered. "That's old Ansul Middlecreek!"

"Who's *he*?"

"Don't you remember? Mama said he's the one that killed Haskell Day—with witchcraft. He's a *stiginnee*!"

"A *stiginnee*? Aw, you don't believe that, do you? Mama says you can tell them by the way they never have to go go to the toilet, and that's where he's been. Look down there." She pointed to the little unpainted house that stood among the trees.

"I don't care *where* he's been! Come on, Shirley! Look! Oh my gosh! He saw you pointing!"

"I'm coming," she said and followed him quickly around the corner of the camp house.

They sat on the porch. Almost everyone was in for the afternoon service and they felt alone. The wind was hot and it blew from the southwest. It blew past them across the dry fields of yellow weeds that spread before them up to the low hills that wavered in the heat and distance. They could smell the dry harshness of the grass and they felt the porch boards hot underneath them. Shirley bent over and wiped her face with the skirt of her dress.

"Come on," she said. "Let's go down to the creek branch before that deacon comes back." She pulled at his sleeve and they stood up.

"Okay," he said and they skirted the outer camp houses and followed the dusty road to the bridge, stepping from tuft to tuft of scorched grass.

Toward evening and suppertime they climbed out of the dry bed of the branch, over the huge boulders to the road and started for the camp grounds. The sun was in their eyes as they trudged up the steep road from the bridge. They had found no water in the branch so they had gone on down to the creek. For the most part it too was dry.

Suddenly they saw a shadow move into the dust before them. They looked up and saw old Ansul Middlecreek shuffling toward them. His cracked shoes raised little clouds of dust that rose around his ankles and made whispering sounds as he moved along.

"Don't look when you go by," the boy whispered intently, and he pushed her behind him. But as they passed by, Shirley looked up.

"Hey, Ansul Middlecreek," she said cheerfully. "*Henks-chay!*" Then with a swish of her skirt she grabbed her brother and they ran. The old man stopped and the puffs of dust around his feet moved ahead as he grumbled, his face still in shadow because he did not turn around. The two didn't stop until they had reached the first gate. Then they slowed down and the boy scolded his sister all the way to their camp. And all through supper he looked at the dark opening of the door and then at Shirley who sat beside him, helping herself with childish appetite to the heavy, greasy food that was set before her.

"You better eat some," she told her brother. "Next meetin's not 'til next month."

Soon after they had left the table she began to complain that her head hurt and their mother got them ready to go home. They took the two little girls and the baby boy from where they were playing under the arbor and cleaned them up before they started out. Their uncle, George Hulegy, would go with them and carry the biggest girl. The mother carried the other one while the boy struggled in the rear with the baby. Shirley followed morosely behind them all as they started down the road that lay white and pale under the rising moon.

She began to fall further behind and shuffled her bare feet into the warm underlayer of dust. The boy gave to his uncle the sleeping child he carried and took Shirley by the hand, surprised that it was so hot and limp.

"Come on, Shirley, come on. Mama, Shirley's got a fever. Don't walk so fast—we can't keep up. Come on, Shirley," he coaxed. "Hurry."

They turned into their lane and followed it until they were on the little hill above the last stretch of road and started down its rocky slope to the sandy road below. Ahead, the house sat wanly under the stars, and Rey, the dog, came out to greet them, sniffing and wriggling his black body and tail.

George Hulegy and the mother were already on the porch as the boy led his sister into the yard. As they reached the porch they saw the lamp begin to glow orange in the window. Then Shirley took hold of the boy's arm and pointed weakly toward the back yard and the form of the storehouse.

"Look, Sonny! Over there, by the storehouse." The boy froze with fear but he saw nothing. "They were three little men," she said vaguely and then she collapsed.

"Mama!" But as he screamed he saw a great yellow dog with large brown spots jump off the other end of the porch with a click of its heavy nails and disappear into the shadows that led to the creek. The boy could hear the brush rustle and a few pebbles scatter as it went. Rey only whined uneasily and did not even look to where the creature had gone.

"What is it? What's wrong?" The two older persons had come quickly onto the porch and the mother bent immediately to help her daughter.

"Oh, Shirley! George! Help me. Oh gosh! She's burning up. Sonny, put back the covers of the big bed. Quick now!"

They were inside now and the boy spoke.

"She saw dwarfs," he said solemnly and the mother looked at George Hulegy. "And there was a big yellow dog that Rey didn't even see."

"Oh, no, no," the mother wailed and leaned over Shirley who had begun to writhe and moan. "Hush, baby, hush. Mama's here. Hush, baby, your Mama's here." She began to sing softly a very old song while George Hulegy took a lantern from behind the stove.

"I'm going to the creek and get some pebbles where the water still runs," he said. "I have to hurry." He closed the screen quietly behind him and the boy watched him as he disappeared with the swinging lantern through the brush and trees, down into the darkness to the ford. Behind him the mother still sang softly as Shirley's voice began to rise, high and thin like a very small child's. The boy shivered in the heat and sat down in the corner to wait helplessly as he tried not to look at the dark space of the window. He grew stiff and tired trying to control his trembling muscles as they began to jump.

Then George Hulegy came in with some pebbles that still were dripping and they left little wet spots of dark on the floor as he placed them above all the doors and windows throughout the house. Finally he placed three round ones at the foot of the bed where Shirley lay twisting and crying with pain and fever.

The mother had managed to start a small fire in the kitchen stove and told the boy to go out and bring in a few pieces of cook wood from the woodpile. He looked at her and couldn't move. He stood stiff and alert and heard George Hulegy, who was bending close over Shirley, muttering some words that he could not understand. He looked at the door but the sagging screen only reflected the yellow lamplight so that he couldn't see through into the darkness; he froze even tighter.

"Hurry, son!"

He looked at Shirley lying on the bed and moving from side to side.

"Sonny, I have to make Shirley some medicine!" His body shook from a spasm. The mother saw and turned to the door.

"I'll get them," she said.

"Mama!"

She stopped and he barged through the door and found the darkness envelop him. As he fixed his wide-open gaze on the woodpile that faintly reflected the starlight and that of the moon which had risen above the trees, he couldn't look to either side nor could he run. When he reached for the first piece of wood, the hysteria that was building inside him hardened into an aching bitter core. He squeezed the rough cool wood to his chest and felt the fibers press into his bare arms as he staggered toward the house and the two rectangles of light. The closer he came the higher the tension inside him stretched until he could scarcely breathe. Then he was inside again and he sat limply in the corner, light and drained of any support. He could feel nothing except that Shirley was lying in the big feather bed across the room, wailing with hurt and a scalding fever.

His mother was hurrying from the kitchen with a tin cup of grass tea when Shirley began to scream, louder and louder until the boy thought that he would never hear another sound as he stood straight and hard, not leaning at all.

She stopped.

In the silence he saw his mother standing above and behind the lamp, casting a shadow on the ceiling, stopped with fear as they heard the other sound. The little girls had come into the room from their bedroom and were standing whimpering in their nightgowns by the door. The mother signaled and they became still and quiet, their mouths slightly open and their eyes wide. They heard nothing.

Then like a great, beating heart the sound rose steadily until they could smell the heat of a monstrous flesh, raw and hot. Steadily it grew to a gagging, stifling crescendo—then stopped. They heard the click of dog's nails on the porch's wooden planks, and afterwards, nothing. In the complete silence the air became cold for an instant and Shirley was quiet.

It was three days now since Shirley had begun to die and everyone knew now and had given up any hope. Even the white doctor could find nothing wrong and all the old Indians nodded their solemn heads when he went away saying that Shirley would be up in a few days, for now, to them, her manner of death was confirmed. He said to send for him if there was any "real" change. No need to move her—there was nothing wrong—nothing physically wrong, he had said. He could not even feel her raging fever. To him Shirley was only sleeping.

Everyone had accepted that Shirley was going to die and they were all afraid to go near her. "There is evil around her," they said. They even convinced the mother to put her in the back room and close off all light and only open it after three days. She would not die until the third day's night, nor would she live to see the fourth day's dawn. This they could know. A very old woman spoke these words to the mother and she could not disbelieve.

On this third day the boy sat and watched the flies as they crawled over the dirty floor, over the specks and splotches, the dust and crumbs. They buzzed and droned about some drops of water, rubbing their legs against themselves, nibbling, strutting, until the drops dried into meaningless little rings while the hot wind blew softly through the open window, stirring particles of dust from the torn screen. A droplet of sweat broke away from above his eyebrow and ran a crooked rivulet down his temple until he wiped it away. In his emptiness the boy did not want his sister to die.

"Mama?"

"What is it, son?"

"Is Shirley going to die?"

"Yes, son."

He watched her as she stood with her back to him. She moved the heavy skillet away from the direct heat and turned the damper so that the flames would begin to die. She moved automatically, as if faster movement would cause her to breathe in too much of the stifling heat. And as she moved the floor groaned under the shift in weight and her feet made whispering sounds against the sagging boards. The flies still flitted about, mindless and nasty, as the boy looked away from them to his mother.

"Does she have to, Mama?"

"Shirley is dying, son."

Again he saw how the flies went about, unaware of the heat, himself, his mother across the room or that Shirley lay in her silence in the back room. He splashed some more water from his glass and they knew he was there but immediately forgot and settled back to their patternless walking about. And even though the table was clean they walked jerkily among the dishes and inspected his tableware. The boy had lived all his life among these creatures, but now he could not stand their nature.

"Darn flies!"

"Well, we won't have to worry when cold weather gets here," she said. "Now go call the kids and eat. I want to get some sewing done this afternoon."

He said nothing and watched her as she went into the other room. He went to the door and leaned out to call the small children. Then he slipped quietly into the back room and closed the door behind him, fastening the latch in the dark. The heat was almost choking and he blinked away the saltiness that stung his eyes. He stood by the door until he could see a little better. High above his head a crack in the shingles filtered down a star of daylight and he stepped to the bed that stood low against the rough planks of the wall. There were no flies in this room and there was no sound.

The boy sat down on a crate and watched the face of his

sister emerge from the gloom where she lay. Straining his eyes, he finally saw the rough army blanket rise and fall, but so slight was the movement that when his eyes lost their focus he could not see it and he quickly put out his hand, but stopped. Air caught in his throat and he stifled a cough, still letting his hand hover over the motionless face. Then he touched the smooth forehead and jerked his hand away as if he had been burned.

He sat and watched his sister's well-formed profile and saw how the skin of the nose and forehead had become taut and dry and now gleamed pale and smooth like old ivory in the semi-darkness. A smell like that of hot wood filled the room, but underneath it the boy could smell the odor of something raw, something evil—something that was making Shirley die.

The boy sat on the empty crate in the darkness through the late afternoon and did not answer when his mother called him. He knew that she would not even try the door to this room. He waited patiently for his thoughts to come together, not moving in the lifeless heat, and let the sweat flow from his body. He smelled the raw smell, and when it became too strong he touched the smooth, round pebbles that had come from the creek where it still flowed, and the smell receded.

For many hours he sat, and then he got up and took down the heavy blanket that had covered the single window and let the moonlight fall across the face of his sister through the opening. He began to force his thoughts to remember, to relive every living moment of his life and every part that Shirley had lived in it with him. And then he spoke softly, saying what they had done, and how they would do again what they had done because he had not given up, for he was alive, and she was alive, and they had lived and would *still* live. And so he prayed to his will and forced his will out through his thoughts and spoke softly his words and was not afraid to look out through the window into the darkness through which came the coolness of the summer night. He smelled its scents and let them touch his flesh and come to rest around the "only sleeping" face of his sister. He stood, watching, listening, living.

Then they came, silently, dark-bellied clouds drifting up from the south, and the wind, increasing, swept in the heavy scent of the approaching storm. Lightning flashed over the low, distant hills and the clouds closed quietly around the moon as the thunder rumbled and the heavy drops began to fall, slowly at first, then irregularly, then increasing to a rhythmic rush of noise as the gusts of wind forced the rain in vertical waves across the shingled roof.

Much later, when the rain had moved ahead and the room became chilly when the water began to drip from the roof and the countless leaves, the boy slipped out of his worn denim pants and took off his shirt and lay down beside his sister. She felt him and woke up.

"You just now gettin' to bed?" she asked. "It's pretty late for that, ain't it?"

"No, Shirley," he said. "Go on back to sleep. It'll be morning pretty soon, and when it gets light again we'll go see how high the water's risen in the creek."

He pulled the cover over him and drew his bare arms beneath the blanket and pulled it over their shoulders as he turned onto his side. Lying thus, he could see in the darkness the even darker shapes of the trees and the storehouse his father had built.

THE WOMAN IN THE GREEN HOUSE

A Story
By Durango Mendoza

He came on horseback, riding slowly up the dirt road from the corner, his old saddle creaking and his body swaying slightly with the gait. The horse's hooves chipped rough crescents into the hard earth beneath the layer of dust with clopping sounds, and it began to plod slower until it stopped before the small green tar paper house.

The sky was high and cloudless above, and the sparse trees and few houses stood quiet and submissive under the afternoon. The man's heavy shoulders sagged forward a little, and the wide-brimmed hat that he wore pulled to one side shadowed his face. It was a broad square face, and the sunlight off the road made it, reddish-brown already, seem even more flushed. He spoke gruffly to his horse, and they started again along the road toward town.

Inside the house the woman moved away from the window and sat down on the edge of the bed. A hot breath of air lifted the filmy curtains above the bed, and she looked down on her children. They were spread apart on the sheeted mattress, and their small faces and limbs glowed with warm dampness.

She picked up a towel and flicked away some flies come to settle and continued to wave it slowly over her children. After a time she lay down beside the youngest who was three and rested her head on her arm. Instinctively, the little boy pushed against her. She spoke softly and rubbed his damp hair back from his forehead.

When they woke up, she sent them out into the yard to play, and soon they disappeared among the weeds toward the old abandoned barn where they often played. The woman moved around the two rooms and gathered up clothing to mend. And all the rest of the afternoon she sat near the door and worked alone. Periodically one of the children would come puffing up to the door wanting water, and would linger only for moments after drinking to lean against her lap to see what she was doing. Then she would become restless and pace around the rooms as if looking for something.

It had been bad at first, and later it seemed to have become less important, but now she could not help but remember, and she waited in anticipation. On some nights she began to let her youngest nurse, although she had no milk to give. She became conscious of her clothes—not their appearance, but how they felt upon her body. Then one day she walked into town without underwear, but had become ashamed and fled back to her house where she spent the rest of the day alternately forgetting her children and then suddenly turning upon them and hugging them to her.

Evening came thick and warm and settled its darkness over the small town and filled the woman's house. The dust upon the roads began to cool, and its harsh daytime odor became richer. The trees and grass seemed to relax, and the sky was the last to darken. Lights came on reluctantly along the sparse streets, and the stars grew brighter and began to stare or glimmer. Atop the water tower the red blinker came on, although few airplanes ever passed and none so low.

The woman filled the wash tub on the back stoop and called her children from the supper table to bathe them. She stood them each in turn in the tub and scrubbed their small bodies as they laughed and splashed or cried when soap got in their eyes. Then they stood around wrapped in towels until she emptied the tub along the fence line and hurried before her into the lamp-lit house. She dressed them in clean underwear and carried the little boy to the bed as the other two scrambled to beat them there.

The night air was still hot, and she fanned them lightly with a piece of cloth as they talked of childish things until they began to mumble and drowse, wanting to stay awake but unable to do so. The youngest had already fallen asleep against his mother and heard nothing, as none of them did except the mother when the man on horseback paused again before their house and then moved on into the darkness.

Above the thin rippled clouds the moon was like a luminous stone in clear water, shining its pale wash into the two rooms of the woman's house.

After the war the man had driven tractor at twenty dollars a week for the man who owned the hardware store and much of the land near the town. He worked alone and could be seen riding the machine slowly back and forth across the wide fields, plowing, discing, and planting throughout the long hot days. He sat slumped a little in the seat, wearing a rumpled dirty hat cocked to one side and grasping the back of the seat to brace himself as he turned to look back over the furrows. He thought often of the war but said little about it or anything else. In the evening he went home to his old mother in the country.

One day as he struggled silently in the heat with a jammed attachment, a chain snapped and lashed him across the forehead, and in the red and black of his pain the war seemed again to crush upon him. It seemed also that the devil laughed beside him and became the one who had struck him.

They found him later lying upon the broken ground with his blood dried and dark upon his face and soaked into the loose earth.

He could not work for a time after the accident, and he rode often by the little green house and puzzled over the woman who lived there. As did most Chicanos in the community, he knew the basic situation of every other Chicano adult and their families. He knew that this woman and her three sisters had gone away to the city and had returned with a child apiece out of wedlock, except for the woman, who had married and had had three children. He knew also that they lived on welfare, for he had seen one day the woman behind the stores grasping the potatoes that her children discovered among the discarded crates and burlap sacks. He had seen how the children acted as if they were playing a game, but what pleased him most was the woman as she stood among them. After that, he watched for them and saw them often along the streets or at church meetings.

Many times as he rode, the war entered his mind and

blurred the minutes until the horse would slow down, then stop, and his big shoulders would seem to hunch forward, and the healing scar on his forehead would tighten with pain.

One day he appeared to the woman before her house, sitting on his horse in the heat and sun like a drooping statue. He heard a screen door slap shut and later saw her standing above him.

You are sick, she was telling him. Come inside. It is the heat and your riding and the cut upon your forehead. Come inside.

She had watched him lying there on his back, and her eyes hid what she thought, if she thought at all, and her posture was timid. Almost reluctantly, she reached out and touched him. She stroked him and felt him begin to swell when he woke up with the war still vague behind his eyes. And then they were inside the little green house, and almost automatically he pulled her upon him.

When the woman woke up, the man still slept. The heat in the room was close, and when she sat up on the edge of the bed, she saw her youngest sitting on a chair with his legs hanging off the side, looking at her through the lattice backing. She started to pick him up, but he slipped away from her and ran outdoors. She saw him through the screen with his small arms bent and his hands held up shoulder high, trotting in the sunlight toward the high grass and the old barn.

To get married they traveled to a town beyond the low surrounding hills and left the children with a friend of the woman's to go to the courthouse. But the youngest would not stop crying and clung to his mother when she tried to leave until finally she diverted him long enough to get away. And when he found out that he had been deceived he cried even louder and would not be approached.

Finally the other children took him outside with them where they were coasting down a hill on a tricycle. They tried to coax him to try it, but he wouldn't until they all struggled to put him on. Then, speeding down the sidewalk hill with the others screaming and laughing beside him, his crying changed to laughter without a pause between them. And when the new couple kissed in the mornings, he stood with the other two and giggled shyly, too. And like them, he was glad when the man left for work. But when he returned at dusk, they became quiet and avoided him.

Those kids, the man told the woman one night while they were in bed, they don't want me here.

Oh, she said, but they aren't used to having a father. Their daddy—

You shut up about their daddy, the man said. I don't want to hear nothing about the son of a bitch.

All right, said the woman, and that night she dreamed of the children's daddy. She dreamed of the times they had had.

In the night the three little ones played in the darkness on their bed, quietly, stopped every so often to listen to the man's rumbling voice as he spoke of the war to their mother. When he was loud, they looked at each other in the darkness.

When fall came the woman began to swell and grew larger through the winter. The children would gather around and feel the tiny kicks in her belly. The man began to help the children dress and wash in the mornings. The little boy thought it was strange. The oldest would become stiff when the man approached her, and the middle boy said nothing and tried to help himself as much as possible.

One morning the children woke up in a cold house. They felt immediately that no one was home, but they didn't stir from the bed. Instead they began to exhale their breath to make round whistling noises. Then sunlight touched the frosted panes, and they saw the old man crouching in the corner. He had been watching them. His long chapped hands hung over his knees and flapped once when he saw that they had seen him. They could not remember ever having seen him before.

The oldest spoke first: Where's Mama, she said.

Where Mama, said the youngest. Where Mama, ol' man.

The old man unfolded himself, but didn't straighten when he stood. Instead he shuffled into the other room where their mother's bed was. They heard him open the door and felt the walls tremble when it slammed. The yellow jewels of sunlight danced in the window frost. As time passed, the frost began to fade and the wind began to blow.

A fat woman came out of the other room. It just wasn't time, she said after she told them.

I felt it kick, said the middle boy.

Yes, said the girl.

But your daddy will be back pretty soon and take you to see your mama.

There, daddy, said the little boy when the man came to the door and entered the house.

The fat woman told him: Your kids are all ready to go see their mother now.

Those ain't my kids, he told her, and went on into the other room.

There, daddy, said the little boy.

You hush your mouth, the girl whispered fiercely. You hear? You just hush up.

The little boy began to whimper, and the fat woman took him on her knee. After a while he pressed against her, and she sat with him there. He looked at his sister and made a face. Suddenly she began to cry, and he jerked and became afraid. But the fat woman held him closer and called him poor baby, and he felt better. The middle boy said nothing and held onto the woman's sleeve and watched his sister standing slumped near the door with her coat on.

THE PASSING

A Story
By Durango Mendoza

Ever since Mama married Miguel we had lived in the country. He had built a tall, single-walled, two-room house on the land of his family above the big bend of Fish Creek, and it stood there, lean and unpainted among the trees back from the road. Even after Mama and I came to live there it remained unpainted. It was built of unfinished sawmill planks and had two stovepipe chimneys sticking through its green Sheetrock roof. Right across the road was the Indian church.

The house stood above a steep, boulder-littered and heavily wooded slope and the creek that ran below. I had developed a swimming hole there, and across the creek on the wooded slopes I played at hunting. It had been almost two years since we had settled there, and I had already explored the surrounding countryside for miles in winter and summer so that I now usually stayed close to the house. Summer had grown old, and I was becoming restless.

One evening as I played cars with pieces of wood in the dust beside the house, Mama saw the boy coming along the road. She stopped gathering the clothes from the line and took the clothes-pins from her mouth. I looked after her gaze and beyond. Through the shadows and trees I saw how the road curved and disappeared quickly into the dusk and woods. I looked back to her when she spoke.

"Sonny, there goes Joe Willow," she said. Then she paused and put the shirt she was holding into the basket at her feet. "He sure does work hard. I hope old Jimmy Bear and Fannie appreciate it, those two."

She shook her head and began to gather the rest of the clothes. I sat back on my heels and wondered at the tone of her voice. I had never really noticed Joe Willow before, but I knew the rest of the family from church meetings. And once I had seen where they lived.

It was about a mile beyond the curve, far back from the road and reached by a rutted drive that skirted the Indian graveyard. I knew the graveyard because near it were some pecan trees from which I gathered the nuts each fall. Their house was very old and unpainted. It sat low and gray under a group of large blackjack oaks and within a grassless yard that was pressed closely by the thick, surrounding woods.

Joe Willow's mother, Fannie, was a short, round woman with mottled brown skin and a high, shiny forehead that wrinkled when she laughed. Jimmy Bear was her second husband, and they used to pass our house often, going to the beer joint in town or to stomp dances. They had once driven an old Dodge, but it no longer ran, and it now sat lopsided and windowless among the weeds beside their lane. Jimmy Bear was a skinny man, but he had a round, protruding belly and wore his belt under it so that it looked as if he carried a basketball inside. He had gaps in his teeth and a rough guttural laugh and walked with a shuffle. Mama told me that Fannie had once had land money but that they had long since used it up.

I remembered the young worker's brother and sister; his sister because of what she had once said when she met me on the path to the toilet at church. "Been to the shit-house?" she had asked. I only knew his brother on sight though, and noticed that he always seemed to keep his black boots shiny and his long hair greased. Mama said he went with Jimmy Bear and Fannie to stomp dances.

The next evening when the young worker passed the gate I got up and ran to hang on it as I watched him pass on up the road. The sun, being low and to his back, sent a long finger of shadow ahead of him. I could hear the crunch and whisper of his footsteps between the squeaks of the bucket he carried until they began to fade with the coming of the breeze through the tall grass alongside the road. The bucket creaked faintly and the breeze dropped for a moment.

I called to him.

"Hello, Joe Willow," I said.

In the stillness my voice carried, and he turned, his shadow pointing into the woods, and lifted his hand. He squinted into the sun and smiled. I waved, and he turned back up the road and soon faded against the shadow and trees.

I watched where the road curved into the woods and knew that to the right the land dropped down to the part of the creek I seldom visited because I had heard that some wolves had been seen there. Beyond it the woods stretched for miles, and the creek merged finally with the river. I remembered once finding a pair of women's underpants, rotten and clinging to some brush near the water there, and scattered among the leaves and twigs were some old, empty beer bottles. The air always seemed heavy there, and the stillness under the drooping trees disturbed me.

I sat on the gate for a while until a deeper darkness crept from the woods and began to fuse with the trees. I heard the trees begin to sigh and settle down for the night, the lonely cooing of a dove, and from somewhere across the creek the hoot of an owl. Then I hurried back to the house in the new coolness and stood near my mom for a while as she moved about the warm iron cookstove preparing supper.

Almost every evening of August that summer the young Indian passed along the road in front of our gate. I saw him several times a week as he came up from the bridge, always carrying a small, empty lard bucket whose handle squeaked faintly as he passed by and out of sight. He walked like someone who is used to walking, slowly, without spirit, but with the strength seen in a young workhorse.

He would come up from the hill, the sun to his back, and his skin, a very reddish brown, would be covered with a fine dust, making his brows appear lighter and thicker than they were. His hair was cut short, but it lacked the uniformity of a regular barber shop haircut, and he wore no hat.

Many evenings I swung back and forth on the gate and waited for him to come by. I had no brothers or sisters as yet, but Mama was expecting Miguel's first child before spring. Miguel was my stepfather, and since he said very little to me and because I couldn't be around Mama all the time, I waited for Joe Willow to pass by, although I seldom spoke except to

reply to his greetings. Often I didn't even show myself at all
and only sat among the grapevines next to the gate until the
darkness sent me home.

I remembered one of the last times I saw him. It was early
in September, and I was sitting on the gate watching the sun
caught on the treetops, noticing how the leaves looked like
embers across its face as it settled into them, when Joe Willow
appeared like a moving post upon the road. I had just gotten
down from the gate and sat on the large rock that propped up
our mailbox when Miguel called for me to eat supper. Instead,
I began to sift sand into little conical piles as I waited. I
looked down the road past the young worker to where the sun
had fallen behind the trees. It looked trapped. The wind was
very soft and smelled of smoke and dust. A few birds chuckled
above me in the trees, and the insects of the evening buzzed
in the weeds below.

Miguel called again and I looked up.

"Howdy, Joe Willow," I said. "You coming home from
work?"

He stopped and grinned.

"That's right," he said. He leaned on the mailbox, and we
said nothing for a few moments until he spoke again. "You're
Miguel's boy, aren't you?"

"Huh-uh. I belong to Rosa."

"Oh." He squatted down. "You know what? I'm the same
way. Everybody calls me Jimmy Bear's boy, but I'm not.
He's not my daddy."

We both shifted around and watched where the sun had
gone down.

"You see what happens when the sun goes down?" He
pointed to the evening star and motioned toward the other
stars that had appeared in the east. "When the daddy goes to
bed, all the little children come out." His teeth gleamed in the
gathering darkness, and I smiled, too.

We had watched the stars for only a moment when Miguel
called again.

"You better get on home," Joe Willow said. "That's your
daddy calling you."

"I'm Rosa's boy," I said.

"I know," he said, "but you better get on back." He looked up again at the deepening sky and laughed softly. "I'll see you some other time—'Rosa's boy.' "

Mama and Miguel were already eating when I stepped quietly into the kitchen. I washed my hands and climbed into my chair. Miguel frowned.

"You hear me callin' you?"

I nodded and looked at Mama.

"Eat now, Sonny," she said.

"He better mind me," Miguel said.

After September came, I started to school and no longer saw Joe Willow pass our gate. One day I asked Mama about him, and she said that he had gone to the free Indian boarding school in the northern part of the state, just south of the Kansas line. And it was when winter was just melting into spring, a few weeks after Mama had returned from the hospital with my baby brother, that I remembered him again.

Just before supper Miguel came into the kitchen, stamping the bits of dirty snow from his overshoes.

"Jimmy Bear's boy's been killed by the Santa Fe train at Chillocco," he said. "But they say they ain't sure how it happened." He warmed his hands over the stove and sat down.

I looked at Mama. She said nothing and rocked the baby. On the stove the beans bubbled softly, and their smell filled the room. I watched the lid on the pot jiggle as the steam escaped, and I heard the wind rattle gently at the window. Miguel struggled with his overshoes and continued:

"Fannie tol' me a railroad man was down the first thing and said they was willin' to pay." He grunted and shoved the overshoes near the stove. "The funeral's Tuesday," he said.

Mama nodded and handed me the baby and got up to put the food on the table. She touched my head, and we sat down to supper.

At the funeral Joe Willow's family cried, and old Fannie even fainted at the grave site when they started to cover him. Jimmy Bear had to struggle to keep her from falling. The dirt sounded on the wooden vault, and the little houses over the older graves looked gray and damp with the people standing among them. I went over to the pecan trees and kicked among the damp mulch looking for good nuts, but I couldn't find any.

That evening after supper I stepped out onto the back stoop to go to the bathroom, and the yellow lamplight behind me threw my shadow onto the patches of snow and earth, enclosing it in the rectangle that the doorway formed. I looked up. The spotty clouds looked like bits of melting snow pressed into the darkness, and the stars were out, sprinkled into the stillness beyond. The black trees swayed, and the cold wind was familiar.

Behind me Mama moved around the kitchen, and I heard the chink and gentle clatter of the plates and pans as she put those things away. I shivered. And I knew that soon, as it did every spring, the clouds would come and it would begin to rain, a cold, heavy drizzle, and the land would turn to mud.

SÁNCHEZ

A Story
By Richard Dokey

That summer tl e son of Juan Sánchez went to work for the Flotill Cannery in Stockton. Juan drove with him to the valley in the old Ford.

While they drove, the boy, whose name was Jesús, told him of the greatness of the cannery, of the great aluminum buildings, the marvelous machines, and the belts of cans that never stopped running. He told him of the building on one side of the road where the cans were made and how the cans ran in a metal tube across the road to the cannery. He described the food machines, the sanitary precautions. He laughed when he spoke of the labeling. His voice was serious about the money.

When they got to Stockton, Jesús directed him to the central district of town, the skid row where the boy was to live while he worked for the Flotill. It was a cheap hotel on Center Street. The room smelled. There was a table with one chair. The floor was stained like the floor of a public urinal and the bed was soiled, as were the walls. There were no drapes on the windows. A pall spread out from the single light bulb overhead that was worked with a length of grimy string.

"I will not stay much in the room," Jesús said, seeing his father's face. "It is only for sleep. I will be working overtime, too. There is also the entertainment."

Jesús led him from the room and they went out into the street. Next to the hotel there was a vacant lot where a building had stood. The hole which was left had that recent, peculiar look of uprootedness. There were the remains of the foundation, the broken flooring, and the cracked bricks of tired red to which the gray blotches of mortar clung like dried phlegm. But the ground had not yet taken on the opaqueness of wear that the air and sun give it. It gleamed

65

dully in the light and held to itself where it had been torn, as earth does behind a plow. Juan studied the hole for a time; then they walked up Center Street to Main, passing other empty lots, and then moved east toward Hunter Street. At the corner of Hunter and Main a wrecking crew was at work. An iron ball was suspended from the end of a cable and a tall machine swung the ball up and back and then whipped it forward against the building. The ball was very thick-looking, and when it struck the wall the building trembled, spurted dust, and seemed to cringe inward. The vertical lines of the building had gone awry. Juan shook each time the iron struck the wall.

"They are tearing down the old buildings," Jesús explained. "Redevelopment," he pronounced. "Even my building is to go someday."

Juan looked at his son. "And what of the men?" he asked. "Where do the men go when there are no buildings?"

Jesús, who was a head taller than his father, looked down at him and then shrugged in that Mexican way, the head descending and cocking while the shoulders rise as though on puppet strings. "*Quien sabe?*"

"And the large building there?" Juan said, looking across the rows of parked cars in Hunter Square. "The one whose roof rubs the sky. Of what significance?"

"That is the new courthouse," Jesús said.

"There are no curtains on the windows."

"They do not put curtains on such windows," Jesús explained.

"No," sighed Juan, "that is true."

They walked north on Hunter past the new Bank of America and entered an old building. They stood to one side of the entrance. Jesús smiled proudly and inhaled the stale air.

"This is the entertainment," he said.

Juan looked about. A bar was at his immediate left, and a bald man in a soiled apron stood behind it. Beyond the bar there were many thick-wooded tables covered with green material. Men crouched over them and cone-shaped lights hung low from the ceiling casting broad cones of light downward upon the men and tables. Smoke drifted and rolled in the light and pursued the men when they moved quickly. There was the breaking noise of balls striking together, the hard wooden rattle of the cues in the racks upon the wall, the humming slither of the scoring disks along the loose wires overhead, the explosive cursing of the men. The room was warm and dirty. Juan shook his head.

"I have become proficient at the game," Jesús said.

"This is the entertainment," Juan said, still moving his head.

Jesús turned and walked outside. Juan followed. The boy pointed across the parked cars past the courthouse to a marquee on Main Street. "There are also motion pictures," Jesús said.

Juan had seen a movie as a young man working in the fields near Fresno. He had understood no English then. He sat with his friends in the leather seats that had gum under the arms and watched the images move upon the white canvas. The images were dressed in expensive clothes. There was laughing and dancing. One of the men did kissing with two very beautiful women, taking turns with each when the other was absent. This had embarrassed Juan, the embracing and unhesitating submission of the women with so many unfamiliar people to watch. Juan loved his wife, was very tender and gentle with her before she died. He never went to another motion picture, even after he had learned English, and this kept him from the Spanish films as well.

"We will go to the cannery now," Jesús said, taking his father's arm. "I will show you the machines."

Juan permitted himself to be led away, and they moved back past the bank to where the men were destroying the building. A ragged hole, like a wound, had been opened in the wall. Juan stopped and watched. The iron ball came forward tearing at the hole, enlarging it, exposing the empty interior space that had once been a room. The floor of the room teetered at a precarious angle. The wood was splintered and very dry in the noon light.

"I do not think I will go to the cannery," Juan said.

The boy looked at his father like a child who has made a toy out of string and bottle caps only to have it ignored.

"But it is honorable work," Jesús said, suspecting his father. "And it pays well."

"Honor," Juan said. "Honor is a serious matter. It is not a question of honor. You are a man now. All that is needed is a room and a job at the Flotill. Your father is tired, that is all."

"You are disappointed," Jesús said, hanging his head.

"No," Juan said. "I am beyond disappointment. You are my son. Now you have a place in the world. You have the Flotill."

Nothing more was said, and they walked to the car. Juan got in behind the wheel. Jesús stood beside the door, his arms at his sides, the fingers spread. Juan looked up at him. The boy's eyes were big.

"You are my son," Juan said, "and I love you. Do not have disappointment. I am not of the Flotill. Seeing the machines would make it worse. You understand, *niño*?"

"*Sí*, Papa," Jesús said. He put a hand on his father's shoulder.

"It is a strange world, *niñito*," Juan said.

"I will earn money. I will buy a red car and visit you. All in Twin Pines will be envious of the son of Sánchez, and they will say that Juan Sánchez has a son of purpose."

"Of course, Jesús *mío*," Juan said. He bent and placed his lips against the boy's hand. "I will look for the bright car. I will write regardless." He smiled, showing yellowed teeth. "Goodbye, *querido*," he said. He started the car, raced the engine once too high, and drove off up the street.

When Juan Sánchez returned to Twin Pines, he drove the old Ford to the top of Bear Mountain and pushed it over. He then proceeded systematically to burn all that was of importance to him, all that was of nostalgic value, and all else that meant nothing in itself, like the extra chest of drawers he had kept after his wife's death, the small table in the bedroom, and the faded mahogany stand in which he kept his pipe and tobacco and which sat next to the stuffed chair in the front room. He broke all the dishes, cups, plates, discarded all the cooking and eating utensils in the same way. The fire rose in the blue wind carrying dust wafers of ash in quick, breathless spirals and then released them in a panoply of diluted smoke, from which they drifted and spun and fell like burnt snow. The forks, knives, and spoons became very black with a flaky crust of oxidized metal. Then Juan burned his clothing, all that was unnecessary, and the smoke dampened and took on a thick smell. Finally he threw his wife's rosary into the flames. It was a cheap one, made of wood, and disappeared immediately. He went into his room then and lay down on the bed. He went to sleep.

When he woke, it was dark and cool. He stepped outside, urinated, and then returned, shutting the door. The darkness was like a mammoth held breath, and he felt very awake listening to the beating of his heart. He would not be able to sleep now, and so he lay awake thinking.

He thought of his village in Mexico, the baked white clay of the small houses spread like little forts against the stillness of the bare mountains, the men with their great wide hats, their wide, white pants, and their naked, brown-skinned feet, splayed against the fine dust of the road. He saw the village cistern and the women all so big and slow, always with child, enervated by the earth and the unbearable sun, the enervation passing into their very wombs like the acceptance, slow, silent blood. The men walked bent as though carrying the air or sky, slept against the buildings in the shade like old dogs, ate dry, hot food that dried them inside and seemed to bake the moisture from the flesh, so that the men and women while still young had faces like eroded fields and fingers like stringy, empty stream beds. It was a hard land. It took the life of his father and mother before he was twelve and the life of his aunt, with whom he then lived, before he was sixteen.

When he was seventeen he went to Mexicali because he had heard much of America and the money to be obtained there. They took him in a truck with other men to work in the fields around Bakersfield, then in the fields near Fresno. On his return to Mexicali he met La Belleza, as he came to call her: loveliness. He married her when he was nineteen and she only fifteen. The following year she had a baby girl. It was stillborn and the birth almost killed her, for the doctor said the passage was oversmall. The doctor cautioned him (warned him, really) La Belleza could not have children and live, and he went outside into the moonlight and wept.

He had heard much of the liveliness of the Sierra Nevada above what was called the Mother Lode, and because he feared the land, believed almost that it possessed the power to kill him—as it had killed his mother and father, his aunt, was, in fact, slow killing so many of his people—he wanted to run away from it to the high white cold of the California mountains, where he believed his heart would grow, his bood run and, perhaps, the passage of La Belleza might open. Two years later he was taken in the trucks to Stockton in the San Joaquin Valley to pick tomatoes, and he saw the Sierra Nevada above the Mother Lode.

It was from a distance, of course, and in the summer, so that there was no snow. But when he returned he told La Belleza about the blueness of the mountains in the warm, still dawn, the extension of them, the aristocracy of their unmoving height, and that they were only fifty miles away from where he had stood.

He worked very hard now and saved his money. He took La Belleza back to his village, where he owned the white clay house of his father. It was cheaper to live there while he waited, fearing the sun, the dust, and the dry, airless silence, for the money to accumulate. That fall La Belleza became pregnant again by an accident of passion and the pregnancy was very difficult. In the fifth month the doctor—who was an atheist—said that the baby would have to be taken or else the mother would die. The village priest, a very loud, dramatic man—an educated man who took pleasure in striking a pose—proclaimed the wrath of God in the face of such sacrilege. It was the child who must live, the priest cried. The pregnancy must go on. There was the immortal soul of the child to consider. But Juan decided for the atheist doctor, who did take the child. La Belleza lost much blood. At one point her heart had stopped beating. When the child was torn from its mother and Juan saw that it was a boy, he ran out of the clay house of his father and up the dusty road straight into a hideous red moon. He cursed the earth, the sky. He cursed his village, himself, the soulless indifference of the burnt mountains. He cursed God.

Juan was very afraid now, and though it cost more money, he had himself tied by the atheist doctor so that he could never again put the life of La Belleza in danger, for the next time, he knew with certainty, would kill her.

The following summer he went again on the trucks to the San Joaquin Valley. The mountains were still there, high and blue in the quiet dawn, turned to a milky pastel by the heat swirls and haze of midday. Sometimes at night he stepped outside the shacks in which the men were housed and faced the darkness. It was tragic to be so close to what you wanted, he would think, and be unable to possess it. So strong was the feeling in him, particularly during the hot, windless evenings, that he sometimes went with the other men into Stockton, where he stood on the street corners of skid row and talked, though he did not get drunk on cheap wine or go to the whores, as did the other men. Nor did he fight.

They rode in old tilted trucks covered with canvas and sat on rude benches staring out over the slats of the tail gate. The white glare of headlights crawled up and lay upon them, waiting to pass. They stared over the whiteness. When the lights swept out and by, the glass of the side windows shone. Behind the windows sometimes there would be the ghost flash of an upturned face, before the darkness clamped shut. Also, if one of the men had a relative who lived in the area, there was the opportunity to ride in a car.

He had done so once. He had watched the headlights of the car pale, then whiten the back of one of the trucks. He saw the faces of the men turned outward and the looks on the faces that seemed to float upon the whiteness of the light. The men sat forward, arms on knees, and looked over the

glare into the darkness. After that he always rode in the
trucks.

When he returned to his village after that season's harvest,
he knew they could wait no longer. He purchased a dress of
silk for La Belleza and in a secondhand store bought an
American suit for himself. He had worked hard, sold his
father's house, saved all his money, and on a bright day in
early September they crossed the border at Mexicali and
caught the Greyhound for Fresno.

Juan got up from his bed to go outside. He stood looking
up at the stars. The stars were pinned to the darkness,
uttering little flickering cries of light, and as always he was
moved by the nearness and profusion of their agony. His
mother had told him the stars were a kind of purgatory in
which souls burned in cold, silent repentance. He had wondered after her death if the earth too were not a star burning
in loneliness, and he could never look at them later without
thinking this and believing that the earth must be the bright-
est of all stars. He walked over to the remains of the fire.
A dull heat came from the ashes and a column of limp smoke
rose and then bent against the night wind. He studied the
ashes for a time and then looked over the tall pine shapes to
the southern sky. It was there all right. He could feel the dry
char of its heat, that deeper, dryer burning. He imagined it,
of course. But it was there nevertheless. He went back into
the cabin and lay down, but now his thoughts were only of
La Belleza and the beautiful Sierra Nevada.

From Fresno all the way up the long valley to Stockton
they had been full with pride and expectation. They had
purchased oranges and chocolate bars and they ate them
laughing. The other people on the bus looked at them, shook
their heads, and slept or read magazines. He and La Belleza
gazed out the window at the land.

In Stockton they were helped by a man named Eugenio
Mendez. Juan had met him while picking tomatoes in the
delta. Eugenio had eight children and a very fat but very
kind and tolerant wife named Anilla. He had helped them
find a cheap room off Center Street, where they stayed while

determining their next course of action. Eugenio had access to a car, and it was he who drove them finally to the mountains.

It was a day like no other day in his life: to be sitting in the car with La Belleza, to be in this moving car with his Belleza heading straight toward the high, lovely mountains. The car traveled from the flatness of the valley into the rolling brown swells of the foothills, where hundreds of deciduous and ever-green oaks grew, their puffballs shapes like still pictures of exploding holiday rockets, only green, but spreading up and out and then around and down in nearly perfect canopies. At Jackson the road turned and began an immediate, constant climb upward.

It was as though his dream about it had materialized. He had never seen so many trees, great with dignity: pines that had gray bark twisted and stringy like hemp; others whose bark resembled dry, flat ginger cookies fastened with black glue about a drum, and others whose bark pulled easily away; and those called redwoods, standing stiff and tall, amber-hued with straight rolls of bark as thick as his fist, flinging out high above great arms of green. And the earth, rich red, as though the blood of scores of Indians had just flowed there and dried. Dark patches of shadow stunned with light, blue flowers, orange flowers, birds, even deer. They saw them all on that first day.

"*¿A dónde vamos?*" Eugenio had asked. "Where are we going?"

"*Bellísima,*" Juan replied. "Into much loveliness."

They did not reach Twin Pines that day. But on their return a week later they inquired in Jackson about the opportunity of buying land or a house in the mountains. The man, though surprised, told them of the sawmill town of Twin Pines, where there were houses for sale.

Their continued luck on that day precipitated the feeling in Juan that it was indeed the materialization of a dream. He had been able in all those years to save two thousand dollars, and a man had a small shack for sale at the far edge of town. He looked carefully at Juan, at La Belleza and Eugenio and said, "One thousand dollars," believing they could never begin to possess such a sum. When Juan handed him the money, the man was so struck that he made out a bill of sale. Juan Sanchez and his wife had their home in the Sierra.

When Juan saw the cabin close up, he knew the man had stolen their money. It was small, the roof slanted to one side, the door would not close evenly. The cabin was gradually falling downhill. But it was theirs and he could, with work, repair it. Hurriedly they drove back to Jackson, rented a truck, bought some cheap furniture and hauled it back to the cabin. When they had moved in, Juan brought forth a bottle of whiskey and for the first time in his life proceeded to get truly drunk.

Juan was very happy with La Belleza. She accepted his philosophy completely, understood his need, made it her own. In spite of the people of the town, they created a peculiar kind of joy. And anyway Juan had knowledge about the people.

Twin Pines had been founded, he learned, by one Benjamin Carter, who lived with his daughter in a magnificent house on the hill overlooking town. This Benjamin Carter was a very wealthy man. He had come to the mountains thirty years before to save his marriage, for he had been poor once and loved when he was poor, but then he grew very rich because of oil discovered on his father's Ohio farm and he went away to the city and became incapable of love in the pursuit of money and power. When he at last married the woman whom he had loved, a barrier had grown between them, for Ben Carter had changed but the woman had not. Then the woman became ill and Ben Carter promised her he would take her West, all the way West away from the city so that it could be as it had been in the beginning of their love. But the woman was with child. And so Ben Carter rushed to the California mountains, bought a thousand acres of land, and hurried to build his house before the rain and snows came. He hired many men and the house was completed, except for the interior work and the furnishings. All that winter men he had hired worked in the snow to finish the house while Ben Carter waited with his wife in the city. When it was early spring they set out for California, Ben Carter, his wife, and the doctor, who strongly advised against the rough train trip and the still rougher climb by horse and wagon from Jackson to the house. But the woman wanted the child born properly, so they went. The baby came the evening of their arrival at the house, and the woman died all night having it. It was this Ben Carter who lived with that daughter now in the great house on the hill, possessing her to the point, it was said about his madness, that he had murdered a young man who had shown interest in her.

Juan learned all this from a Mexican servant who had worked at the great house from the beginning, and when he told the story to La Belleza she wept because of its sadness. It was a tragedy of love, she explained, and Juan—soaring to the heights of his imagination—believed that the town, all one hundred souls, had somehow been infected with the tragedy, as they were touched by the shadow of the house itself, which crept directly up the highway each night when the sun set. This was why they left dead chickens and fish on the porch of the cabin or dumped garbage into the yard. He believed he understood something profound and so did nothing about these incidents, which, after all, might have been the pranks of boys. He did not want the infection to touch him, nor the deeper infection of their prejudice because he was Mexican. He was not indifferent. He was simply too much in love with La Belleza and the Sierra Nevada. Finally the incidents stopped.

Now the life of Juan Sánchez entered its most beautiful time. When the first snows fell he became delirious, running through the pines, shouting, rolling on the ground, catching the flakes in his open mouth, bringing them in his cupped hands to rub in the hair of La Belleza, who stood in the doorway of their cabin laughing at him. He danced, made up a song about snowflakes falling on a desert and then a prayer which he addressed to the Virgin of Snowflakes. That night while the snow fluttered like wings against the bedroom

window, he celebrated the coming of the whiteness with
La Belleza.

He understood that first year in the mountains that love
was an enlargement of himself, that it enabled him to be
somehow more than he had ever been before, as though certain
pores of his senses had only just been opened. Whereas before
he had desired the Sierra Nevada for its beauty and contrast
to his harsh fatherland, now he came to acquire a love for it,
and he loved it as he loved La Belleza; he loved it as a woman.
Also in that year he came to realize that there was a fear or
dread about such love. It was more a feeling than anything
else, something which reached thought now and then, particularly in those last moments before sleep. It was an absolutely minor thing. The primary knowledge was of the
manner in which this love seemed to assimilate everything,
rejecting all that would not yield. This love was a kind of
blindness.

That summer Juan left La Belleza at times to pick the
crops of the San Joaquin Valley. He had become good friends
with the servant of the big house and this man had access to
the owner's car, which he always drove down the mountain
in a reckless but confident manner. After that summer Juan
planned also to buy a car, not out of material desire, but
simply because he believed this man would one day kill
himself, and also because he did not wish to be dependent.

He worked in the walnuts near the town of Linden and
again in the tomatoes of the rich delta. He wanted very much
to have La Belleza with him, but that would have meant
more money and a hotel room in the skid row, and that was
impossible because of the pimps and whores, the drunks and
criminals and the general despair, which the police always
tapped at periodic intervals, as one does a vat of fermenting
wine. The skid row was a place his love could not assimilate,
but he could not ignore it because so many of his people were
lost there. He stayed in the labor camps, which were also bad
because of what the men did with themselves, but they were
tolerable. He worked hard and as often as he could and gazed
at the mountains, which he could always see clearly in the

morning light. When tomato season was over he returned to La Belleza.

Though the town would never accept them as equals, it came that summer to tolerate their presence. La Belleza made straw baskets which she sold to the townspeople and which were desired for their beauty and intricacy of design. Juan carved animals, a skill he had acquired from his father, and these were also sold. The activity succeeded so well that Juan took a box of these things to Jackson, where they were readily purchased. The following spring he was able to buy the Ford.

Juan acquired another understanding that second year in the mountains. It was, he believed, that love, his love, was the single greatness of which he was capable, the thing which ennobled him and gave him honor. Love, he became convinced, was his only ability, the one success he had accomplished in a world of insignificance. It was a simple thing, after all, made so painfully simple each time he went to the valley to work with his face toward the ground, every time he saw the men in the fields and listened to their talk and watched them drive off to the skid row at night. After he had acquired this knowledge, the nights he had to spend away from La Belleza were occupied by a new kind of loneliness, as though a part of his body had been separated from the whole. He began also to understand something more of the fear or dread that seemed to trail behind love.

It happened late in the sixth year of their marriage. It was impossible, of course, and he spent many hours at the fire in their cabin telling La Belleza of the impossibility, for the doctor had assured him that all had been well tied. He had conducted himself on the basis of that assumption. But doctors can be wrong. Doctors can make mistakes. La Belleza was with child.

For the first five months the pregnancy was not difficult, and he came almost to believe that indeed the passage of La Belleza would open. He prayed to God. He prayed to the earth and sky. He prayed to the soul of his mother. But after the fifth month the true sickness began and he discarded prayer completely in favor of blasphemy. There was no God

and never could be God in the face of such sickness, such
unbelievable human sickness. Even when he had her removed
to the hospital in Stockton, the doctors could not stop it, but
it continued so terribly that he believed that La Belleza
carried sickness itself in her womb.

After seven months the doctors decided to take the child.
They brought La Belleza into a room with lights and instruments. They worked on her for a long time and she died there
under the lights with the doctors cursing and perspiring
above the large wound of her pain. They did not tell him of
the child, which they had cleaned and placed in an incubator,
until the next day. That night he sat in the Ford and tried
to see it all, but he could only remember the eyes of La
Belleza in the vortex of pain. They were of an almost eerie
calmness. They had possessed calmness, as one possesses the
truth. Toward morning he slumped sideways on the seat and
went to sleep.

So he put her body away in the red earth of the town
cemetery beyond the cabin. The pines came together overhead and in the heat of midday a shadow sprinkled with
spires of light lay upon the ground so that the earth was cool
and clean to smell. He did not even think of taking her back
to Mexico, since, from the very beginning she had always
been part of that dream he had dreamed. Now she would be
always in the Sierra Nevada, with the orange and blue flowers,
the quiet, deep whiteness of winter, and all that he ever was
or could be was with her.

But he did not think these last thoughts then, as he did
now. He had simply performed them out of instinct for their
necessity, as he had performed the years of labor while waiting
for the infant Jesús to grow to manhood. Jesús. Why had he
named the boy Jesús? That, perhaps, had been instinct too.
He had stayed after La Belleza's death for the boy, to be
with him until manhood, to show him the loveliness of the
Sierra Nevada, to instruct him toward true manhood.
But Jesús. Ah, Jesús. Jesús the American. Jesús of the Flotill.
Jesús understood nothing. Jesús, he believed, was forever

lost to knowledge. That day with Jesús had been his own liberation.

For a truth had come upon him after the years of waiting, the ultimate truth that he understood only because La Belleza had passed through his life. Love was beauty, La Belleza and the Sierra Nevada, a kind of created or made thing. But there was another kind of love, a very profound, embracing love that he had felt of late blowing across the mountains from the south and that, he knew now, had always been there from the beginning of his life, disguised in the sun and wind. In this love there was blood and earth and, yes, even God, some kind of god, at least the power of a god. This love wanted him for its own. He understood it, that it had permitted him to have La Belleza and that without it there could have been no Belleza.

Juan placed an arm over his eyes and turned to face the wall. The old bed sighed. An image went off in his head and he remembered vividly the lovely body of La Belleza. In that instant the sound that loving had produced with the bed was alive in him like a forgotten melody, and his body seemed to swell and press against the ceiling. It was particularly cruel because it was so sudden, so intense, and came from so deep within him that he knew it must all still be alive somewhere, and that was the cruelest part of all. He wept softly and held the arm across his eyes.

In the dark morning the people of the town were awakened by the blaze of fire that was the house of Juan Sánchez. Believing that he had perished in the flames, several of the townspeople placed a marker next to the grave of his wife with his name on it. But, of course, on that score they were mistaken. Juan Sánchez had simply gone home.

La Raza in The Fields Today

THE PLUM PLUM PICKERS

By Raymond Barrio

Dawn.

Outside, the coolest night.

Outside, the soft, plush, lingering sheen of nightlight.

Within his breezy air-conditioned shack Manuel Gutierrez lay half asleep in the middle of the biggest apricot orchard in California's Santa Clara Valley, biggest in all the world, nothing but apricot trees all around, in one of a long double row of splintered boards nailed together and called a shack. A migrant's shack. He struggled to come awake. Everything seemed to be plugged up. A distant roar closed in steadily. He awoke in a cold sweat. He sat up abruptly in the cold darkness.

The roar grew louder and louder. He leaned forward, hunched in his worn, torn covers, and peered through the grimy window. A huge black monster was butting through trees, moving and pitching about, its headlights piercing the armor of night, then swinging away again as the roaring lessened. Manuel smiled. The roar of a tractor. He rubbed the sleep from his eyes. He stretched his aching arms and shoulders. He thought of Lupe and the kids back in Drawbridge.

On the very brink of the full onslaught of summer's punishing heat, with the plums and pears and apricots fattening madly on every vine, branch, bush, and limb in every section of every county in the country, pickers were needed right now immediately on every farm and orchard everywhere and all at once. The frantic demand for pickers increased rapidly as the hot days mounted. That sure looked good out there. What a cool job that was. Driving a tractor at night. Maybe he could get Ramiro to teach him to drive one.

Manuel well knew what his physical energy was.

His physical energy was his total worldly wealth.

No matter how anxious he was to work, he did have his limit. He had to rest his body. The finger joint he'd injured still hurt. He missed Lupe's chatter. He'd signed up with that shrewd contractor, Roberto Morales, that fat, energetic *contratista*, manipulator of migrating farm workers, that smiling middleman who promised to deliver so many hands to the moon at such and such a time at such and such an orchard at such and such a price, for such a small commission. A tiny percentage. Such a little slice. Silvery slavery—modernized.

Roberto Morales, an organization man, was a built-in toll gate. A parasite. A collector of drops of human sweat. An efficiency expert. Had he not been Mexican, he would have made a fantastic capitalist, like Turner, the company owner. He was Turner upside down. Sucking blood from his own people. With the help and convenient connivance of Turner's insatiable greed.

The agricultural combine's imperative need to have its capital personally plucked when ripe so as to materialize its honest return on its critical investment in order to keep its executives relaxed in blue splendor in far-off desert pools was coupled to the migrant workers' inexorable and uncompromising need to earn pennies to fend off stark starvation.

Good money.

Good dough.

Good hard work.

Pick fast.

Penny a bucket.

Check off.

Get the count right.

Cotsplumsprunespeachesbeanspeas.

Pods.

The seed of life.

And:—don't complain . . .

Manuel lay back in the blackness. As the light of day started creeping imperiously across its own land, he thought that these powerful orchard land owners were awfully generous to give him such a beautiful hostel to stop in overnight. The skylight hotel. There the land stood. A heaving, sleeping mother earth. A marvelous land. Ripening her fruit once again. Once more. Ripening it fatly and pregnantly for the thousandth time. It must be plucked, said the wise man. For it cannot hang around on limbs a minute extra. At no man's convenience. As soon as the baby's ready. Lush and full of plump juices. Hugging its new seed around its own ripeness. The plum and the cot and the peach and the pear must plummet again to earth, carrying the seed of its own delicate rebirth and redestruction back home to earth again. A clever mother earth who in her all-but-unbelievable generosity was capable of giving man fivefold, tenfold the quantity of fruit he could himself eat, five times fifty, and yet the pickers were never paid enough to satisfy their hunger beyond their actual working hours. And yet it was called a moral world. An ethical world. A good world. A happy world. A world full of golden opportunities. Manuel simply couldn't figure it out.

What was wrong with the figures?

Why was mother earth so generous? And men so greedy?

You got twenty-five cents a basket for tomatoes. A dollar a crate for some fruit. You had to work fast. That was the whole thing. A frantic lunatic to make your barely living wage. If you had no rent to pay, it was OK. You were ahead, *amigo*. Pay rent, however, stay in one place, and you couldn't migrate after other easy pickings. The joy of working was looking over your dreams locked to hunger.

Manuel studied the whorls in the woodwork whirling slowly, revealed in the faint crepuscular light penetrating his shack. His cot was a slab of half-inch plywood board twenty-two inches wide and eight feet long, the width of the shack, supported by two two-by-four beams butted up against the wall at both ends beneath the side window. The shack itself was eight by twelve by seven feet high. Its roof had a slight pitch. The rain stains in the ceiling planks revealed the ease with which the rain penetrated. Except for two small panes of glass exposed near the top, most of the window at the opposite end was boarded up. A single, old, paint-encrusted door was the only entry. No curtains. No interior paneling. Just a shack. A shack of misery. He found he was able to admire and appreciate the simplicity and the strength of the construction. He counted the upright studs, level, two feet apart, the double joists across the top supporting the roof. Cracks and knotholes aplenty, in the wall siding, let in bright chinks of light during the day and welcome wisps of clear fresh air at night. The rough planking of the siding was stained dark. The floor was only partly covered with odd sections of plywood. Some of the rough planking below was exposed, revealing cracks leading down to the cool black earth beneath. A small thick table was firmly studded to a portion of the wall opposite the door. A few small pieces of clear lumber stood bunched together, unsung, unused, unhurried, in the far corner. An overhead shelf, supported from the ceiling by a small extending perpendicular arm, containing some boxes of left-over chemicals and fertilizers, completed the furnishings in his temporary abode.

It was habitable.

He could raise his family in it.

If they were rabbits.

The first rays of a bright new day clinked in through the small rectangle of panes. The ray hovered, then peaked, finally rested on the covers pushed up by his knees. He recalled his mountain trips with his uncle to the great forbidding *barrancas* near Durango in central Mexico, and stopping to rest in the middle of the wild woods, and coming unexpectedly upon a crumbling, splintered hulk of a shack that was all falling apart. It barely gave them shelter from the sudden pelting storm they were trying to escape, but shelter it was—and how beautiful that experience was, then, for they were free, daring, adventurers, out in the wilderness, alone with nothing between them and God's own overpowering nature. They belonged to nothing. To no one but themselves. They were dignity purified. No one forced them to go or stay there. They were delighted and grateful to the shack for the protection it afforded them, even though it was hardly more than a ratty pile of splinters. It had been far worse than this one he was now occupying—but also somehow far more beautiful in his memory.

And now here he was. Shut up in this miserable shack. Thinking how it sickened him inside because it was more a jail cell than a shelter. He didn't care how comfortable and convenient the growers made the shacks. They were huts of slavery. What he wanted was an outlet for his pride. A sudden fierce wave of anger made him want to cross the shack with his fists. There had to be some way to travel over the unbridgeable gulf. Why was necessity always the bride of hunger? To be free . . . ah, and also to be able to eat all one wanted. My heart, *mi corazon*, why did work always have to blend with such misery?

The welcome warmth of the sun's early rays, penetrating more, warmed his frame. But it was a false, false hope. He knew it. The work that lay ahead of him that day would drain and stupefy and fatigue him once again to the point of senseless torpor, ready to fall over long before the work day was done. And that fatigue wasn't merely so bad to bear as the deadly repetitious monotony of never changing, never resting, doing the same plucking over and over and over again. But he had to do it. He had no choice. It was all he could do. It had to be done if he wanted the money. And he had to have money if he wanted to feed his family. The power in his arms was his only capital. Not very much, true, but it was the only sacrifice he could offer the money gods, the only heart he could offer on the pyramid of gold.

His life. *La gran vida.*

Wide awake now, fully refreshed, his whole body lithe and toned, Manuel was ashamed to find himself eager to start his work, knowing that he would do well, but ashamed because he could think of nothing he would rather do more. The final step.

The final the final the final the final the final the final step.

To want to work oneself to death. *A la muerte.* It wasn't the work itself that bothered him. It was the total immersion, the endless, ceaseless, total use of all his energies and spirit and mind and being that tore him apart within. He didn't know what else he was good for or could do with his life. But there had to be something else. He had to be something more than a miserable plucking animal. Pluck pluck pluck. Feed feed feed. Glug glug glug.

Dressing quickly, rolling up his blanket roll and stuffing it into a corner to use again that night, Manuel stepped coolly out into the morning sweetness and breathed the honey-scented air and joined the thickening throng of fellow pluckers milling about the large open barn serving as a cookout. Feeding all the pickers was another of the fat man's unholy prerogatives, for he cheated and overpriced on meals, too. Roberto Morales, the fat man, the shrewd *contratista*, was a bully man, busily darting his blob about, exhorting his priceless pickers to hurry, answering questions, giving advice in the cool half-light, impatiently, pushing, growling orders. Manuel, in order to avoid having to greet him, scowled at his toes when Roberto came trouncing by, saying, "*Apurense, compañeros*, hurry, hurry, hurry, *amigos*." Sure. *Amigos. Si. Si.* They all gulped their food down, standing. Just like home. Paper plates, plastic cups. Wooden spoons. And bits of garbage flying into large canisters. Then in the cool, nightlike morning air, like a flood of disturbed birds, they all picked up their pails and filed into the orchard.

The apricots were plump.

Smooth.

A golden syrupy orange.

Manuel popped two into his mouth, enjoying their cool natural sweetness after the bitter coffee. He knew he should not eat too many. His stomach muscles would cramp. Other pickers started pulling rapidly away from him. Let them. Calmly he calculated the struggle. Start the press sure, slow, and keep it going steady. Piecework. Fill the bucket, fill another, and still another. The competition was among a set of savages, as savage for money as himself, savages with machetes hacking their way through the thickets of modern civilization back to the good old Aztec days, waiting to see who'd be first in line to wrench his heart out. Savage beasts, eager to fill as many buckets as possible in as short a time as possible, cleaning out an entire orchard, picking everything in sight clean, tons of fruit, delivering every bit of ripe fruit to the accountants in their cool air-conditioned orifices.

The competition was not between pickers and growers.

It was between pickers—Jorge and Guillermo.

Between the poor and the hungry, the desperate and the hunted, the slave and the slave, slob against slob, the depraved and himself. You were your own terrible boss. That was the cleverest part of the whole thing. The picker his own bone picker, his own willing built-in slave driver. God, that was good! That was where they reached into your scrotum and screwed you royally and drained your brain and directed your sinews and nerves and muscles with invisible fingers. To fatten their coffers—and drive you to your coffin. That sure was smart. Meant to be smart. Bookkeepers aren't dumb. You worked hard because you wanted to do that hard work above everything else. Pick fast pick hard pick furious pick pick pick. They didn't need straw bosses studying your neck to see if you kept bobbing up and down to keep your picking pace up. Like the barn-stupid chicken, you drove yourself to do it. You were your own money monkey foreman, monkey on top of your own back.

You over-charged yourself.

With your own frenzy.

Neat.

You pushed your gut and your tired aching arms and your twitching legs pumping adrenalin until your tongue tasted like coarse sandpaper.

You didn't even stop to take a drink, let alone a piss, for fear you'd get fined, fired, or bawled out.

And then, after all that effort, you got your miserable pay.

Would the bobbing boss's sons stoop to that?

His fingers were loose and dexterous now. The plump orange balls plopped pitter patter like heavy drops of golden rain into his swaying, sweaty canvas bucket. His earnings depended entirely on how quickly he worked and how well he kept the pressure up. The morning sun was high. The sweet shade was fragrant and refreshing and comfortable under the leafy branches. The soil, too, was still cool and humid. It was going to be another hot one.

There.

Another row ended.

He swung around the end of the row and for a moment he was alone, all by himself. He looked out far across the neighboring alfalfa field, dark green and rich and ripe. Then he looked at the long low Diablo Range close by, rising up into the misty pale blue air kept cool by the unseen bay nearby. This was all his. For a flowing, deceptive minute, all this rich, enormous terrain was all his. All this warm balmy baby air. All this healthful sunny breeze. All those hills, this rich fertile valley, these orchards, these tiled *huertas*, these magnificent farms all, all his ... for his eyes to feast upon. It was a moment he wished he could capture forever and etch permanently on his memory, making it a part of living life for his heart to feast joyously on, forever. Why couldn't he stop picking? Why? Why couldn't he just put the bucket down and open his arms and walk into the hills and merge himself with the hills and just wander invisibly in the blue? ...

But here he was—a mere straw among the enormous sludge of humanity flowing past, a creature of limb and his own driving appetites, a creature of heed and need. Swinging around another end run he placed his ladder on the next heavy limb of the next pregnant tree. He reached up. He plucked bunches of small golden fruit with both hands. He worked like a frenzied windmill. He cleared away an arc as far as the circumference of his plucking fingers permitted. A living model for da Vinci's outstretched man. Adam heeding God's moving finger. He moved higher. He repeated another circle. Then down and around again to another side of the tree, until he cleared it, cleared it of all visible, viable, delectable, succulent fruit. It was sweet work. The biggest difference between him and the honey-gathering ant was that the ant had a home.

Several pickers were halfway down the next row, well in advance of him. He was satisfied he was pacing himself well. Most of the band was still behind him. The moving sun, vaulting the sky dome's crackling earth, pounded its fierce heat into every dead and living crevice. Perspiration poured down his sideburns, down his forehead, down his cheeks, down his neck, into his ears, off his chin. He tasted its saltiness with the tip of his dry tongue. He wished he'd brought some salt tablets. Roberto Morales wasn't about to worry about the pickers, and Manuel wasn't worried either. Despite the heat, he felt some protection from the ocean and bay. It had been much, much worse in Texas, and much hotter in Delano in the San Joaquin Valley and worst of all in Satan's own land, the Imperial Valley.

No matter which way he turned, he was trapped in an end-less maze of apricot trees, as though forever, neat rows of them, neatly planted, row after row, just like the blackest bars on the jails of hell. There had to be an end. There had to be. There—trapped. There had to be a way out. Locked. There had to be a respite. Animal. The buckets and the crates kept piling up higher. Brute. He felt alone. Though sur-rounded by other pickers. Beast. Though he was perspiring heavily, his shirt was powder-dry. Savage. The hot dry air. The hot dry air sucking every drop of living moisture from his brute body. Wreck. He stopped and walked to the farthest end of the first row for some water, drank the holy water in great gulps so he wouldn't have to savor its tastelessness, letting it spill down his torn shirt to cool his exhausted body, to replenish his brute cells and animal pores and stinking follicles and pig gristle, a truly refined wreck of an animal, pleased to meetcha. Predator.

Lunch.

Almost too exhausted to eat, he munched his cheese with tortillas, smoked on ashes, then lay back on the cool ground for half an hour. That short rest in the hot shade restored some of his humor and resolve. He felt his spirit swell out again like a thirsty sponge in water.

Then, up again. The trees. The branches. The briarly branches. The scratching leaves. The twigs tearing at his shirt sleeves. The ladder. The rough bark. The endlessly unending piling up of bucket upon box upon crate upon stack upon rack upon mound upon automator. A beast. A ray of enemy sun penetrated the tree that was hiding him and split his forehead open. His mind whirred. He blacked out. Luckily he'd been leaning against a heavy branch. His feet hooked to the ladder's rung. His half-filled bucket slipped from his

grasp and fell in slow motion, splattering the fruit he'd so
laboriously picked. To the ground. Roberto happened by and
shook his head. "Whatsamatter, can't you see straight,
pendejo?" Manuel was too tired even to curse. He should have
had some salt pills.

Midafternoon.

The summer's fierce zenith passed overhead. It passed,
then dropped. It started to light the ocean behind him, back
of the hills. Sandy dreams. Cool nights. Cold drinks. Soft
guitar music with Lupe sitting beside him. All wafting through
his feverish moments. Tiredness drained his spirit of will.
Exhaustion drained his mind. His fingers burned. His arms
flailed the innocent trees. He was slowing down. He could
hardly fill his last bucket. Suddenly the whistle blew. The
day's work was at last ended.

Ended!

The *contratista* Roberto Morales stood there.

His feet straddled. Mexican style. A real robber. A mythical
version of a Mexican general. A gentlemanly, friendly, polite,
grinning, vicious, thieving brute. The worst kind. To his own
people. Despite his being a fellow Mexican, despite his torn,
old clothing, everyone knew what kind of clever criminal he
was. Despite his crude, ignorant manner, showing that he
was one of them, that he'd started with them, that he grew
up with them, that he'd suffered all the sordid deprivations
with them, he was actually the shrewdest, smartest, richest
cannibal in forty counties around. They surely couldn't blame
the *gueros* for this miscarriage. He was a crew chief. How
could anyone know what he did to his own people? And what
did the *gueros* care? The Anglo growers and *guero* executives,
smiling in their cool filtered offices, puffing their elegant thin
cigars, washed their clean blond bloodless dirtless hands of
the whole matter. All they did was hire Roberto Morales.
Firm, fair, and square. For an agreed-upon price. Good. How
he got his people down to the pickings was no business of
theirs. They were honest, those *gueros*. They could sleep at
night. They fulfilled their end of the bargain, and they cheated
no one. Their only crime, their only soul-grime was that they

didn't give a shit how that migratory scum lived. It was no concern of theirs. Their religion said it was no concern of theirs. Their wives said it was no concern of theirs. Their aldermen said it was no concern of theirs.

Whenever Roberto Morales spoke, Manuel had to force himself not to answer. He had to keep his temper from flaring.

"Now," announced Morales at last, in his friendliest tone, "now, I must take two cents from every bucket. I am sorry. There was a miscalculation. Everybody understands. Everybody?" He slid his eyes around, smiling, palms up.

The tired, exhausted pickers gasped as one.

Yes. Everyone understood. Freezing in place. After all that hard work.

"Any questions, men?"

He was still grinning, knowing that this would mean a loss of two or three dollars out of each picker's pay that day, a huge windfall for Morales.

"You promised to take nothing!" Manuel heard himself saying. Everyone turned in astonishment to stare at Manuel.

"I said two cents, *hombre*. You got a problem or what?"

"You promised."

The two men, centered in a huge circle of red-ringed eyes, glared at each other. Reaching for each other's jugular. The other exhausted animals studied the tableau through widening eyes. It was so unequal. Morales remained calm, confident, studying Manuel. As though memorizing his features. He had the whole advantage. Then Manuel, with his last remaining bit of energy, lifted his foot and clumsily tipped over his own last bucket of cots. They rolled away in all directions around everyone's feet.

Roberto Morales' eyes blazed. His fists clenched. "You pick them up, Gutierrez."

So. He knew his name. After all. For answer, Manuel kicked over another bucket, and again the fruit rolled away in all directions.

All the other pickers moved toward their own buckets still standing beside them on the ground, awaiting the truck gatherer. They took an ominous and threatening position over them, straddling them with their feet.

Without looking around, without taking his eyes off Manuel, Roberto Morales said sharply, "All right. All right, men. I shall take nothing this time."

Manuel felt a thrill of power course through his nerves.

He had never won anything before. He would have to pay for this, for his defiance, somehow, later. But he had shown defiance. He had salvaged his money savagely and he had earned respect from his fellow slaves. The gringo *hijos de la chingada* would never know of this little incident, and would probably be surprised, and perhaps even a little mortified, for a few minutes. But they wouldn't give a damn, these Anglos. It was bread, *pan y tortillas* out of his own children's mouths. But they still wouldn't give a single damn. Manuel had wrenched Morales' greedy fingers away and removed a fat slug of a purse from his sticky grasp. And in his slow way, in his stupid, accidental, dangerous way, Manuel had made an extravagant discovery. And that was—that a man counted for something. For men, Manuel dimly suspected, are built for something more important and less trifling than the mere gathering of prunes and apricots, hour upon hour, decade upon decade, insensibly, mechanically, antlike. Men are built to experience a certain sense of honor and pride.

Or else they are dead before they die.

THE TALE OF LA RAZA

By Luis Valdez

The revolt in Delano is more than a labor struggle. Mexican grape pickers did not march 300 miles to Sacramento, carrying the standard of the *Virgen de Guadalupe*, merely to dramatize economic grievances. Beyond unionization, beyond politics, there is the desire of a New World race to reconcile the conflicts of its 500-year-old history. *La Raza* is trying to find its place in the sun it once worshipped as a Supreme Being.

La Raza, the race, is the Mexican people. Sentimental and cynical, fierce and docile, faithful and treacherous, individualistic and herd-following, in love with life and obsessed with death, the personality of the *raza* encompasses all the complexity of our history. The conquest of Mexico was no conquest at all. It shattered our ancient Indian universe, but more of it was left above ground than beans and tortillas. Below the foundations of our Spanish culture, we still sense the ruins of an entirely different civilization.

Most of us know we are not European simply by looking in a mirror—the shape of the eyes, the curve of the nose, the color of skin, the texture of hair; these things belong to another time, another people. Together with a million little stubborn mannerisms, beliefs, myths, superstitions, words, thoughts—things not so easily detected—they fill our Spanish life with Indian contradictions. It is not enough to say we suffer an identity crisis, because that crisis has been our way of life for the last five centuries.

That we Mexicans speak of ourselves as a "race" is the biggest contradiction of them all. The *conquistadores*, of course, mated with their Indian women with customary abandon, creating a nation of bewildered halfbreeds in countless shapes, colors and sizes. Unlike our fathers and mothers, unlike each other, we *mestizos* solved the problem with poetic license and called ourselves *la raza*. A Mexican's first loyalty—when one of us is threatened by strangers from the outside—

95

is to that race. Either we recognize our total unity on the basis of *raza*, or the ghosts of a 100,000 feuding Indian tribes, bloods and mores will come back to haunt us.

A little more than 60 years ago the Revolution of 1910 unleashed such a terrible social upheaval that it took 10 years of insane slaughter to calm the ghosts of the past. The Revolution took Mexico from the hands of New World Spaniards (who in turn were selling it to American and British interests) and gave it, for the first time and at the price of a million murders, to the Mexicans.

Any Mexican deeply loves his *mestizo patria*, even those who, like myself, were born in the United States. At best, our cultural schizophrenia has led us to action through the all-encompassing poetry of religion, which is a fancy way of saying blind faith. The Virgin of Guadalupe, the supreme poetic expression of our Mexican desire to be one people, has inspired Mexicans more than once to social revolution. At worst, our two-sidedness has led us to inaction. The last divine Aztec emperor Cuauhtemoc was murdered in the jungles of Guatemala, and his descendants were put to work in the fields. We are still there, in dry, plain American Delano.

It was the triple magnetism of *raza*, *patria*, and the Virgin of Guadelupe which organized the Mexican American farmworker in Delano—that and Cesar Chavez. Chavez was not a traditional bombastic Mexican revolutionary; nor was he a *gavacho*, a gringo, a white social worker type. Both types had tried to organize the *raza* in America and failed. Here was Cesar, burning with a patient fire, poor like us, dark like us, talking quietly, moving people to talk about their problems, attacking the little problems first, and suggesting, always suggesting—never more than that—solutions that seemed attainable. We didn't know it until we met him, but he was the leader we had been waiting for.

Although he sometimes reminds one of Benito Juarez, Cesar is our first real Mexican American leader. Used to hybrid forms, the *raza* includes all Mexicans, even hyphenated Mexican-Americans; but divergent histories are slowly making the *raza* in the United States different from the *raza* in

Mexico. We who were born here missed out on the chief legacy of the Revolution: the chance to forge a nation true to all the forces that have molded us, to be one people. Now we must seek our own destiny, and Delano is only the beginning of our active search. For the last hundred years our revolutionary progress has not only been frustrated, it has been totally suppressed. This is a society largely hostile to our cultural values. There is no poetry about the United States. No depth, no faith, no allowance for human contrariness. No soul, no *mariachi*, no chili sauce, no *pulque*, no mysticism, no *chingaderas*.

Our *campesinos*, the farmworking *raza*, find it difficult to participate in this alien North-American country. The acculturated Mexican Americans in the cities, *ex-raza*, find it easier. They have solved their Mexican contradictions with a pungent dose of Americanism, and are more concerned with status, money and bad breath than with their ultimate destiny. In a generation or two they will melt into the American pot and be no more. But the farmworking *raza* will not disappear so easily.

The pilgrimage to Sacramento was no mere publicity trick. The *raza* has a tradition of migrations, starting from the legend of the founding of Mexico. Nezahualcoyotl, a great Indian leader, advised his primitive *Chichimecas*, forerunners of the Aztecs, to begin a march to the south. In that march, he prophesied, the children would age and the old would die, but their grandchildren would come to a great lake. In that lake they would find an eagle devouring a serpent, and on that spot, they would begin to build a great nation. The nation was Aztec Mexico, and the eagle and the serpent are the symbols of the *patria*. They are emblazoned on the Mexican flag, which the marchers took to Sacramento with pride.

Then there is the other type of migration. When the migrant farm laborer followed the crops, he was only reacting to the way he saw the American *raza*: no unity, no representation, no roots. The pilgrimage was a truly religious act, a rejection of our past in this country and a symbol of our unity and new direction. It is of no lasting significance that Governor Brown was not at the Capitol to greet us. The unity of thousands of *raza* on the Capitol steps was reason enough for our march. Under the name of HUELGA we had created a Mexican American *patria*, and Cesar Chavez was our first *Presidente*.

Huelga means strike. With the poetic instinct of the *raza*, the Delano grape strikers have made it mean a dozen other things. It is a declaration, a challenge, a greeting, a feeling, a movement. We cried *Huelga!* to the scabs, *Huelga!* to the labor contractors, to the growers, to Governor Brown. With the Schenley and DiGiorgio boycotts, it was *Huelga!* to the whole country. It is the most significant word in our entire Mexican American history. If the *raza* of Mexico believes in *La Patria*, we believe in *La Huelga*.

The route of the pilgrimage was planned so that the *huelga* could reach all the farmworkers of the San Joaquin Valley. Dependent as we were on each farmworking town for food and shelter, we knew the *raza* would not turn us down. *"Mi casa es suya"*—"My house is yours"—is the precept of Mexican hospitality.

The Virgin of Guadalupe was the first hint to farmworkers that the pilgrimage implied social revolution. During the Mexican Revolution, the peasant armies of Emiliano Zapata carried her standard, not only because they sought her divine protection, but because she symbolized the Mexico of the poor and humble. It was a simple Mexican Indian, Juan Diego, who first saw her in a vision at Guadalupe. Beautifully dark and Indian in feature, she was the New World version of the Mother of Christ. Even though some of her worshippers in Mexico still identify her with Tonatzin, an Aztec goddess, she is a Catholic saint of Indian creation—a Mexican. The people's response was immediate and reverent. They joined the march by the thousands, falling in line behind her standard. To the Catholic hypocrites against the pilgrimage and strike the Virgin said *Huelga!*

The struggle for better wages and better working conditions in Delano is but the first, realistic articulation of our need for unity. To emerge from the mire of our past in the United

States, to leave behind the divisive, deadening influence of poverty, we must have bargaining power. We must have unions. To the farmworkers who joined the pilgrimage, this cultural pride was revolutionary. There were old symbols— Zapata lapel buttons—and new symbols standing for new social protest and revolt; the red thunderbird flags of the NFWA, picket signs, armbands.

There were also political rallies in the smallest towns of the San Joaquin Valley. Sometimes they were the biggest things that had ever happened in town. Every meeting included a reading of *El Plan de Delano*, a "plan of liberation" for all farmworkers in the language of the picket line: " . . . our path travels through a valley well known to all Mexican farmworkers. We know all of these towns . . . because along this very same road, in this very same valley, the Mexican race has sacrified itself for the last 100 years . . . This is the beginning of a social movement in fact and not in pronouncements . . . We shall unite . . . We shall strike . . . Our PILGRIMAGE is the MATCH that will light our cause for all farmworkers to see what is happening here, so that they may do as we have done . . . VIVA LA CAUSA! VIVA LA HUELGA!"

The rallies were like religious revivals. At each new town, they were waiting to greet us and offer us their best—*mariachis*, embraces, words of encouragement for the strike, prayers, rosaries, sweet cakes, fruit and iced tea. Hundreds walked, ran or drove up to the march and donated what little money they could afford. The countless gestures of sympathy and solidarity were like nothing the *raza* had ever seen.

The NFWA is a radical union because it started, and continues to grow, as a community organization. Its store, cafeteria, clinic, garage, newspaper and weekly meeting have established a sense of community the Delano farmworker will not relinquish. After years of isolation in the barrios of Great Valley slum towns like Delano, after years of living in labor camps and ranches at the mercy and caprice of growers and contractors, the Mexican American farmworker is developing his own ideas about living in the United States. He wants to be equal with all the working men of the nation, and he does not mean by the standard middle-class route. We are repelled by the human disintegration of peoples and cultures as they fall apart in this Great Gringo Melting Pot, and determined that this will not happen to us. But there will always be *raza* in this country. There are millions more where we came from, across the thousand miles of common border between Mexico and the United States. For millions of farmworkers, from the Mexicans and Filipinos of the West to the Afro-Americans of the South, the United States has come to a social, political and cultural impasse. Listen to these people, and you will hear the first murmurings of revolution.

THE ORGANIZER'S TALE

By Cesar Chavez

It really started for me 16 years ago in San Jose, California, when I was working on an apricot farm. We figured he was just another social worker doing a study of farm conditions, and I kept refusing to meet with him. But he was persistent. Finally, I got together some of the rough element in San Jose. We were going to have a little reception for him to teach the gringo a little bit of how we felt. There were about 30 of us in the house, young guys mostly. I was supposed to give them a signal—change my cigarette from my right hand to my left —and then we were going to give him a lot of hell. But he started talking and the more he talked, the more wide-eyed I became and the less inclined I was to give the signal. A couple of guys who were pretty drunk at the time still wanted to give the gringo the business, but we got rid of them. This fellow was making a lot of sense, and I wanted to hear what he had to say.

His name was Fred Ross, and he was an organizer for the Community Service Organization (CSO) which was working with Mexican Americans in the cities. I became immediately really involved. Before long I was heading a voter registration drive. All the time I was observing the things Fred did, secretly, because I wanted to learn how to organize, to see how it was done. I was impressed with his patience and understanding of people. I thought this was a tool, one of the greatest things he had.

It was pretty rough for me at first. I was changing and had to take a lot of ridicule from the kids my age, the rough characters I worked with in the fields. They would say, "Hey, big shot. Now that you're a *politico*, why are you working here for 65 cents an hour?" I might add that our neighborhood had the highest percentage of San Quentin graduates. It was a game among the *pachucos* in the sense that we defended ourselves from outsiders, although inside the neighborhood there was not a lot of fighting.

After six months of working every night in San Jose, Fred assigned me to take over the CSO chapter in Decoto. It was a tough spot to fill. I would suggest something, and people would say, "No, let's wait till Fred gets back," or "Fred wouldn't do it that way." This is pretty much a pattern with people, I discovered, whether I was put in Fred's position, or later, when someone else was put in my position. After the Decoto assignment I was sent to start a new chapter in Oakland. Before I left, Fred came to a place in San Jose called the Hole-in-the-Wall and we talked for half an hour over coffee. He was in a rush to leave, but I wanted to keep him talking; I was that scared of my assignment.

Those were hard times in Oakland. First of all, it was a big city and I'd get lost every time I went anywhere. Then I arranged a series of house meetings. I would get to the meeting early and drive back and forth past the house, too nervous to go in and face the people. Finally I would force myself to go inside and sit in a corner. I was quite thin then, and young, and most of the people were middle-aged. Someone would say, "Where's the organizer?" And I would pipe up, "Here I am." Then they would say in Spanish—these were very poor people and we hardly spoke anything but Spanish— "Ha! This *kid*?" Most of them said they were interested, but the hardest part was to get them to start pushing themselves, on their own initiative.

The idea was to set up a meeting and then get each attending person to call his own house meeting, inviting new people—a sort of chain letter effect. After a house meeting I would lie awake going over the whole thing, playing the tape back, trying to see why people laughed at one point, or why they were for one thing and against another. I was also learning to read and write, those late evenings. I had left school in the 7th grade after attending 67 different schools, and my reading wasn't the best.

At our first organizing meeting we had 368 people: I'll never forget it because it was very important to me. You eat your heart out; the meeting is called for 7 o'clock and you start to worry about 4. You wait. Will they show up? Then the first one arrives. By 7 there are only 20 people; you have everything in order, you have to look calm. But little by little they filter in and at a certain point you know it will be a success.

After four months in Oakland, I was transferred. The chapter was beginning to move on its own, so Fred assigned me to organize the San Joaquin Valley. Over the months I developed what I used to call schemes or tricks—now I call them techniques—of making initial contacts. The main thing in convincing someone is to spend time with him. It doesn't matter if he can read, write or even speak well. What is important is that he is a man and, second, that he has shown some initial interest. One good way to develop leadership is to take a man with you in your car. And it works a lot better if you're doing the driving; that way you are in charge. You drive, he sits there, and you talk. These little things were very important to me; I was caught in a big game by then, figuring out what makes people work. I found that if you work hard enough you can usually shake people into working too, those who are concerned. You work harder and they work harder still, up to a point and then they pass you. Then, of course, they're on their own.

I also learned to keep away from the established groups and so-called leaders, and to guard against philosophizing. Working with low-income people is very different from working with the professionals, who like to sit around talking about how to play politics. When you're trying to recruit a farmworker, you have to paint a little picture, and then you have to color the picture in. We found out that the harder a guy is to convince, the better leader or member he becomes. When you exert yourself to convince him, you have his confidence and he has good motivation. A lot of people who say OK right away wind up hanging around the office, taking up the workers' time.

During the McCarthy era in one Valley town, I was subjected to a lot of redbaiting. We had been recruiting people for citizenship classes at the high school when we got into a quarrel with the naturalization examiner. He was rejecting people on the grounds that they were just parroting what they learned in citizenship class. One day we had a meeting about it in Fresno, and I took along some of the leaders of our local chapter. Some redbaiting official gave us a hard time, and the people got scared and took his side. They did it because it seemed easy at the moment, even though they knew that sticking with me was the right thing to do. It was disgusting. When we left the building they walked by themselves ahead of me as if I had some kind of communicable disease. I had been working with these people for three months and I was very sad to see that. It taught me a great lesson.

That night I learned that the chapter officers were holding a meeting to review my letters and printed materials to see if I really was a Communist. So I drove out there and walked right in on their meeting. I said, "I hear you've been discussing me, and I thought it would be nice if I was here to defend myself. Not that it matters that much to you or even to me, because as far as I'm concerned you are a bunch of cowards." At that they began to apologize. "Let's forget it," they said. "You're a nice guy."

But I didn't want apologies. I wanted a full discussion. I told them I didn't give a damn, but that they had to learn to distinguish fact from what appeared to be a fact because of fear. I kept them there till two in the morning. Some of the women cried. I don't know if they investigated me any further, but I stayed on aother few months and things worked out.

This was not an isolated case. Often when we'd leave people to themselves they would get frightened and draw back into their shells where they had been all the years. And I learned quickly that there is no real appreciation. Whatever you do, and no matter what reasons you may give to others, you do it because you want to see it done, or maybe because you want power. And there shouldn't be any appreciation, understandably. I know good organizers who were destroyed, washed out, because they expected people to appreciate what they'd done. Anyone who comes in with the idea that farmworkers are free of sin and that the growers are all bastards either has never dealt with the situation or is an idealist of the first order. Things don't work that way.

For more than 10 years I worked for the CSO. As the organization grew, we found ourselves meeting in fancier and fancier motels and holding expensive conventions. Doctors, lawyer and politicians began joining. They would get elected to some office in the organization and then, for all practical purposes, leave. Intent on using the CSO for their own prestige purposes, these "leaders," many of them, lacked the urgency we had to have. When I became general director I began to press for a program to organize farmworkers into a union, an idea most of the leadership opposed. So I started a revolt within the CSO. I refused to sit at the head table at meetings, refused to wear a suit and tie, and finally I even refused to shave and cut my hair. It used to embarrass some of the professionals.

At every meeting I got up and gave my standard speech: We shouldn't meet in fancy motels, we were getting away from the people, farmworkers had to be organized. But nothing happened. In March of '62 I resigned and came to Delano to begin organizing the Valley on my own.

I drew a map of all the towns between Arvin and Stockton —86 of them, including farming camps—and decided to hit them all to get a small nucleus of people working in each. For six months I traveled around, planting an idea. We had a simple questionnaire, a little card with space for name, address and how much the worker thought he ought to be paid. My wife, Helen, mimeographed them, and we took our kids for two- or three-day jaunts to these towns, distributing the cards door-to-door and to camps and groceries.

Some 80,000 cards were sent back from eight Valley counties. I got a lot of contacts that way, but I was shocked at the wages the people were asking. The growers were paying $1 and $1.15, and maybe 95 percent of the people thought they should be getting only $1.25. Sometimes people scribbled messages on the cards: "I hope to God we win" or "Do you think we can win?" or "I'd like to know more." So I separated the cards with the pencilled notes, got in my car and went to those people.

We didn't have any money at all in those days, none for gas and hardly any for food. So I went to people and started asking for food. It turned out to be about the best thing I could have done, although at first it's hard on your pride. Some of our best members came in that way. If people give you their food, they'll give you their hearts. Several months and many meetings later we had a working organization, and this time the leaders were the people.

None of the farmworkers had collective bargaining contracts, and I thought it would take ten years before we got that first contract. I wanted desperately to get some color into the movement, to give people something they could identify with, like a flag. I was reading some books about how various leaders discovered what colors contrasted and stood out the best. The Egyptians had found that a red field with a white circle and a black emblem in the center crashed into your eyes like nothing else. I wanted to use the Aztec eagle in the center, as on the Mexican flag. So I told my cousin Manuel, "Draw an Aztec eagle." Manuel had a little trouble with it, so we modified the eagle to make it easier for people to draw.

The first big meeting of what we decided to call the National Farm Workers Association was held in September 1962, at Fresno, with 287 people. We had our huge red flag on the wall, with paper tacked over it. When the time came, Manuel pulled a cord ripping the paper off the flag and all of a sudden it hit the people. Some of them wondered if it was a Communist flag, and I said it probably looked more like a neo-Nazi emblem than anything else. But they wanted an explanation, so Manuel got up and said, "When that damn eagle flies—that's when the farmworkers' problems are going to be solved."

One of the first things I decided was that outside money wasn't going to organize people, at least not in the beginning.

I even turned down a grant from a private group—$50,000 to go directly to organize farmworkers—for just this reason. Even when there are no strings attached, you are still compromised because you feel you have to produce immediate results. This is bad, because it takes a long time to build a movement, and your organization suffers if you get too far ahead of the people it belongs to. We set the dues at $42 a year per family, really meaningful dues, but of the 212 families we got to pay, only 12 remained by June of '63. We were discouraged at that, but not enough to make us quit.

Money was always a problem. Once we were facing a $180 gas bill on a credit card I'd got a long time ago and was about to lose. And we *had* to keep that credit card.

One day my wife and I were picking cotton, pulling bolls, to make a little money to live on. Helen said to me, "Do you put all this in the bag, or just the cotton?" I thought she was kidding and told her to throw the whole boll in so that she had nothing but a sack of bolls at the weighing.

The man said, "Whose sack is this?" I said, well, my wife's, and he told us we were fired. "Look at all that crap you brought in," he said.

Helen and I started laughing. We were going anyway. We took the $4 we had earned and spent it at a grocery store where they were giving away a $100 prize. Each time you shopped they'd give you one of the letters of M-O-N-E-Y or a flag: you had to have M-O-N-E-Y plus the flag to win. Helen had already collected the letters and just needed the flag. Anyway they gave her the ticket. She screamed, "A flag? I don't believe it," ran in and got the $100. She said, "Now we're going to eat steak." But I said no, we're going to pay the gas bill. I don't know if she cried, but I think she did.

It was rough in those early years. Helen was having babies and I was not there when she was at the hospital. But if you haven't got your wife behind you, you can't do many things. There's got to be peace at home. So I did, I think, a fairly good job of organizing her. When we were kids, she lived in Delano and I came to town as a migrant. Once on a date we had a bad experience about segregation at a movie theater, and I put up a fight. We were together then, and still are. I think I'm more of a pacifist than she is. Her father, Febela, was a colonel with Pancho Villa in the Mexican Revolution. Sometimes she gets angry and tells me, "These scabs—you should deal with them sternly," and I kid her, "It must be too much of that Febela blood in you."

The Movement really caught on in '64. By August we had a thousand members. We'd had a beautiful 90-day drive in Corcoran, where they had the Battle of the Corcoran Farm Camp 30 years ago, and by November we had assets of $25,000 in our credit union, which helped to stabilize the membership. I had gone without pay the whole of 1963. The next year the members voted me a $40-a-week salary, after Helen had to quit working in the fields to manage the credit union.

Our first strike was in May of '65, a small one but it prepared us for the big one. A farmworker from McFarland named Epifanio Camacho came to see me. He said he was sick and tired of how people working the roses were being treated, and was willing to "go the limit."

I assigned Manuel and Gilbert Padilla to hold meetings at Camacho's house. The people wanted union recognition, but the real issue, as in most cases when you begin, was wages. They were promised $9 a thousand, but they were actually getting $6.50 and $7 for grafting roses. Most of them signed cards giving us the right to bargain for them. We chose the biggest company, with about 85 employees, not counting the irrigators and supervisors, and we held a series of meetings to prepare the strike and call the vote. There would be no picket line; everyone pledged on their honor not to break the strike.

Early on the first morning of the strike, we sent out 10 cars to check the people's homes. We found lights in five or six homes and knocked on the doors. The men were getting up and we'd say, "Where are you going?" They would dodge. "Oh, uh . . . I was just getting up, you know."

We'd say, "Well, you're not going to work, are you?" And they'd say no. Dolores Huerta, who was driving the green panel truck, saw a light in one house where four rose workers lived. They told her they were going to work, even after she reminded them of their pledge. So she moved the truck so it blocked their driveway, turned off the key, put in it her purse and sat there alone.

That morning the company foreman was madder than hell and refused to talk to us. None of the grafters had shown up for work. At 10:30 we started to go to the company office, but it occurred to us that maybe a woman would have a better chance. So Dolores knocked on the office door, saying, "I'm Dolores Huerta from the National Farm Workers Association."

"Get out!" the man said, "you Communist. Get out!" I guess they were expecting us, because as Dolores stood arguing with him the cops came and told her to leave. She left.

For two days the fields were idle. On Wednesday they recruited a group of Filipinos from out of town who knew nothing of the strike, maybe 35 of them. They drove through escorted by three sheriff's patrol cars, one in front, one in the middle and one at the rear with a dog. We didn't have a picket line, but we parked across the street and just watched them go through, not saying a word. All but seven stopped working after half an hour, and the rest had quit by mid-afternoon.

The company made an offer the evening of the fourth day, a package deal that amounted to a 120 percent wage increase, but no contract. We wanted to hold out for a contract and more benefits, but a majority of the rose workers wanted to accept the offer and go back. We are a democratic union so we had to support what they wanted to do. They had a meeting and voted to settle. Then we had a problem with a few militants who wanted to hold out. We had to convince them to go back to work, as a united front, because otherwise they could be canned. So we worked—Tony Oredain and I, Dolores and Gilbert, Jim Drake and all the organizers—knocking on doors till two in the morning, telling people, "You have to go back or you'll lose your job."

And they did. They worked.

Our second strike, and our last before the big one at Delano, was in the grapes at Martin's Ranch. The people were getting a raw deal there, being pushed around pretty badly. Gilbert went out to the field, climbed on top of a car and took a strike vote. They voted unanimously to go out. Right away they started bringing in strikebreakers, so we launched a tough attack on the labor contractors, distributed leaflets portraying them as really low characters. We attacked one so badly that he just gave up the job, and he took 27 of his men out with him. All he asked was that we distribute another leaflet reinstating him in the community. And we did. What was unusual was that the grower would still talk to us. The grower kept saying, "I can't pay. I just haven't got the money." I guess he must have found the money somewhere, because we were asking $1.40 and we got it.

We had just finished the Martin strike when the Agricultural Workers Organizing Committee (AFL-CIO) started a strike against the grape growers, DiGiorgio, Schenley liquors and small growers, asking $1.40 an hour and 25 cents a box. There was a lot of pressure from our members for us to join the strike, but we had some misgivings. We didn't feel ready for a big strike like this one, one that was sure to last a long time. Having no money—just $87 in the strike fund—meant we'd have to depend on God knows who.

Eight days after the strike started—it takes time to get 1,200 people together from all over the Valley—we held a meeting in Delano and voted to go out. I asked the membership to release us from the pledge not to accept outside money, because we'd need it now, a lot of it. The help came. It started because of the close, and I would say even beautiful, relationship that we've had with the Migrant Ministry for some years. They were the first to come to our rescue, financially and in every other way, and they spread the word to other benefactors.

We had planned, before, to start a labor school in November. It never happened, but we have the best labor school we could ever have, in the strike. The strike is only a temporary condition, however. We have over 3,000 members spread out over a wide area, and we have to service them when they have problems. We get letters from New Mexico, Colorado, Texas, California, from farmworkers saying, "We're getting together and we need an organizer."

It kills you when you haven't got the personnel and resources. You feel badly about not sending an organizer because you look back and remember all the difficulty you had in getting two or three people together, and here *they're* together. Of course, we're training organizers, many of them younger than I was when I started in CSO. They can work 20 hours a day, sleep four and be ready to hit it again; when you get to be 39 it's a different story.

The people who took part in the strike and the march have something more than their material interest going for them. If it were only material, they wouldn't have stayed on the strike long enough to win. It is difficult to explain. But it flows out in the ordinary things they say. For instance, some of the younger guys are saying, "Where do you think's going to be the next strike?"

I say, "Well, we have to win in Delano."

They say, "We'll win, but where do we go next?"

I say, "Maybe most of us will be working in the fields."

They say, "No, I don't want to go and work in the fields. I want to organize. There are a lot of people that need our help."

So I say, "You're going to be pretty poor then, because when you strike you don't have much money." They say they don't care much about that.

And others are saying, "I have friends who are working in Texas. If we could only help them."

It is bigger, certainly, than just a strike. And if this spirit grows within the farm labor movement, one day we can use the force that we have to help correct a lot of things that are wrong in this society. But that is for the future. Before you can run, you have to learn to walk.

There are vivid memories from my childhood—what we had to go through because of low wages and the conditions, basically because there was no union. I suppose if I wanted to be fair I could say that I'm trying to settle a personal score. I could dramatize it by saying that I want to bring social justice to farmworkers. But the truth is that I went through a lot of hell, and a lot of people did. If we can even the score a little for the workers then we are doing something. Besides, I don't know any other work I like to do better than this. I really don't, you know.

THE NUN'S TALE

By Sister Mary Prudence

The Virgin of Guadalupe, the Virgin of Guadalupe
She was on our beautiful banner, and the man,
The farm worker from Delano who carried her,
Led the March. We were going to Modesto.
We were going to show the justice of our cause.
A man with a six-foot cross walked behind.

Six miles in two hours, then we stopped
Under the shade of a railway depot
And while we rested we talked.
The people were glad to see us there—
Glad to see the habits of the Church.
I wonder if they know they are the Church?

Young Joey asked if I were tired,
How far we had to go, four miles
I said, and I was tired and Joey said
But we'll walk all those four miles
However tired, for if we sacrifice we win.
This is what the march put into Joey's head.

Then we came to Manteca, and in Manteca,
I learned why the *jefes* spoke so seriously.
I learned what it means to be a minority—
Someone had threatened our lives, and
The policemen thought we should stay,
Stay in Manteca park and not march.

Cesar Chavez, at night, when we were all together
Asked us to tell why we came to march.
This was our poverty—How could I tell? We had
Only ourselves, only our support to give.
We "Anglos" received much, gave little.
How could I tell them that?

Because we wore the habits of the Church
A farmer offered what he could. No,
We are part of the farm workers, we said,
What you give to us, goes to them.
He knew what the workers needed,
But he was afraid, and we were sorry for him.

"The growers are Catholics," said another,
He would not pray, "They can pray for themselves,
They sure don't pray for us."
Cesar Chavez, on Sunday, led a palm procession;
We sang songs in Spanish. Celebrated the Mass.
This is how it was meant to be.

But they are bitter on both sides,
And as we left Manteca, one other man, not with us,
Began to heckle, "Sister, you are ruining
The image of the Church." The image?
And what about the Gospel of the Church? I thought.
And what about the duties of the Church, to God's people?

Fresh air and sun and cool water
This is my memory, and burning feet,
Smiles, and the suffering but always
A determination and a hope; this is the beauty
Of it I thought, the beauty in our being here.
Together, we manifest the brotherhood of man.

EL TEATRO CAMPESINO—ITS BEGINNINGS

By Luis Valdez

El Teatro Campesino is somewhere between Brecht and Cantinflas. It is a farmworkers' theater, a bilingual propaganda theater, but it borrows from Mexican folk humor to such an extent that its "propaganda" is salted with a wariness for human caprice. Linked by a cultural umbilical cord to the National Farm Workers Association, the Teatro lives in Delano as a part of a social movement. We perform for the grape strikers at weekly meetings, seek to clarify strike aims, and go on tour throughout the state publicizing and raising funds for the *Huelga*.

Our most important aim is to reach the farmworkers. All the actors are farmworkers, and our single topic is the *Huelga*. We must create our own material, but this is hardly a limitation. Neither is our concentration on the strike. The hardest thing at first was fixing limits, some kind of dramatic form within which to work. Working together, we developed what we call *"actos"*—10- to 15-minute skits, sometimes with and sometimes without songs. We insist on calling them *actos* rather than skits, not only because we talk in Spanish most of the time, but because "skit" seems too light a word for the work we are trying to do.

Starting from scratch with a real-life incident, character, or idea, everybody in the Teatro contributes to the development of an *acto*. Each is intended to make at least one specific point about the strike, but improvisations during each performance sharpen, alter, or embellish the original idea. We use no scenery, no scripts, and no curtain. We use costumes and props only casually—an old pair of pants, a wine bottle, a pair of dark glasses, a mask, but mostly we like to show we are still strikers underneath, armbands and all. This effect is very important to our aims. To simplify things, we hang signs around our necks, sometimes in black and white, sometimes in lively colors, indicating the characters portrayed.

Practicing our own brand of *commedia dell' arte*, we improvise within the framework of traditional characters associated with the strike. Instead of Arlecchinos, Pantalones, and Brighellas, we have *Esquiroles* (scabs), *Contratistas* (contractors), *Patroncitos* (growers), and *Huelguistas* (strikers). We have experimented with these four types in dozens of combinations. Being free to act as they will, to infuse a character type with real thought and feeling, the farmworkers of the Teatro have expressed the human complexity of the grape strike. This is where Brecht comes in. As propaganda, the Teatro is loyal to an *a priori* social end: the winning of the strike. We not only presume Our Cause is just; we know it.

Every member of the Teatro, however, *knows* it differently. We vary in age from 18 to 44, with drastically different degrees of education, but we are all drawn into the Teatro by a common enthusiasm to express what we individually know and feel. The freedom to do so lifts our propaganda into Brecht-like theater: Our Just Cause is many-faceted, like human nature.

The Teatro appeals to its actors for the same reason it appeals to its audience. It explores the meaning of a social movement without asking its participants to read or write. It is a learning experience with no formal prerequisites. This is all-important because most farmworkers have never had a chance to go to school and are alienated by classrooms, blackboards, and the formal teacher-student approach.

By contrast, our Cantinflas-inspired burlesque is familiar to the farmworkers. It is in the family; it is *raza*; it is part of the Mexican people. They know that the Teatro discusses the *Huelga*, but the actors are fellow farmworkers and strikers, not teachers. If the Teatro has a point to make, it is just a step ahead of the audience, and the audience takes the step easily.

In a Mexican way, we have discovered what Brecht is all about. If you want unbourgeois theater, find unbourgeois actors to do it. Your head could burst open at the simplicity of the act, not the thought, but that's the way it is in Delano. Real theater lies in the excited laughter (or silence) of recognition *in the audience*, not in all the paraphernalia on the stage. Minus actors, the entire Teatro can be packed into one trunk, and when the Teatro goes on tour, the spirit of Delano goes with it.

The Teatro toured with the pilgrimage from Delano to Sacramento. Part of the purpose of the *peregrinación* then was to "turn on" the farmworkers of the San Joaquin Valley, to expose them to our growing *Huelga* movement. The Teatro performed nightly at all the rallies we held in more than 20 farmworker towns. The response of the audience to the Teatro in all of these towns was a small triumph, within the greater triumph of the NFWA march.

Perhaps the best key to the "theater" of the Teatro Campesino is a description of our most successful performance on the pilgrimage. It occurred in Freeport, a small town just nine miles southwest of Sacramento. We were to arrive at the Capitol in two days, and Governor Brown had just refused to meet with us on Easter Sunday. He had previously promised he would meet the pilgrimage somewhere on the road, but that was off too.

The Teatro Campesino decided to bring the governor to the rally that same night. We revamped an old skit we had on Governor Brown and which also involved the "DiGorgio Fruit Corp." and "Schunley." The "Schunley" character was dropped because Schenley Industries had recognized the NFWA as its workers' sole bargaining agent two days before. We replaced "Schunley" with another grower type, a "Mr. Zunavuvich," which—believe it or not—sounds incredibly like the name of a ranching family in Delano. To supplement Zunavuvich, and to hit at another DiGiorgio interest, we introduced a new character, "Bank Amerika."

When the time for the Teatro came, the DiGorgio character—complete with sign, dark glasses, and cigar—leaped onto the one-and-a-half-ton truck used as a stage for the nightly rallies, and was quickly booed and reviled by the farmworker audience of over 300. Threatening them with loss of their jobs, blackballing, and deportation, DiGorgio blustered and guffawed his way through all the booing, and announced that his old high school buddy, the Governor, was coming to speak to them that same night, and in Spanish. At this point, a car with a siren and a loudspeaker drove up behind the audience, honking and moving toward the platform. An authoritative voice commanded the workers to move out of the way, and the outside rally was momentarily halted as "Governor Brown" was pulled out of the car by his cronies and pushed onto the stage. The "Governor" protested all the way that he couldn't speak Spanish, but DiGorgio, Zunavuvich, and Bank Amerika convinced him to try:

"*No Huelga*," they exhorted, "just say *no Huelga!*"

"And *no boycoteo*," insisted DiGorgio.

The "Governor"—played by long, thin, dark Augustín Lira wearing a huge fake paunch—not only spoke Spanish, though brokenly at first; he spoke so ardently that he turned into a Mexican. This is the turning point of the acto. DiGorgio and his friends were forced to drag the metamorphosed Governor off the stage, as he shouted "*Huelga! Huelga!*" all the way down, to the laughter and applause of the farmworker audience.

It has never been easy to measure the actual effect of the Teatro as serious social propaganda, but we do receive indirect reports occasionally. After one Bakersfield performance we were told that two scabs vowed never to come to Delano as strikebreakers again, and they cited the Teatro's satire as the reason for their change of heart. More encouraging than anything is that farmworkers on the march kept asking, "Is there going to be a Teatro tonight?"

The first striker to join the Teatro was Augustín Lira, then 21. Irrepressible songwriter and guitar player, Augie was born in Torreón, Coahuila, Mexico. He had been a farmworker all his life, following the crops from Texas to California with his mother and seven brothers and sisters. He was picking grapes in the Fresno area when the strike started in Delano. He joined it in the second week. Proud and rebellious, he expresses a fierce loyalty to the *raza* through his gentle and sensitive songs.

Other early members of the group were Errol Franklin, a

native of Cheyenne, Wyoming, who worked as a horsebreaker, fisherman, apple picker, tomato picker, short-order cook, waiter, and longshoreman; Felope Cantu, a comic genius born and raised in Nuevo León, Mexico; Gilbert Rubio, third in a family of 13, born and raised in Lubbock, Texas, and who got his chance to act as the rotten, smelly grape in the *Tres Uves* acto.

These men are only a few of the many farmworkers who have participated in the Teatro. Unfortunately for the Teatro, actors, encouraged to express themselves, often showed leadership potential and were put to work doing other things for the association. Some of our best natural talents were sent to organize or boycott in Los Angeles, San Francisco, and as far away as Texas.

The Teatro by its mere existence condemns the real loss of human talent, the deadening of the human spirit, the brutalization of mind and body caused by the callous, feudal exploitation that is farm labor today. More than that, it affords us the opportunity to laugh as free men. The Teatro Campesino lives and grows in that laughter.

The Barrios, a Growing Awareness

THE BARRIO

By Ronald Arias

For many Americans home is still the ghetto.

The Chinatowns, Little Sicilies and Little Polands of the early century have long disappeared or have become tourist attractions. In their place are other "havens" for newcomers to the city. Hardly tourist spots, these pockets of poverty, tin-can alleys and rat nests are today the most serious and explosive fact in urban reality.

One newcomer to ghetto life is Ignacio Gonzalez, a young Los Angeles roofer's helper who recently moved from San Antonio, Texas, with his wife and three children.

"When I came here I wanted something better for my kids," Gonzalez said. "But now I don't know what to do."

A small, dark-eyed man, Gonzalez was sitting on the porch of his four-room house in the East Los Angeles ghetto called "Maravilla," or "Paradise." Behind him the windows were broken or cracked, the woodwork unpainted and splitting.

He explained he had only a sixth-grade education, and was now working part-time. Looking out across the littered street to the distant freeway, Gonzalez seemed sadly resigned about his future. "Maybe we'll always live here. Who knows? It costs money to live like a *gabacho* (Anglo-white)."

For Gonzalez and thousands of others the ghetto is no longer "just a temporary place" before moving into better areas. It has become a permanent home.

Why do people remain in the ghettoes? Broadly speaking, the answer lies in the differences between the dominant "white" society and the minority ghetto world. Jobs, schooling, income, family size, color and cultural values are a few of the obvious differences. In part, they are the causes of boiling frustration.

One attempt towards understanding the problem of housing segregation was made by the Mexican-American Study Project at the University of California, Los Angeles. The project was mainly concerned with the least known of the "big" minorities—the Mexican Americans. Concentrated primarily in five Southwestern states—California, Colorado, New Mexico, Texas and Arizona—they number today close to an estimated seven million.

So far, said Project Director Leo Grebler, there has been a vast ignorance prevailing outside the Southwest about the Mexican Americans. "And while people in the Southwest are more aware of this minority, false stereotypes and indifference to its problems are still widespread."

Most every town and city in the Southwest has its "little Mexico" or barrio. They range in size from a cluster of Arizona desert shacks to the sprawling Boyle Heights area in the heart of Los Angeles.

Many of these barrios began as original settlements around a square, or plaza. Gradually they were encircled by the larger city. Other barrios sprouted from former agricultural labor camps and communities. These were usually located on the fringes of the city.

As the cities grew, occupations in these areas changed. The worker now found his job in a factory instead of a field. Or else he would split his time between city and field.

There are still good reminders of what these farming ghettoes used to be. The shack towns on the outskirts of Fresno, California, are examples.

But in many areas, especially in Texas, the Mexican Americans have traditionally been the majority—in numbers if not in political power. Laredo and Rio Grande City are such places.

In other words, there is an enormous variety in the kinds of Mexican American ghettoes. Some form entire towns, some are seedlings of a few houses, just beginning, and still others can trace their origins back to sixteenth-century Spanish colonization.

And yet together—through a common language and cultural background—they are distinct. Largely because of their heritage, they remain shut off from the mainstream of American society. In this sense, they face problems similar to any disadvantaged minority.

The UCLA project for the first time showed statistically just how heavy these lines of segregation are in the Southwest. Based on census figures from 35 Southwestern cities, it examined housing segregation among the three largest population groups—Anglo whites, Negroes and Mexican Americans.

Results showed without exception that Negroes were much more segregated than Mexican Americans. But in such cities as Dallas, Denver, Houston, Los Angeles, Phoenix and San Antonio the degree of separation for both groups has remained high.

Segregation between Negroes and Mexican Americans was also seen to be severe.

The least amount of segregation was found between Anglos and Mexican Americans. This was especially so in Laredo, Texas; Colorado Springs, Colorado; and Galveston, Texas. Of all 35 cities, Sacramento was found to have the least separation between Anglos and Mexican Americans.

Among the Mexican Americans there is also some segregation between native born and foreign born.

A major effort of the study focused on an "exploratory" analysis of the causes of residential segregation. It was exploratory because the reasons segregation exists are complex and difficult to measure. As the researchers explained, some facts of life are hard to analyze through mere statistics.

Perhaps the most important factor—discrimination—is the one that so far has gone unexplained. Though discriminatory practices are documented against both minorities, the authors of the study, Joan W. Moore and Frank G. Mittelbach, conclude that they cannot statistically account for discrimination.

This is probably because it often goes under other names, such as prejudice, dislike or hate. Perhaps it is just snobbishness or lack of sympathy for the minority person. Whatever the reasons, discrimination exists.

Without hazarding imperfect guesses, the study found four important factors in accounting for segregation:

*The larger the city, the greater is the separation between Negroes and Anglos, Mexican Americans and Anglos, and Mexican Americans and Negroes.

*The greater the number of large family households among the two minorities, the more severe is the segregation.

*Income does little to explain the segregation between Mexican Americans and Negroes.

*Separation of either minority from the dominant groups is greater in cities with a larger nonwhite population than their Mexican American population.

Whatever the causes may be, the barrios remain. They are places few people point to with pride—even though there are hundreds of examples existing in the midst of American affluence.

MARÍA TEPACHE

A Story
By Amado Muro

In San Antonio, I got off a Southern Pacific freight train near the tracks that spidered out from the roundhouse turntable. When I quit the train it was almost five o'clock, and the sky was dark with the smoky pall of thunderheads. I was tired and chilled and hungry. I hoped to find something to eat and then get on to Houston.

Nearby was a small white-frame Mexican grocery with a corrugated tin porch held up by a few warped scantlings. The window displayed lettuce heads and coffee in paper sacks, and near the door was a wire bin of oranges. A dog lay on the porch before the door. I went in and asked a buxom, gray-haired woman with a round face and untroubled eyes if she could spare some day-olds.

"Ay, Señora Madre de San Juan, I just fed four hoboes and I can't feed no more," she said.

I started out the door then, but she called me back. She stared at me, her dark eyes becoming very round. "*Hijole, paisanito*, what spider has stung you—you look sad and burdened like the woodcutter's burro," she said. "Well, I don't blame you. When bread becomes scarce so do smiles."

The gray-haired woman wore a blue dress that was cut straight and came to her knees, and she had on huaraches. She told me her name was María Rodriquez, but she said people all called her María Tepache because she liked *tepache* with big pineapple chunks in it so well. We talked of different things—about where she came from was one. She came from a Durango village populated mostly, she said, by old men, old women, and goats.

"I was born in one of those homes where burros sleep with Christians," she said. "I can read and eat with a spoon, but I'm not one of those women meant to live in homes that would be like cathedrals if they had bells. In our adobe hut

village, we lived a primitive life with no more light than the
sky gives and no more water than that of the river. But my
father never stopped feeding me because he couldn't give me
bonbons or clothing me because he couldn't dress me in
silks."

She asked me where I was from, her face intent with
strong interest. When I told her, she appeared surprised.
"¡*Valgame* San Crispin! I'd never had guessed it," she said.

When I asked why, she smiled and said: "Most Chihuahua
people don't talk so fast as we of Durango. But you talk fast,
and with the accent *Santa María de todo el mundo*."

After that she put on a *cambaye* apron with a big bow in
back, and led me to the back of the store where all the living
was done. "This is your humble kitchen—come in," she
invited.

The place was like all the homes of poor Mexicans that
I'd seen in Texas. There was a broken-legged woodstove,
a shuck tick bed, a straight-back chair, a mirror with the
quicksilver gone, and a table covered with oilcloth frayed
and dark at the edges. Beyond the stove and to one side was
an old cupboard with the doors standing open. The kitchen's
bare floor was clean, and the walls were painted wood with
only a calendar picture of Nicolás Bravo that hung crookedly
from its nail as decoration. On a tiny shelf in a corner was a
gilt-framed picture of María Guadalupana and a crucified
Christ.

The window had burlap curtains, and Doña María explained why she put them up long ago. "In a place where
there aren't any curtains on the windows you can't expect
children to turn out well," she said.

She lit a coal-oil lamp, and set it on the table. Outside it
was beginning to rain. Wind blew the rain in through the
window and made the lamp burn unevenly and smoke the
chimney. The chimney blackened until only a ring around
the base gave off light. Doña María closed the window and
afterward stood near the lamp and told me she was a widow.
Standing there very still with heavy lashes lowered, she
spoke of her husband and her voice was husky. The dog that

had lain on the porch was curled on the floor by the bed, his head resting on his outspread paws and his eyes watching her.

"In our village my husband was an *adobero*, and he came here to earn *dólarotes* in the pecan mills," she said. "I wasn't one of those model Mexican wives who leave their wills in the church, but we were happy together and I never worried that he'd fall in love with another *chancluda* prettier than me. He couldn't read or write, but I went through the fourth grade at the Justo Sierra School and I taught him about numbers so he could count the stars with our first son. When our *centavos* married and multiplied, he talked about going back to Mexico. '*¡Ay Mariquita!* If we can go back someday I swear I'll climb Popocatepetl on my hands,' he told me. 'We could go to Puebla on the other side of the volcanoes, and buy land near the *magueyes* and *milpas*. We'll buy three cows, and each will give her three *litros*. Our *chilpayates* will never dance the *Jarabe Moreliano* with hunger.'"

Her face softened in a reflection of faraway dreaminess. She said her husband made Puebla sound like Bagdad, and talked of singing to her with twenty *mariachis*.

"Now I live with no more company than my own sins," she said. "I pass my life tending the store, and mending the clothes of my many grandchildren." She broke off and lowered her lids over her eyes, veiling them. Her mouth grew set, a thin, straight line; she passed her hands over her forehead as though awakening from sleep. Her gray hair was in a tangled cloud about her face, and she looked older than I'd thought at first seeing her. But when she looked up toward me, she was smiling again and her dark eyes were calm and reflective. "My grandchildren are less brutes than I," she said. "All of them know how to speak the gringo."

I hung my crumpled crush hat on a nail behind the kitchen door and went out in the backyard to split stovewood. The backyard was cluttered with piled-up packing boxes and crates, and the grass was yellow with sand. There was a stumpy cottonwood near the water tap, and a row of sweetpeas clinging to a network of strings tacked on the fence. The cottonwood leaves had turned yellow, but they were still flat with green streaks showing in them. Every once in a while the wind would shake the branches and a flurry of dry leaves and dust funneled up near me.

I split wood, carried out ash buckets, and brought water in a zinc pail. While I worked, Doña María bent over a larded frying pan and told me about her father.

"He was a shepherd and a good man—never ambitious for the *centavos*," she said. "He was happy and contented with no more ambition than not to lose a lamb and go down to Santiago Papasquiaro two or three times a year to hear the *mariachis* play in the plaza and listen to the church bells."

When I finished the chores, night was coming and the rain was heavier. There was lightning, vivid flashes that scarred the sky, and I could see San Antonio's lights golden as oil lamps beyond the new Braunfels Bridge. The rain fell through the yellow lamplight streaming from the kitchen window, and cars, their lamps wet gems, moved slowly across the high bridge. Their headlights seemed to draw the raindrops, like moths. I looked at them for a moment, rain spattering off my shoulders, then went inside.

Doña María had finished setting the table. She wiped sweat from her forehead with a fold of her apron, and began to fan herself. Then she motioned me to a plate filled with refried beans, rice, and *blanquillos*.

"*Esa es mecha*," she said. "It will make you feel like shouting, '*Yo soy Mexicano*,' in the middle of a crowded street. Eat—one can think of nothing good when he's hungry."

I ate so fast I grew short of breath. Doña María watched me with her arms wrapped in her apron and crossed over her chest. She looked solemn except for a faint flicker of a smile at the corner of her mouth. The dog sat on his haunches beside her bare legs.

When I finished, she gave me an *ixtle* shopping bag filled with *tamales de dulce*, *nopalitos*, a milk bottle of *champurrado*, and a *tambache* of flour tortillas wrapped in a piece of newspaper. I tried half-heartedly to refuse it. But she insisted I take it.

"I have enough for today, perhaps tomorrow, and another day too," she said. "After that, God will say."

When I thanked her, she smiled her mild smile and told me to say the prayer of San Luisito every day.

"May the Indian Virgin who spoke with Juan Diego protect you and cover you with her mantle," she said when I went out the door, "and may you become rich enough to drink chocolate made with milk and eat *gorditas* fried in Guadalajara butter."

Egton had abruptly … relate it. But he pushed [

…

… he was still to obey … him as if … and another …

When I married," … the same … his right side and you …

"Now you don't … of S.I.T … upon you …

"… I am going on … Wherefore … that they protect, you, and cover you with his justice," she said, when I went out the door; "and … you become … myself to that … blessed time … blood, and said, when … the faith of … Guardian love letter.

MY NAME IS JESÚS

By Jesús Ascension Arreola, Jr.

My name is Jesús.
The last one I don't know.
Does that make a difference?
My last one I don't know;
My first one was a gift.
I didn't earn either one.

My name is foreign,
Yet I was home born.
I am not an abortion.
Nor am I a prince,
    or a juggler of balls.
I am a little world.

The Universe is my eyes.
The planets are my arms and legs.
My Sun is my love.
The cold and the hate that
    cling to the ship of hope are
    supplied by you.

But what do I say?
That I talk with an accent?
You listen to my voice, yes,
    but not to my words.
For each man must say something
    in protest of the cold.

My name is man.
My skin is brown;
    but is yours warm?
And that makes a difference.
We're all here.
My name is Jesús.

And what is yours?
Is it in the phone book?
I'll bet you live someplace.
But then, someone lives in Tasmania.
Are you vaccinated against love?
Or have you developed an antidote.

I suppose you've volunteered for heaven.
Made arrangements for your cloud.
Will you look for your neighbor?
You might have to look hard.
Only your name will get you there,
And my name is Jesús.

THEIR HERITAGE—POVERTY

By Manuel Aragon

It was election time again and the old politician was making his rounds. He came to the barrio and made his usual speech. As he left, he saw a little boy selling newborn puppies for a dollar each. "What fine puppies," he told the boy. "I'll be back soon to buy one from you."

Two years later, the politician returned and found the boy still in business. "Those puppies have grown into beautiful dogs," he said. "Here is your dollar for one of them."

"Not a chance," said the boy. "They are worth a lot more now that their eyes are open."

Alfredo Sánchez often makes his Bryn Mawr, California, neighbors laugh over a good *cuento*. His stories always have a lesson and they respect him. After all, he earns almost $4,000 a year and drives a '63 Chevy.

In Bryn Mawr, a Mexican American community sixty miles east of Los Angeles, Alfredo is considered a success.

One-third of his neighbors live on less than $40 a week earned in the packing sheds. Some drive old cars fifty miles through the desert to Coachella for their jobs. Another third are on welfare.

Unlike Bryn Mawr across the country in Pennsylvania, this California town is not a pleasant place to live in. Cool, orderly orange groves surround it, but there are no paved streets, rain gutters, sewers, street lights, or recreational areas. Two-thirds of its homes are dilapidated. Cracked plaster, leaky roofs, sagging porches, and bad plumbing are the rule. Alfredo and his neighbors are poor, and now they, too, have opened their eyes.

The people of Bryn Mawr, like Mexican Americans throughout the Southwest, are beginning to see and grudgingly admit the widespread poverty of their group. They have long felt it . . . privately. Now, their poverty is also publicly recorded in cold, hard statistics.

A special report published by the UCLA Mexican-American Study Project spells out the dismal details of poverty among the seven million Spanish surname people who live in Arizona, California, Colorado, New Mexico, and Texas. The report, titled *The Burden of Poverty*, reads like a handicap sheet for young Mexican Americans.

People with Spanish surnames, for example, are more likely to be poor than other whites, and less likely to finish high school than any other group including Negroes. Very few Mexican Americans get to college.

The study reveals that almost two-thirds of the Mexican Americans who live in rural areas like Bryn Mawr are poor. Of the one million Mexican Americans who live in rural towns or villages over 600,000 are poor. Almost as many rural Mexican Americans live in poverty as the total population of San Francisco.

The UCLA report also shows that rural Mexican Americans cannot escape their poverty by moving to the cities where 80 percent of all Mexican Americans live. In the cities, one out of every three Mexican Americans lives in abject poverty . . . in gross figures, 1,500,000—a population equal to the entire state of Arkansas or Nebraska.

Compared with Negroes, another group far down on the economic scale, Mexican Americans appear to have a slightly higher family income. But in fact, because Mexican American families are usually larger, the amount of money per person is less for Mexican Americans than for any other group.

In California, for example, Mexican Americans have an average income of $1,380 per person per year as against $1,437 for the Negro, a difference of $57. The white majority population of California has a per capita average annual income of over $2,110, about $700 more than either Mexican Americans or Negroes.

Larger families and lower per capita income result in worse housing for Mexican Americans than for anybody else. The UCLA Mexican-American Study Project proves that substandard housing and overcrowding are by far most prevalent among Mexican Americans.

Extremely poor housing puts the individual under unbearable stress and frustration and destroys his self-confidence and initiative. More than 1,700,000 Mexican Americans live in such housing.

Graciela Olivarez, an outstanding Mexican American and member of the National Advisory Council for the War on Poverty, has pointed out that the poverty of the Mexican Americans' parents is inherited by their children. Of more than 2,000,000 poor Mexican Americans, over half are children. According to Mrs. Olivarez, it looks like the poor children of today will live in poverty as adults tomorrow.

In Tucson, Arizona, several years ago, participants in a national poverty conference heard one account from a 19-year-old Mexican American girl from Colorado:

> Six years before the conference she had taken an overdose of sleeping pills because she was "tired of working and depressed" at the age of 13.
> "I got a car, the car broke down. I couldn't pay for it and they wanted to sue me, so I forged a check." Married at 15, she was left to support her child alone since her husband was sent to jail.
> "I started working the town, I got paid for it—they call it hustling . . . I needed the money . . . to go out and hustle, I had to be under the influence of narcotics."

A few weeks after the Tucson conference, Diana was found dead of an accidental overdose of narcotics.

Larry Wycoff of the *San Antonio News* reported another poverty victim: little 8-year-old Lucie was barred from the Mackey-Cable Elementary School. Her father could not afford to pay a two-dollar fee for school supplies demanded by the school principal.

Another report shows that even if she gets into school, Lucie and other young Mexican Americans in San Antonio will be shortchanged. Her school will put up one-third less money per student than other schools in the city. Of her teachers, one in four will have a substandard degree, and the odds are five to one against her going on to college.

Yet, her chances for college may be better than those of Mexican Americans in California. According to Educational

Opportunity Program (EOP) reports for 1970, 18 percent of Californians are members of minority groups—blacks, Mexican Americans, Indians, and Asians. But only 5 percent of minority students go on to state colleges. Negroes, not in any sense a privileged group, still greatly outnumber the Mexican Americans in colleges. At UCLA in 1966, for example, the Negro students outnumbered the Mexican Americans by ten to one, although, largely due to the benefits of the EOP, the number of Mexican American enrollments is increasing each semester.

The great disparity between the ability of Mexican Americans and Negroes to get into college reflects what happens in the earlier school years. Negro youngsters stay in school longer than Mexican Americans though both groups suffer heavy losses through the first nine grades. By and large, the schools have not solved the problems of giving a good education to children whose first language is Spanish.

The unresponsiveness of the schools and the pressures at home for more money result in a devastating number of dropouts or, more properly, force-outs, since these circumstances tend to push the kids out of school. The lack of schooling among Mexican Americans will have increasingly severe economic consequences since the educational requirements for employment are climbing and will continue to do so.

The real income of some Mexican Americans has dropped in the last few years despite the general prosperity of the nation. This fact was discovered by a special census of East Los Angeles, a Mexican American barrio, recently released by the Department of Commerce.

A major reason for this drop, one tied directly to education, was a decline from 27 percent in 1960 to 24 percent in 1965 of Mexican Americans holding professional, technical, and managerial positions or jobs as craftsmen and foremen.

In other words, Mexican Americans are losing their weak hold on the better paying jobs.

It is clear that the grease pencil of poverty will continue

to cross off young hopes and adult ambitions, that the poverty of the Mexican Americans will get worse during the 1970's unless the downward trend is reversed by massive corrective programs.

EL TEATRO CAMPESINO TODAY and EL TEATRO URBANO

By James Santibañez

To the Chicano, the symbol of life in California's San Joaquin Valley is the soil. Out of its richness and fertility come the grapes, oranges, lettuce, barley, and other crops that sustain much of the state and much of the world.

From Bakersfield and Merced in the south to Stockton and Tracy in the north, local communities owe their existence to the soil. Visalia, Tulare, Delano, and other similar towns serve as focal points for the surrounding farm areas.

The backbone of the valley's prosperity is the farmer who grows the many fruits and vegetables. But if the farmer, or grower, is the backbone, the blood and sinew are supplied by the farmworker, usually a migrant, who labors long and hard to make the dream of a "Golden State" a reality. Without him, there would be no $4 billion-a-year agribusiness. Without him, the soil, perhaps, would revert to its condition of 150 years ago—an arid, wind-sucked land covered with sagebrush and inhabited mainly by the coyote, bobcat, and ring-tailed pheasant.

The migrant worker gets up at five a. m., is picked up in a roadside barrio at six a. m. and loaded into a bus, truck, or van with other workers. He is driven five, ten, or thirty miles to the fields to work the day under a hot sun. A break in the midmorning, thirty minutes for lunch, and a ten-minute break in the afternoon provide his only rest periods. He spends the rest of the day either hunched down cutting lettuce, carrying a ladder from one orange tree to another, or picking grapes from the vines. After a ten-hour workday, he is taken back to his desolate barrio.

His life is a stunted and impoverished existence of hard work, weariness, and sweat. His vacuous social life is broken only by an occasional trip to the nearest town. From year to year, his life is uncertain, his work sporadic. During the harvest season of three or four months, he has plenty of work—often at wages approximating $1.50 an hour, sometimes—if he is lucky—more. But the rest of the year he lives from day to day, week to week, and month to month until he finds new work. He usually must move to where jobs are available or he and his family will not eat.

This is why in the summer of 1965 Cesar Chavez began to attempt to organize the farmworker in the heart of the San Joaquin Valley. In Delano he led the first strike against the grape growers of the area. There were moments of bitter confrontation between the growers and the strikers. And there were moments of tense waiting while the antagonists of the strikers prepared for the next encounter.

During a lull, Cesar Chavez, Luis Valdez, and Augustín Lira discussed ways in which the energies of the workers could be best utilized. Chavez, the organizer, urged Luis Valdez and Augustín Lira to keep the workers interested in the strike, to keep their morale high. Valdez, who was to become known as the founder of El Teatro Campesino, had the idea of mimicking the growers who would come to harass the strikers. Valdez and his group would imitate the actions of the growers on the picket lines.

Thus was born El Chicano Teatro—the Chicano Theater.

Its first two years were spent performing for the Chicano community. Its plays were mostly improvised, bilingual, combining hilarious comedy, music, song, and Brechtian social satire.

In 1967, the group with its growing numbers put on the play called *The Three Grapes* (*Tres Uves*) to a mixed audience in Santa Barbara. The scenes depicted the relationships between the grower, the striker, and other characters involved in the drama. Songs were an important part of the play and were sung at the appropriate times. For most of the novice actors, it was a difficult time. Some of the roles they played were both foreign and obnoxious to them, but they learned to cope with these difficulties and to go on with the play.

The Three Grapes

Players:

Esquirol:	Scab; wears sign around his neck.
Huelgista:	Striker; has his neck on the block.
Patroncito:	Little Boss.
Contratista:	Middleman—the most hated man. Usually a Mexican who lives off the skills of others and who hires or fires them at will.
Private Guard:	Gringo.
Farmworker:	Portrayed pruning with scissors, picking fruit from a tree, or bending down and cutting lettuce.

Tours began for El Teatro Campesino. One of the earliest was to Sacramento, with Cesar Chavez and his *Huelga* march. Then, others: San Jose, Los Gatos, San Francisco, Los Angeles, in California; and to the Southwest and East. In 1968, it won an Obie (Off-Broadway) award which cited the Teatro "for creating a workers' theatre to demonstrate the politics of survival." In 1969, it appeared at the World Theatre Festival in Nancy, France, and a review in *Le Monde* read, "They do not appear to be acting at all . . . They do not go to the people; they come from the people."

But the Teatro is still that of the farmworker. It is El Teatro Campesino. Its origin and strength lie in the toil and sweat of the farm laborer. It comes directly from the strike. It has its roots in *Huelga*. It is an expression of the cause and struggle of the Chicano. El Teatro Campesino's motto: "Don't say it; do it." It responds to reality. It has become part of the movement of *La Raza*.

The seasons play an important part in the existence of the farmworker. In the play *La Quinta Temporal* the Teatro is concerned with the varying effects that each of the seasons has on the farmworker. The characters of Don Sotaco and Don Coyote were first portrayed by Augustín Lira, the four seasons by Luis Valdez, Daniel Valdez, and others in the cast.

The grower is played by a gringo member of the group. The fifth season, *La Quinta Temporal*, represents social justice.

La Quinta Temporal

Players:

Don Sotaco: Comes from Mexico looking for work.

Don Coyote: All-purpose Anglo.

Grower: Gringo.

First Season: Summer. The fruits of summer slip through Don Sotaco's hands and into the grower's pockets.

Second Season: Autumn. With no more work, Don Sotaco's difficulties increase.

Third Season: Winter, who gets money from the grower who is going to Acapulco.

Fourth Season: Spring, who tells Don Sotaco to get the hell out of here. This is the moment when Don Sotaco begins to fight for his rights.

Fifth Season: *La Quinta Temporal* (Social Justice). Help comes from the Church, from the Mexican Americans (*La Raza*), and the unions.

The climax of the play is reached when Don Sotaco signs the contract between the growers and the workers who are represented by the unions.

The Teatro also presents a puppet show depicting the two cultures that make up the Chicano community. The main purpose of the play is to express the feeling and fact that our ancient civilization was driven underground by conquest. Music by the band, *Banda Calavera*, adds to the strength of the theme. By wearing masks and garments representing those of skeletons, the members of the band show both defiance of death and a hope for the rebirth of our culture as they parade and play their instruments.

Los Bandidos is a play portraying the stereotyped Mexican.

Los Bandidos

Players:

Honest Harry:	Proprietor of a Mexican Curio Shop. Sign: "Honest Harry—Used Mexican."
Farmworker:	Wears large sombrero, is dirty, eats beans, tortillas, chile, lives in an old shack, speaks no English, and his work is called *el hale*.
Miss Martinez:	Pronounced *Martin es* (looking for a cheap used Mexican).
Pachuco:	Cop-killer, wears dark glasses, has urban shuffle, likes fights and dances, gets arrested (is handcuffed), is economical, lives on hamburgers, soft drinks, pot, and glue, has built-in inferiority complex, owns a knife, is self-supporting (steals).
Revolutionario:	Present-day Mexican revolutionary. Drinks tequila, eats raw meat, smells like a horse, was made in Mexico in 1910, wears sarape, and yells *Viva Villa!*
Mexican American:	Wears suit and tie, well-bred, clean, has college education, functions on school board and in political machines, and is patriotic. Cash value, $15,000. Likes Langendorf Bread, TV dinners; on ceremonial occasions eats Mexican food. His only malfunction is that he gives out an exhaust.

The play *Pancho Villa* is about the modern Chicano family and the inability of the Chicano to accomplish anything in the gringo culture. It is this feeling of helplessness which Pancho Villa symbolizes.

Pancho Villa

Players:

Pancho Villa: Oldest brother without a body.
Middle son: Returns from the service, lives in the land of opportunity.
Joaquin: Pachuco who is on welfare.
Father: A wino, exploited, came from the Revolution.
Mother: All-suffering, all-forgiving.
Daughter: Frightened by her bodiless brother.

Pancho Villa was assassinated, in 1923, during the Mexican Revolution, and it is recorded that he was beheaded. To the imagination, the act was brutal and horrible, but also suggestive of a cosmic and tragic significance. The cosmic character of the Chicano is symbolized in the play.

These plays portray *La Raza* and *La Causa*—the cause, in its broadest sense now that the urgency of the grape strike is over—that is now in progress. *La Raza* Movement has its roots in our culture's past: our Indian and Spanish cultures. We are Chicanos. Anything that has to do with our culture is part of that Movement. The struggle to organize the farmworkers in the San Joaquin and Salinas Valley is part of the Movement. So are the efforts that are being expended through the Southwest from Rio City Valley of Texas, Colorado, Arizona, Nevada, and California to the Oregon border. The Movement has become a thorn in the side of the Anglo whose multimillion-dollar business has controlled the Southwest since 1915. The independent farmer has been gradually pushed out of the picture and replaced by the migrant worker who travels the Southwest in search of work, picking the fruits and vegetables of big business. Exploited, transitory, and deprived, he lives a barren existence.

Of these things the actors of the Teatro Chicano tell—and sing.

During the next two years conflicts within the group

emerged as to what direction the Teatro should take. Should it separate itself completely from the *campesino*—the field worker—to develop as a distinct theatrical unit? Or should it remain with the worker and *Huelga*? The Teatro could successfully depict the lives of the farmworkers in their environment and in their culture. But how could it portray the urban community with all the aspects that the Mexican American experiences in the political, social, and economic world?

The outgrowth of these different interests was the creation of El Teatro Urbano in San Jose, California, under the direction of Daniel Valdez. El Teatro Urbano is a bilingual theater group with many of its members high school and college students, as well as people who have made the theater their way of life.

The group describes itself: "El Teatro Urbano was formed because of the need to make our own people aware of the inadequacies of the Educational System . . . This system created a need for us to get together to relate to our people the racism, bias, and lack of understanding which was created by the Educational System. There was also a need to relate to our people the attitude with which the police, the judges, and various government agencies (welfare, unemployment, government funded programs) were dealing with our people in the barrio. Out of these needs then, we created a Teatro to work with and for the RAZA.

"El Teatro Urbano uses the theater as a tool of expression, as well as a tool of education, which makes our form of theater different from what you find in the "ON BROADWAY" tradition. It is our goal to reach a level of professionalism only to present a new medium to offer a solution to the one-sided viewpoint which the system perpetuates through television, movies, and theater. These forms of media present the oppressors' point of view and not that of the oppressed . . . Thus we hope that through this form of education we can make our RAZA aware and alert of the dangers of the American System."

Working with Daniel Valdez are his wife Armenia and a friend of the director, Ricardo Valdez.

As a reviewer for the Los Angeles *Herald-Examiner* observed of El Teatro Campesino, the urban group also possesses an "elemental aliveness ... They do everything—sing, polemicize, satirize—with a direct, nearly primitive gusto."

While guitar and bass are featured in their music, theirs is not a simple rendition of quiet Mexican folk music nor a laborious reading of complex orchestrations. Their music is free, with no touch of self-consciousness; it soars with a simple, bold, and captivating strength.

At this moment in the 1970's the impetus of the Teatro Chicano is directed toward the struggle for basic economic and social change in the fields, in the urban centers, in the schools. El Teatro Campesino and El Teatro Urbano are the first of the Teatro Chicano. New groups are forming—in Colorado, New Mexico, Arizona, Texas. They will be heard. A new theatrical medium has been created.

BARRIOLOGY EXAM

By Antonio Gómez

Among those publications which compromise with neither Chicano nor *gabacho*, which rise above the brainwashing of the Anglo educational system, is *Con Safos—Reflections of Life in the Barrio*, published quarterly in Los Angeles. Here, as in *La Raza, El Grito, Regeneración, El Gallo, El Grito del Norte, El Malcriado*, and other publications of the Chicano Press Association, the Chicano is finding a medium in which to develop his own literary forms and to interpret the rebirth of his culture.

A *Con Safos* editorial reads, "The *Con Safos* emphasis is on the literary and aesthetic forms that most accurately reflect our barrios and our people in the barrios. Further, it is the C/S goal to help develop and formulate art forms that are truly ours. We have no literary genre that is our own. We have no body of visual arts that reflect our life experience. . . . We have no defined or formalized aesthetics that delineate our ethnic relevance within the dominant culture of the United States . . .

"Not until our art forms are thus created, crystallized and formalized can we assure ourselves of this ethnic relevance in the spectrum of human experience."

One of the most popular features of *Con Safos* has been a series of Barriology Exams by Antonio Gómez, Art Coordinator of the magazine . . .

BARRIOLOGY EXAM

By Barriologist Emeritus—Antonio Gómez

1. Laurel and Hardy were popularly known in the barrio as

2. Duck _____ describes a hair style worn by barrio dudes in the 50's.

3. According to baby care practices of barrio women, tickling a baby will produce what defect?

4 Barrio tradition among youth has often demanded that students
   A. excel in school
   B. do poorly in school
   C. keep the group norm
   D. none of the above is applicable

5. *Pedichi* and *moocher* have what in common?

6. Eating watermelon and drinking beer simultaneously is, according to barrio lore,
   A. sexually stimulating
   B. bad for one's stomach
   C. good for hangovers
   D. not an ethnic diet

7. What slang name refers to the older barrio dudes?

8. Large brown market bags have been used in barrio households for what purpose? How about ½ gallon milk cartons?

9. Complete the following children's chant:

   > *De tin marin*
   > *de do pinque*
   > *cucara macara*
   >
   > _____

10. Lowered, channeled, chopped, primed all refer to what barrio art form?

11. "Chanate" refers to what two things in barrio slang?

12. Barrio baby care practices require what procedure when a child's *mollera* falls?

13. If you had to assure someone of your sincerity or truthfulness, you would be most likely to say *lo juro por* ____

14. Many young men in the barrio have traditionally wanted to go airborne. What does this mean?

15. *Sopa* made from tortillas is called _____

16. Juarez, Chihuahua, is across from what USA city, and what was the name of the strip of land from this city that was recently returned to Mexico?

17. Someone who is described as a *lechusa* is a
    A. lettuce peddler
    B. leech
    C. milkman
    D. night person

18. The first Chicano to have a big hit record was the person who sang DONNA; what was his name?

19. A green carder is a person who_____

20. Barrio myth has it that one who eats a great deal of salt will become like what kind of animal?

21. *Capirotada* is the traditional food during what time of year?

22. Those people referred to as *manitos* come from what part of the USA?

23. In *rebote*, when one is going to play the next game, the expression for this is _____ and that person must perform what function in the game that is in progress?

24. In the old barrio when a child would accidentally drop a piece of candy or food, he had to perform what ritual in order to pick it up and eat it?

25. The accidental dropping of silverware in a barrio household predicts what event according to popular belief?

26. According to the best in barrio tradition, if a bill collector comes to a house to collect money, the woman of the house will_____

27. Miniskirts were worn originally in the barrio by whom?

28. *Halfers* when used by the youths of the barrio refers to what practice?

29. Complete the following children's chant:

> *Pelon Pelonete*
> *Cabeza de quete*
> *Vendiendo Tamales*

_____

30. Bicarbonate of Soda is popularly known in the barrio as

_____

ANSWERS TO BARRIOLOGY EXAM

1. *El gordo y el Flaco.*
2. Ducktail.
3. A speech defect.
4. C. Keep the group norm.
5. Both describe one who asks for handouts.
6. B. Bad for one's stomach.
7. *Veteranos*—adults who have been through barrio warfare and usually no longer take part in gang hassles.
8. Trash bags and garbage containers.
9. *Titere fue*—a chant used by children to select players for a game—similar to "one potato, two potato," etc.
10. A customized car.
11. Coffee and black or dark person.
12. (*Mollera* refers to the soft spot on a baby's head.) Pick up the child by his feet and let him hang, head down—this in order to restore the shape of the head.
13. *Mi Madre*—"I swear by my mother."
14. To join the paratroopers has been a sign of masculinity and courage.
15. *Chilaquiles.*
16. El Paso—El Chamisal.
17. D. Night person—literally means owl, but it has been used to describe people who stay out at night and are up to "no good."
18. Richie Valens.
19. Has immigrated to the USA

20. A burro with large ears.
21. During Lent.
22. New Mexico.
23. *Tiene el teles*—that person must keep score and referee the game in progress.
24. He would pick it up, dust it off and kiss it towards Heaven. This act would cleanse it from contamination of the devil.
25. Guests will be arriving.
26. Hide and not answer.
27. The *Cholas* or *Pachucas* in the early 1940's.
28. A demand by one to share in food, candy, etc., that his friend has.
29. *De cinco y de siete*—a children's taunt.
30. *Soda del Martillo*—Arm and Hammer Soda.

RATE YOURSELF ON THE CON SAFOS BARRIOLOGY QUOTIENT SCALE

Barriology Examination Questions answered correctly:

25 to 30	Chicano Barriologist, *o muy de aquellas.*
20 to 24	High Potential, *o ya casi*
15 to 19	Mexican American, *o keep trying ese*
10 to 14	*Vendido, o* culturally deprived
5 to 9	*Pobrecito*
0 to 4	*Pendejo*

Education, a Way In or Out

THE EDUCATION OF MEXICAN AMERICANS

By Philip D. Ortego

A Need for Bilingual Education

Without doubt the single most significant manifestation of the educational problems of Mexican Americans focuses in large part on language. However, to attack only this aspect of the problems will result in the kinds of failures that have too frequently characterized many such attempts.

Unfortunately, on the basis of "unsuccessful" attempts, far too many educators are prone to generalize that since they've tried and failed to solve the educational problems of Mexican Americans, either the students are unteachable or nothing will work. This "experiential fallacy" is at work in far too many school situations in the Southwest. The end result is frustration, stagnation, and alienation.

The education of Mexican Americans cannot be reduced to language only, for there is no one language problem but as many problems as there are Mexican American children with linguistic disadvantages. The truth is that the disadvantages are more the product of a thoroughly lexocentric, or linguistically chauvinistic, society than they are real; they are the product of ignorance about language and its communicative and social function; they are the product of distortion of Mexican American culture and history.

It must be pointed out, however, that the problems of Mexican Americans relate specifically to American life in spite of their linguistic ties to another culture. That many Mexican Americans do not speak American English makes them no less Americans, for their interests, attitudes, and aspirations differ little from those of other Americans. But at the moment, what best characterizes Mexican Americans in the Southwest is that most of them have a limited and inadequate education.

The educational statistics on Mexican Americans are shocking. For example, their dropout rate is more than twice the rate of the national average, and estimates of the average number of school years completed by Mexican Americans (7.1 years) are significantly below figures of Anglo children (12.1 years) and Negro pupils (9.0 years). A 1964 survey revealed that in Texas 39 percent of its Mexican Americans had less than a fifth-grade education; and Mexican Americans 25 years of age and older have as little as 4.8 years of schooling. Almost half of the Mexican Americans in Texas are essentially still functional illiterates. In California, 50 percent of Spanish-speaking students drop out of school by the time they reach the eighth grade.

The percentage of Mexican American children entering first grade knowing enough English to move forward with their peers is slight. More startling, though, is that many Mexican American youngsters never get to the first grade. Four out of five of those who do fall two grades behind their Anglo classmates by the time they reach fifth grade. Consequently, more than 50 percent of Mexican American high school students drop out between grades 10 and 11.

This situation can only be viewed as shamefully tragic, especially for a people whose ancestral roots on this continent —both Indo and Hispanic—go back to more than a century before the establishment of Jamestown. The odyssey of Mexican Americans has been long and arduous and, indeed, without public attention or apparent concern. They have truly been, as George I. Sánchez called them in 1940, "forgotten people," or as the NEA Tucson meeting of 1966 identified them, "the invisible minority."

Existing Programs for Mexican Americans

For the most part, education programs (with the exception of pilot or experimental model programs) make no allowance for the fact that many Mexican American children come to school knowing little English or knowing only Spanish. From the start, Mexican American children are burdened with the disadvantage of being unable to deal with the national language. Spanish-speaking children have been herded into schools which are conducted in a language they don't understand, via which they are expected to learn all the standard subjects, including reading.

Sad to say, Mexican American children have been seriously traumatized by what has all too often been a demoralizing and degrading learning experience. Even when the teachers have the best intentions, their lack of facility in the Spanish language has often created the most debilitating complexes in the children. What is needed, of course, is proper and adequate preparation of teachers in linguistic principles. The teacher needs to fully comprehend the nature of language and its psychol-social function in human beings, especially children.

Spanish-speaking Mexican American children have been relegated to classes for the retarded simply because many teachers equate linguistic disadvantage with intellectual ability. In California alone, Mexican Americans account for more than 40 percent of the so-called "mentally retarded." As Harold Howe, former U. S. Commissioner of Education, pointed out in his address to the National Conference on Educational Opportunities for Mexican Americans, the notion of Anglo cultural superiority is reflected in hundreds of ways in American society, and this notion of Anglo cultural superiority is a much larger factor in the lack of achievement among Mexican Americans than we are willing to admit.

In the last year, walkouts by Mexican American students have taken place in numerous communities of the Southwest. One of the issues in these walkouts has been the custodial manner that emphasizes attendance and discipline at the expense of learning. Many Mexican Americans are beginning to suspect that the only reason for wanting to keep them in school is to improve the average daily attendance, the basis for most Federal funding and support. However, most school districts receiving Federal funds can only point to showcase programs, some of them so abominably put together that one wonders how they continue to be funded.

Moreover, few Mexican American educators are to be found on the rosters of these programs. Of course, the "harvest of shame" in the Southwest includes the fact that in most of the Schools of Education or Teachers Colleges few, if any, Mexican Americans are on the teaching faculties, let alone represented in the decision-making activities dealing with the education of Mexican Americans.

Just as the "come and get it" approach to the common curriculum and the problems of Mexican Americans has failed to come to grips with one of the most fundamental problems underlying learning difficulties, so too has the approach to readying the child for the common curriculum failed. Projects such as Head Start, Follow-Through, and other preschool compensatory educational programs have attempted to resolve the problems, reasoning that preschoolers who are recipients of such programs—short or long term, well designed or inefficient—will now be fluent in English and ready enough to begin formal instruction in English in a common and traditional curriculum. Six months of preschool alone is hardly enough time to overcome the disadvantages that confront children from a non-English-speaking background. The fact of the matter is, as Herschel T. Manuel put it:

> The special difficulties with which we are struggling are those of children who must learn a second language outside of the home; of children who in addition suffer the disadvantages of poverty; of children who have to adjust to patterns of living in the larger community different from those of the immediate environment; and of children whose migrant parents have no secure place in the community.

More recently, the technology of linguistics has led to what might be termed the "technorriculum," that is, the curriculum heavily invested in gadgetry like tape recorders, slide projectors, et cetera, in the hope that somehow technology may help overcome what has been otherwise deemed impossible. Unfortunately, the gadgets are only as good as the teacher who uses them. Thus, thousands of schools which hurriedly acquired the technological hardware have still not improved the education of Mexican Americans significantly, nor does it appear that they are likely to.

At the moment there is much ado about English-as-second-language (ESL) programs both as compensatory education and as part of experimental bilingual programs. While these programs are perhaps the most meritorious thus far, they are nevertheless characterized by the erroneous insistence that to speak English with an accent is unacceptable. This is, as *El Grito* calls it, "insidious arrogance." After all, such people as Lyndon Baines Johnson, Werner Von Braun, Ted Kennedy, Otto Preminger, and others speak with colorful accents, all of which are perfectly acceptable. Perhaps *El Grito's* conclusion is correct: "In the United States today any accent is acceptable except that of a Mexican American who speaks English with a Mexican accent."

Languages in Conflict

It is indeed a striking contradiction, as Armando Rodriguez, Chief of the Mexican American Affairs Unit for the U. S. Office of Education, has pointed out, that "we spend millions of dollars to encourage school children to learn a foreign language and, at the same time, frown upon Mexican American children speaking Spanish in school."

In most schools of the Southwest, Mexican American students are still expressly forbidden to speak Spanish except in Spanish classes, and even then their Spanish is considered tainted by Anglo teachers of Spanish. The rationale behind the "English only" rule is that by *speaking* English the students will *learn* English. As one school administrator remarked, "If these people want to be Americans, they should speak English." For many lexocentric Anglo-Americans this settles the question, the logic being that once a Spanish-speaking child is forbidden the use of

Spanish he will then speak fluent idiomatic English like all other Americans.

Unfortunately, this insistence on "English only" tends to produce hostility and resentment on the part of Spanish-speakers who are pressed into thinking of their language as "inferior." And the more Spanish-speaking students are reprimanded for the crime of speaking the only language they feel comfortable with, the more they are alienated from society, from their families, and even from themselves. Thus, the Spanish-speaking child who encounters stern and imposing prohibitions against using his language is not only traumatized by a conflict he does not readily understand but is forced into a position of repudiating his cultural identity or else perishing in the educational process.

The fact of the matter is that in many parts of the Southwest Mexican American students are still being punished for breaking the "English only" rules. In Brownsville, Texas, for example, Mexican American students have been fined for speaking Spanish in the schools. Some Southwest schools have resorted to corporal punishment of students who break the "English only" rules. Not until recently have such rules been challenged by Mexican Americans, and then only after actual or threatened Mexican American student uprisings.

Commenting on the elimination of the "English only" rules in San Antonio, one school official remarked that not only should Spanish be allowed in the schools but that Mexican American pupils should be "motivated to improve their fluency in standard Spanish in such conversation." The obvious inference is that even the *Spanish* of Mexican Americans is poor at best. It is precisely this attitude which has led to remarks that Mexican Americans are "illiterate in two languages." While this may be true, the pejoration is intended to degrade the quality of the Spanish spoken by Mexican Americans. Thus, even the Mexican American border dialect of Spanish (as well as the Mexican American border dialect of English) is reduced to an inferior position on some tenuous linguistic scale. Again, ignorance of the central role of language in the life of human beings continues to foster linguistic prejudices.

Not only have Mexican Americans been made to feel inferior in Anglo-American society because of their lack of English, but they have been made to feel inferior in their Spanish-speaking environment as well. To avoid identity crises, teachers of Mexican Americans must not only become more aware of Mexican American heritage and culture, but they must rid themselves of outmoded concepts about language in order to help the more than 3 million Spanish-speaking children of the Southwest. For as Harold Howe put it: "It is time we stopped wasting (our linguistic resources) and instead enabled youngsters to move back and forth from one language to another without any sense of difficulty or strangeness."

About 5 percent of American school children score below 75 on IQ tests, and are therefore considered mentally retarded. However, 13 percent of Mexican American youngsters fall below 75 when tested. About 25 percent of all children score between 75 and 90 on IQ tests, but 50 percent of Mexican Americans fall in this range. Fifty percent of all children score between 90 and 100, but only 25 percent of Mexican American children score this high. Again, only 12 percent of Mexican American children score above 100 compared to 20 percent of all others.

The percentage of Mexican American children classified with inferior IQ's is two and one-half times the percentage of Mexican Americans in the population. Those who inveigh against bilingual education usually point to the results of these questionable tests to support their contention about the intellectual potential and capability of Spanish-speaking Americans. On the basis of IQ tests in the English language, Mexican American youngsters have been categorically considered intellectually inferior to their Anglo counterparts.

Only recently have educators become aware that the right instruments are lacking for measuring intelligence and achievement potential of Mexican Americans, despite the fact that as long ago as 1935 Herschel T. Manuel had pointed out the deficiencies of the Stanford-Binet in testing Spanish-speaking Mexican American children. As a consequence, many Mexican Americans have come to internalize the effects of low IQ scores. The effect on their children has been devastating, for they are facing in their homes the same negative valuation they encounter in the schools.

The illusory IQ has oftentimes been responsible for the assignment of Mexican American youngsters to sections for the mentally retarded or slow learners. Enlightened educators now see the distinct relationship between the degree of retardation and the extent to which a knowledge of the language used in the testing is required. The implications of the Rosenthal and Jacobson experiment in a lower-class community of the South San Francisco Unified School District (*Pygmalion in the Classroom*) are far-reaching, indeed, for it appears that a teacher's perception and expectation of her students *does* demonstrably affect pupil performance. (In fact, the findings of current studies indicate that teacher attitudes toward minority students may be influenced by the kind of professional training they get.) It now appears that IQ tests have been used to identify *presumed* differences in innate ability of students perhaps simply to make the administration of schools easier and more statistically efficient.

Thus, the concept of "equal educational opportunity" in America is tainted by an educational tradition and philosophy that caters not to the lower classes but to the more affluent. Americans have been too quick to endorse the Platonic concept of hierarchical superiority measured and manifested in statistical terms. The concept of intelligence has been refracted so peculiarly by American educators that the result has been the IQ, the *point d'appui* which sustains their entire perspective.

The findings of the special advisory committee to the California State Board of Education, created at the insistence of the California Association of Mexican American Educators, are startling. Mexican American children classified as mentally retarded after IQ tests in English have done remarkably better with tests in Spanish. Some of the children tested had spent as long as three years in special classes for slow learners simply because of low IQ scores. The study by the special advisory committee found that the "special" classes themselves had a "retarding influence." After retesting, one Mexican American student showed an improvement of 28 points while the group's average rose 13 points from 70 to 83. The report of the committee asserts that Mexican American students are placed apparently in remedial or special classes "solely on their inability to function in what to them is a foreign language." Thus, with respect to the IQ performance of Mexican American children, the educational system focuses on their spurious weakness rather than on their capabilities.

Until more precise instruments than IQ tests are developed, all attempts to assess the intelligence of Spanish-speaking Mexican Americans must be considered invalid and questionable. The simple-minded assumptions about the nature of intelligence, like the simple-minded assumptions about the nature of language, must be eliminated. The academic rejection of Mexican American pupils simply because they don't demonstrate the ability they are supposed to, as determined by Anglo-American scales of value, must yield to more promising contentions about human beings.

The Dropout Problem of Mexican Americans

Mexican Americans have a higher dropout rate than any other comparable group in the nation. One of the principal reasons for the high dropout rate of Mexican Americans has been simply that Mexican American youngsters tend to be overage in grade levels. By the time they get to the point where they are able to function in English and do the required first-grade work, they should chronologically be in the second grade. Thus, many Mexican American youngsters are one or two grades behind right up to the time they get to high school—if they make it *that* far.

There is no doubt that the high dropout rate of Mexican Americans is directly linked to tests and measurements. Of the many Mexican American children who were found to be overage in grade levels in a study at Arizona State University, their median performance on most tests was about one standard deviation below the Anglo groups. The study also pointed out that on achievement tests the apparent retardation varied from subject to subject but with progressive retardation in reading with advancing grades.

Not only do Mexican American children enter school at a measureable disadvantage but the disadvantage becomes more pronounced as they move up through the grades. With such factors reinforcing the "failure-syndrome" and "negative self-concept," little wonder that Mexican American youngsters leave school in such great numbers. Unfortunately, the Mexican American who drops out has been the poor reader, the underachiever, and the low performer right from the beginning.

The lack of emphasis on education in the home cannot be considered a significant factor in the high dropout rate of Mexican Americans. Studies have concluded that there is little difference between Mexican American families and other families in the emphasis on education. The conclusion can only be that the academic failure of Mexican Americans is the result of inadequate school programs rather than of low achievement or aspiration levels.

Without laboring the point, the evidence clearly demonstrates the extremely low education level of Mexican Americans. In most counties of Colorado, for instance, over 50 percent and as high as 82 percent of Mexican Americans have no more than an eighth-grade education. If one simply looks at the enrollment figures of Texas alone, the evidence is most distressing. Though there was some slight gain in Mexican American educational levels in Texas during the decade 1950 to 1960, the prospects for keeping Mexican

American youths in school beyond the eighth grade anywhere in the Southwest are slim indeed.

In the five southwestern states of Arizona, California, Colorado, New Mexico, and Texas, Mexican Americans complete three to four grades less than Anglos, except for Texas where the gap is six grades less. If Mexican Americans are to attain significant places in American society, their levels of educational attainment must be increased at a far more rapid pace than at present. Federal funds to states and school districts must be increased and the regulations concerning their expenditure must be explicit. Schools must be encouraged to cooperate in Federal programs for Mexican Americans, programs which should relate to the needs of the learners, taking into account their assets, attitudes, skills, personalities, and background. A new breed of teacher is needed, sensitive to the diverse educational problems of Mexican Americans. At educational ground zero, Mexican American youngsters are being wiped out. The dropout cycle of Mexican Americans can be broken, but it will take a lot of doing.

Considering the high dropout rate of Mexican American students, little wonder that there are so few of them in colleges. Some recent studies point out that only 2 percent of the California State College population is Mexican American. Of these less than one-half of one percent go on to graduate. And although Mexican Americans make up more than 14 percent of the public school population of California, less than one-half of one percent are enrolled in the nine campuses of the University of California. For example, at UCLA last year there were only 300 Mexican American students out of a student population of 29,000; there were only 70 three years ago out of a student population of 25,000. Out of approximately 25,000 students at the University of California at Berkeley in 1966 only 78 were Mexican Americans.

These are shocking statistics considering the fact that there are over a million Mexican Americans in California alone. And despite the fact that Mexican Americans comprise amost half the population of New Mexico, less than 8 percent of them attend the state universities. At the University of New Mexico, for instance, only 10 percent of the student population is Mexican American, yet they account for 15 percent of the freshman dropout rate. And only 6 percent of them graduate.

In his testimony before a Senate Subcommittee, Vicente T. Ximenes, a member of the Equal Employment Opportunity Commission and former Chairman of the Interagency for Mexican American Affairs (which has all of a sudden developed a hang-up in the semantics of its name), pointed out that Mexican Americans in the Southwest are "historically and deliberately" denied the benefits of higher education. Out of 83,053 students enrolled at UCLA, the University of Colorado at Boulder, the University of Texas at Austin, and the Universities of Arizona and New Mexico for 1968–1969, the total enrollment of Spanish surnamed students in these colleges was only 3,370, considerably less than one-half of one percent of the total enrollment. Of these, only 600 were graduated in the spring of 1969.

To Mexican Americans it seems almost ironic that the American dream is so firmly rooted in education—a process which has rejected them so traumatically that they have come to feel like strangers in their own land. An accident of history and geography has created an ethnic isolation where literacy has become the exception rather than the rule. If education is truly the answer to the blight of poverty, then indeed there must be a new coalition between the forces of government and the forces of poverty to bring about the long overdue transformation of the American Southwest in terms of the American dream.

The education of Mexican Americans must involve a coalition of *all* facets of society, but especially between the community and the school. The quaint and antiquated concept of the college as the guardian of some universal wisdom belongs to an era and tradition of elitism that doesn't square with the concepts of American democracy. Indeed, it may be the colleges themselves which are impeding progress for

American minority groups. The university can no longer just talk about equality; it must become the bastion of that equality. It must, at the very least, make a percipient thrust in that direction.

In a democracy, the university should be the last place for elitist doctrines. Yet it is Newman's elitist and inegalitarian idea of a university which pervades the thinking of most college professors and administrators. The groves of academe must not be allowed to become the Tuileries of blueblooded intellectual aristocrats. The solution to the educational problems of Mexican Americans should be no febrile attempt, but one borne of recognition and deliberation of the problems confronting American society as it approaches the twenty-first century.

Some organizations like the Latin American Educational Foundation of Colorado award grants and loans to Spanish-named students, but the effort is meager compared to the vast numbers of Spanish-speaking Americans who need financial assistance to get to college and to stay there. Mexican American students of predominantly barrio and *colonia* backgrounds enter the almost exclusively middle-class, Anglo-American environment of colleges to their own detriment and eventual alienation. University of California President Charles H. Hitch must be applauded for establishing the post of special assistant to the President in charge of Mexican American affairs at all nine campuses, a step which Mexican Americans view as a sign of progress.

Mexican Americans and the Future

Most Mexican Americans see the need for bilingual education as the most pressing issue in Mexican American education, and the most challenging. But the promise of bilingual education has been more palliative than corrective. Though a number of schools were quick to establish model programs, the first fruits of bilingual education have been about as palpable as the fruit of the desert. Unfortunately, the concept of bilingual education has run the gamut of confusion and misunderstanding. Thoroughly lexocentric Anglos insist that "segregating children from homes where 'Spanglish' is spoken into classes taught in any other language but English would only widen this barrier of language, not bridge it."

But the aim of bilingual education is to create functionally literate individuals in both Spanish and English by capitalizing on the linguistic skills the Spanish speaker already has. It calls for new teaching techniques; language arts programs must be redesigned to satisfy the needs of the children. The English language is introduced in the curriculum in small regulated doses at first, then in increasingly larger time units until the target language becomes the medium of instruction and the child's first language becomes simply a co-equal linguistic tool.

One must concede that the old "English only" concept has not worked to alleviate the mounting problems of Mexican American education. As Armando Rodriguez has pointed out, "Bilingualism must come to be accepted as a blessing—not a problem. It must be cultivated—not neglected."

For the first time, bilingual education articulates a Mexican American alternative to Mexican American problems. Mexican Americans are beginning to see their roles in American society not in terms of Anglo equivalents but in terms of their own cultural identity and linguistic heritage. Bilingual education satisfies this alternative by stressing the multistrands of American heritage. Indeed, the American Southwest owes more of its past to Cabeza de Vaca than it does to the Pilgrims. Bilingual education will illuminate the dark side of the American historical moon by showing the relationship between Spanish-speaking Americans and their Spanish-speaking brethren of Spanish America and Spain as well as stressing the relationship between English-speaking Americans and England. Thus, bilingual education involves acquainting the Mexican American not only with the Anglo-American part of his political identity but with the significance of his Spanish American past. No, not denigrating that past as has been the case thus far, but elevating it to its proper historical level. For brown-faced Mexican American children to see only white faces in their textbooks is to perpetuate a kind of academic colonialism that has hitherto created cultural cripples—Mexican Americans who were made to feel like marginal people, creatures in a cultural and linguistic no-man's land.

Unfortunately, bilingual education exists at the moment in only 14 model programs throughout the country. Also, the ratio of Mexican American teachers tapped into EPDA (Educational Professions Development Act) has been minimal, and of the Anglo teachers in the programs few are conversant in Spanish despite the fact that current estimates for bilingual teachers by 1970 place the need at 100,000 fluent in both Spanish and English. Even on the staffs of many EPDA Institutes, one finds at best only a token Mexican American. Of course, the directors of these institutes are primarily Anglos. This is what irritates many Mexican Americans, and why they see in the current Federal programs for Mexican Americans only educational boondoggles.

For example, it seems strange that the 28 Mexican American youngsters from a San Antonio elementary school who were selected for a bilingual demonstration program for the New York City Board of Education in its MNYE-TV studios were herded there by an Anglo teacher. Less palatable is the fact that the director of the Bilingual Education Program of the Southwest Educational Development Laboratory is not a bilingual Mexican American.

Mexican Americans wonder how these Anglos, who have not been successful so far with the old programs, are going to be any more successful with new programs. Interestingly enough, these Anglo educators account for the low performance norms of Mexican American children in the model bilingual programs by pointing to the child's poor "socio-economic background, which differs tremendously from that of middle-class Anglo-Saxon pupils for whom the norms are set."

The rejoinder to any criticism is that Mexican American pupils "who do *not* participate in the program do considerably worse on standardized achievement tests than those who do take part."

Mexican Americans are not saying that *only* Mexican Americans can teach Mexican Americans. On the contrary, they are saying that *bilingual* Mexican American or Anglo-American teachers represent a *better* approach to filling the teacher needs of bilingual education. However, since Mexican American children need Mexican American models in their classrooms, it makes good sense to utilize bilingual Mexican American teachers. It goes without saying, of course, that the success of bilingual education depends on the teacher, whether Mexican American or Anglo.

The time to look upon the Mexican American as the poor, uneducated, tortilla-eating peon who is a victim of some fate stemming from Quetzalcoatl's disapproval is over. Mexican Americans are descendants of a proud race. As Americans they deserve their rightful place in the American sun.

WE'RE SUPPOSED TO BELIEVE WE'RE INFERIOR

By Ronald Arias

"Why did he cut your hair?"

"He said it was too long."

Shamefaced and almost in tears, Mexico-born John Garcia took his seat in class. His head was bald in spots. He tried to hide the black tufts of hair that stuck out all over. There was an awkward silence. Garcia's humiliation was to serve as a warning to the other boys.

"Haircutting never works," Miss Maria Talavera, Garcia's English teacher, complained later. "All this does is force them out of school. They've had this kind of treatment since the first grade. Why should they want to stay in?" she added.

Miss Talavera teaches ninth grade in a largely Mexican American junior high school in East Los Angeles.

She pointed out that Anglo youngsters are never given such treatment as the one Garcia received from the vice-principal.

"There's one blond and freckled kid in my class with longer hair than any of the Mexican kids. Nobody will ever touch him, though," Miss Talavera said.

When questioned about the incident, a downcast Garcia said he hated most of his teachers. "If they're out to get me, why should I like them? Why should I like the math teacher who called me a dirty Mexican?"

Miss Talavera, 23 and also a Mexican American, explained that most classes were overcrowded—about 40 pupils to a teacher. Attention is consequently poor or harsh.

"Most of the teachers take an unsympathetic attitude towards these kids and their cultural background," she said. "Poor students in this atmosphere become worse and eventually drop out. Of course, nearly all are poor to begin with."

John Garcia will probably drop out. Or else he will transfer to another school "for disciplinary reasons." His situation is typical in the crowded barrios.

173

In the city's two predominantly Mexican American high schools the average dropout rate is above 20 percent. And average transfer rates are far above 50 percent of the student body. This means that a teacher will face essentially a different class at the end of the school year than he faced at its beginning.

In predominantly Anglo schools these averages are genally reduced by half or more.

"Forced-out" is another term often applied to the barrio school dropout. Usually beginning school with little more than a pidgin-grasp of English, he works slowly in class and rarely catches up to the "Anglo norm." All textbooks, exams and I. Q. tests, which present other stumbling blocks, are geared to the Anglo student. After failing several grades and accepting the image of inferiority, the Mexican American youth will long to be free of school.

"They don't respect me at school," one student complained. "Why should I stay in a place that calls me dumb?"

Miss Talavera emphasized the tendency of many teachers to stereotype the Mexican American child. "Right off, he's considered stupid. And the only remedy is to keep him busy in manual arts or shop classes," she explained. "All this, because he can't speak English well and maybe comes from a broken home."

It is hardly a surprise that a high dropout rate exists throughout the Southwest among Mexican Americans. This has a telling effect on their earning capacities.

Results of the recent Mexican American Study Project at UCLA show a startling pattern concerning education and income.

The study found that on the average, Spanish-surnamed persons (88 percent Mexican American) had much less schooling and income than white Anglos.

In California, for example, those of Spanish surnames receive a median education of 8.5 years and go on to receive an average yearly income of $4,381. The corresponding figures for the Anglo group are 12.1 and $5,806.

In Texas, Spanish-surnamed persons finish an average of

4.8 years of school and receive an income of $2,400. For the Anglo population the figures are 10.8 years and $4,768.

The severest cases of low income and education are found among rural migrant workers. In the Southwest and Pacific states alone, these workers total over 75,000—almost entirely of Mexican descent. Their average annual income drops below $1,000, and their schooling is generally from one to four years.

Admittedly, the plight of the migrant's child is the worst. He rejoices with little more than some shade and a handful of strawberries. School is still something he knows during summers only. In most cases he remains illiterate.

Theodore W. Parsons, in a 1966 Stanford doctoral dissertation, gave some distressing examples of discrimination in an agricultural town. After 40 days of personal observation in a 58 percent Mexican American elementary school in Central California, Parsons cited:

> *A teacher, asked why she had called on "Johnny" to lead five Mexicans in orderly file out of the schoolroom, explained: "His father owns one of the big farms in the area and . . . one day he will have to know how to handle the Mexicans."
>
> *Another teacher, following the general practice of calling on the Anglos to help Mexican pupils recite in class, said in praise of the system: "It draws them (Anglos) out and gives them a feeling of importance."
>
> *The president of the Chamber of Commerce declared in praise of the school principal: "He runs a good school. We never have any trouble in our school. Every kid knows his place . . . we believe that every kid has to learn to respect authority and his betters."
>
> *The principal stated: "Once we let a Mexican girl give a little talk of some kind and all she did was mumble around. She had quite an accent too. Afterwards we had several complaints from parents, so we haven't done anything like that since . . . That was about 12 years ago."

Discrimination goes beyond the schools. Especially in cities, this unwritten rule of the majority envelopes entire communities. Housing segregation is often the direct cause for ghetto school zoning. The harsh truth of this system is that the most up-to-date facilities are designed for middle- and upper-class Anglo districts.

Can the quality of a school, then, be disregarded? Can a

new approach to teaching the Mexican American youth be taken? Can a curriculum—perhaps bilingual in part—be scaled for him and not just for the Anglo student?

If the children of the barrio are ever to be released from the poverty traps of the ghetto, they must first be given full opportunity for education of good quality.

THE LIVES OF LOS SIETE

Prepared by the Research Organizing Cooperative of San Francisco (ROC)

On Saturday, November 7, 1970, six young men were acquitted by a San Francisco jury of a charge of a Violation of Section 187 of the Penal Code of the State of California, to wit: Murder, a felony.

So read the charge.

"Hoodlums" and "Latin hippie types," the San Francisco *Chronicle* had called them. "A bunch of punks," the Mayor had said.

But others, especially those in San Francisco's largely Latino Mission District, knew *Los Siete de la Raza* (the Seven of the Race) as students at the College of San Mateo, as organizers for the outstanding "College Readiness Program," and as serious young men working and studying to improve their abilities to help others.

Curiously, in a land where the Constitution guarantees all people to a speedy and just trial, the six remained in jail for 18 months before allowed that trial.

As with the killing of Ruben Salazar in Los Angeles, many citizens of all races were incensed by the overt hostility, prejudice, and sadism reflected by the needless incident, as well as by the pretrial conviction by the news media.

Perhaps the story is best told in the publication *Basta Ya!—The Story of Los Siete de la Raza*, prepared by the RESEARCH ORGANIZING COOPERATIVE (ROC), which is presently working to provide legal defense for the community, a free health clinic, a food co-op, a youth group, and other community groups.

"What happened on May 1, 1969?" asks the ROC. "Everyone agrees on a bare outline of facts.

"Brodnik and McGoran [police officers] were dressed in plain clothes and they were driving an old, battered, unmarked '58 Dodge. They came upon a few Latinos. One, police claim, was transferring a television set into a car from the home of José Rios, 18, one of their friends. As 225-pound, 6-foot-4 McGoran later told the Grand Jury, 'Anyone moving a TV set from their car to their house is automatically a robbery suspect.'

"The cops stopped and questioned them. McGoran had his gun tucked into his waist holster, hidden by a sweater. Scuffling broke out. Shots were fired and seconds later Brodnik lay dead on the sidewalk, with a bullet from Mc-Goran's gun in him. McGoran was injured. A week later, six of the seven were captured. The seventh, Gio López, remains free. . .

"Seven Latino brothers have been charged with murder. Four of them were not even on the street when the incident occurred. According to McGoran himself, two were upstairs in the house when the shooting took place. Nelson Rodriquez and Tony Martínez *were not even in the city at the time*. Nelson was in San Mateo, and Tony was in class at the College of San Mateo. . .

"Lieutenant Charles Ellis, the head of San Francisco's Homicide Detail, all but admitted that most of *Los Siete* were not involved when he told the *Chronicle* on May 5 that 'new information has narrowed the six original suspects to three.' But the police case rested on McGoran's testimony with its hodge-podge of conflicting statements."

After the trial, the attorney for *Los Siete*, Charles Garry, commented, "McGoran should be put on trial for perjury and attempting to commit murder of these six beautiful persons."

Rodolfo Martínez said, after the verdict, "Our only victory was a symbolic one since it gave a rallying point to *La Raza*. We did not get a fair trial."

The ROC asks, "If *Los Siete* are not thieves and murderers, who are they? Where did they come from, and how did they come to be victims of the police? What are their lives about?

"And if the police are not the defenders of 'law and order,' what are they? For whose benefit do they occupy the Mission district? And what purpose do they serve by making the

Mission a difficult, desperate place to live? These are the questions we will be answering. . .''

> I remember the last time I really felt hungry was the last time my mother was pregnant. I remember that we only ate green bananas . . . green bananas, that's how poor our countries are.
> —a member of the 20th-Street Gang

> It has been almost eight years since we came to this great northern country searching for a better life, after having endured so many sacrifices. . . . Our purpose was always to work in order that our family could benefit from all the advantages that this country offers which do not exist in Central America.
> —father of José Rios, one of *Los Siete*

> Mario was pretty messed up about what direction he was going in until he met Ralph Ruiz [of the College Readiness Program], who talked to him about going to college. Mario decided to go, but this caused a lot of laughter among his teachers. . . . "If you can't even make it in high school," they told him, "how you gonna make it in college?"
> —a friend of Mario Martínez

When the Martínez family arrived in the United States from El Salvador in 1961, everything was new to them. But they had great hopes for their future, especially for the children. For wasn't this the "land of opportunity"? And couldn't their children get the education they needed to get ahead? Their sons, Tony and Mario, had always been first or second in school, and they had confidence in them.

The parents of most of *Los Siete* felt the same way when they came here in the early 1960's from El Salvador, Nicaragua, and Honduras (all in Central America). Of the seven, only Gio López was born in the United States.

None of these families expected life to be easy for them here. They knew that they would have to work hard, and they were ready to. When the Rios family came in 1962, with their seven children, Mr. Rios started out by washing dishes, and Mrs. Rios worked in a hospital laundry. They spent the weekends picking fruit in the valleys. With the entire family working a long day, they would still earn only fifteen or twenty dollars. But every extra dollar helped.

Mr. Martínez came to California by himself in 1961.

He faced discrimination and he did not speak the language. But he was able to find a job in a body and fender shop in the Mission district, where he worked twelve hours a day. After seven months he was able to save enough to bring his family together again in San Francisco.

The families of *Los Siete* were willing to work hard, because they believed that here their children would be able to get a good education and make a better life.

Gradually and painfully, they discovered that this was not so. The children were not learning anything in school, and their teachers didn't care. The children dropped out.

Why?

For those children—for most children from black, brown, Asian, or American Indian homes—school is a terrifying obstacle course. Their language and culture are ridiculed or ignored. The teachers discourage the children from learning. And they are pushed into a dead-end program by the "tracking system."

It is not easy to learn a new language. So when Gary ("Pinky") Lescallet or BeBe Melendez came into the public schools knowing little or no English, we might have expected the schools to give them a lot of help.

But the schools gave them no help at all. The schools did not try to teach them English. Nor did the schools allow for the fact that they did not speak English. One of the friends of *Los Siete*, Francisco Flores, recalls pleading with his teachers when he was in elementary school: "Give it to me in Spanish; I can do it." But no, he was told, you have to learn English. This is America.

So they were not allowed to study arithmetic or geography in Spanish while they were learning English. The teachers and the administrators take the view that it is all or nothing. Either you learn English immediately and instantly—or we teach you nothing. This is the response to the schoolchildren (one-third of the students in San Francisco) who come from homes where Spanish, Chinese, or some other foreign language is spoken.

Studies have shown that the Spanish-speaking children

make remarkable progress when the schools begin by teaching them to read *in Spanish*. Then, a year or two later, they can gradually be introduced to English and make the transition successfully. This makes sense. Instead of making the child face two problems at once—learning to read and learning English—you allow the child to focus his or her energies on one problem at a time.

Instead, the schools humiliate the child and convince him that he is a failure. They may hold him back in the first grade for two, three, even four years, while the other children his age advance. Or else they automatically pass him through the system—first grade to second grade, second to third, third to fourth—even though he is learning nothing.

The language barrier is only the first obstacle facing the "Third World" child in school. Even more important is the attitude of his teachers. Many teachers have only to see the color of the skin, or hear the accent, to "know" that a child has no future. She "knows" how much to expect of the child—and children quickly understand when they are not expected to do well.

Mrs. Martínez, the mother of Tony and Mario, two of the seven, explained how her children were discouraged in this way:

"They left school not because they were lazy, like everyone thought, or that they had no ambitions. They did so because they got no moral or physical help from their teachers, and were discouraged. If you want to know what happened to Tony, he said he wanted to be an engineer.

"The professor asked, why did he want to do that? It was a big profession and required lots of work and study, and especially an aptitude to do the work, and if he wanted to do carpentry, he could start right away earning money.

"My son said his ambitions went far beyond being a carpenter, and he didn't want to be a carpenter, because that's what his father was... and he saw that his father has to struggle very hard in order for him to get a better education.

"I remember my son was sad, and said to his father, he had been talking with his teacher concerning his aspirations, his

ambitions, and that he wanted to be an engineer. And his
teacher said it was a very hard career which cost much money.
His father said: Don't worry about that, because I am willing
to work in the body shop with all my energy so you can have
a good career. I don't want you to end up like me. . . working
every Saturday. It is very hard. And I want you to have a
profession that will help your *Raza*.

"I think the professors have been educated into a system,
so they push these boys to end up without a profession—in
a factory where all they do is mass production. And they
don't advance—especially our *Raza*.

"The teachers wanted the boys to give in to their system,
their ideas, until they lost their own character. And each one
has his own character. Mario has a character and he likes to
be honest. And when he saw that no one listened, he lost
confidence then, and didn't want to finish school because it
was a waste of time. . .

"My sons didn't want to go to school because the teachers
were never with them. . ."

Often the teachers do not even realize they are holding
back their pupils. They "want" the children to learn. But
they do not believe that brown or black children can do as
well as whites. And one way or another, they communicate
this feeling to the children.

An experiment that took place in a working-class elementary school in South San Francisco proved this. The teachers
were told that an objective test had identified some "late
developers" in their classes. They were told that certain
children who had been doing only average work would soon
show a dramatic improvement in their classroom performance.

Actually the children were just average children, selected
at random. But once the teachers believed that these children
were about to do better, the children *did* do better. The
teachers "knew" they were not ordinary children and treated
them more patiently and respectfully—and the children
responded: in one year they gained an average of 28 points
in their "IQ" test scores. But is not just the attitude of
individual teachers. The oppression of black and brown

children in the schools is made systematic by the tracking system.

What is the "tracking system"? Since 1960 there have been two standard "tracks" in the elementary and high schools of California. One is for children who are considered "college material," the other for those who are "not academically inclined." If your child is placed on the "college" track, he will be in a classroom with other children who are headed for college. What he is taught will prepare him for college.

If your child is placed on the "vocational" track, he will be taught different materials, by teachers who know that he is not likely to go to college. And they are right. Once he is put on this track he hasn't much chance of getting off.

Why is there a tracking system? In America today, the number of good jobs is limited, and there are many jobs that are poorly paid. If everyone got a good education, it would be hard to find people to fill the poorer jobs. Moreover, people who have good jobs now are not satisfied just to have good jobs. They want to make sure their children have them too. But in a fair competition for the good jobs, privileged kids of average ability would be edged out by brighter working-class and Third World kids.

So, for various reasons, children, in many school systems, are placed very early in their school careers—usually by the third grade—on either the college track or the other track, on the basis of seemingly "objective" reading and "IQ" tests. But in fact these tests are far from objective.

In the first place, the tests are only given in English. Of course, a child who has only recently learned to speak English will not do as well on such a test. One result is that many perfectly normal children who speak Spanish have been shunted into classes for the *mentally retarded*. Recently, all of the Spanish-surnamed children in these were retested in Spanish. The results, San Francisco school officials "reluctantly admitted," showed that 45 percent—almost half—of these children were of normal intelligence or better. (San Francisco *Chronicle*, January 24, 1970)

"One child who was tested in English and scored 67 IQ,"

wrote the *Chronicle*, "was retested in Spanish and scored 128 IQ, well above the average quotient (score) of 100."

But still there are no plans for using Spanish IQ tests throughout the school system. The *Chronicle* explained the reason for this: "The school district will stand to lose a lot of money by transferring the retested children out of the special program since the district gets about $550 extra a year from the state for each child enrolled [in 'mentally retarded' classes]."

Even if a brown child spoke English perfectly the tests would still discriminate against him. So-called "intelligence tests" measure "intelligence" by comparing a child's test scores with those of an average group of white, privileged, city children of the same age. But the "IQ" test is based in part on things that a child living in a higher-income city neighborhood is more likely to know about.

When it comes right down to it, IQ tests measure income, not intelligence. It may be news to some parents that the IQ tests discriminate in this way. But teachers, professors, and testers have known it all along.

In theory it is possible for a child to get onto the college track even if he starts on the lower track. But it is very difficult. Because these tests are one of the most important signals that tell teachers what to expect of a child.

Tony and Mario's teachers, BeBe and Pinky's, Gio, José, and Nelson's teachers expected nothing of them and gave them nothing. By the seventh grade Nelson, Tony, Mario, and José Rios, who were in the Burbank School, were already on a familiar road to nowhere.

Los Siete came together again at Jefferson High School. But now these young men were mainly interested in "high living." One boy remembers how quickly his family learned, on coming to the United States, that buying things, owning things, is the source of respect and honor here. And so the brothers wanted to be on top of it all... clothing, cars, girl friends, everything.

Partly, they were responding to the pressures they were under, the pressures you feel when you're young and you don't have enough money. "We got a four-room house for a family of eight; what happens is the family disintegrates," one of their friends pointed out.

> We start going to the street because we can't stand our house, because the house is four rooms and there's eight people in it, and we can't stand this. And what happens in the streets? We start taking dope . . . we start drinking.

A gap grows between the young people and their fathers: "He works from seven o'clock in the morning, man, to three o'clock at night," Oscar Rios says.

> Instead of us being grateful to him, we were turned against him . . . they blind you, that you have parents, here. You know, you go out and get stoned and don't come back; and your poor parents are struggling. And you don't see those things. Like we've been here nine years and both my parents have been working, and nine years they have been trying to give us a better life.

Partly, too, the "high living" of the young is a response to their confusion about just who they are. "You see these hundred people out there in Dolores Park?" asks Francisco Flores, one of the young men who hung around the 29th Street area with *Los Siete*.

> . . . And you know what most of these hundred people are? They are Latinos. Why are they in the park? Because they have been smoking grass . . . And why have they been smoking grass? Because the school don't teach them nothing that is relevant to them, that they can say, "This is my own."
> I was in the fifth grade and they used to teach us about the folk culture of the United States, and they used to have square dances . . . square dancing . . . you know, in Mexico we never do square dancing. In the schools they teach us how to do the jarabi tapatia . . .
> But when we come here they teach us square dancing. And they don't teach us anything about our culture, or any of the things that are part of us. In this country, they alienate us from our culture . . .

Los Siete did not learn these lessons from books. They learned from struggle. The College Readiness Program, of which they became a part, engaged them in struggle, and exposed the real enemies of their people. . .

At first the Readiness Program recruited mainly blacks. But two Latino students, high school dropouts from South San Francisco, were brought into the program in the spring of 1967—Ralph Ruiz and Jackie Montoya. They, in turn, seized the opportunity to recruit more Latino and Chicano students to the program. One of Ralph's first recruits, in the summer of 1967, was Mario Martínez.

Mario's mother recalls that "when he was finally admitted to San Mateo, he was so happy—we were all so happy at last. And the friends he brought home, he pulled into this program. And he got more enthusiastic and happy every day, and we celebrated. And I saw him talk to his friends, and at meetings, and my son always talked about the same thing—that you people now have the opportunity. We are not going to stay like this, without a profession, or go to the factories like the teachers want."

Mario himself says, "This program was teaching us what the system had been hiding from us. We started learning the truth about the system, and about our people. We started learning about our identity."

Mario became deeply involved in bringing brown people into the program, starting with his brother Tony and his friend Nelson Rodriquez. And they joined him in recruiting others. They didn't just talk to people who were already in high school—they went to the brothers who hung around the streets and pool halls of the Mission district. "If *Los Siete* hadn't come into the pool hall as one of us," said one who is now a student at CSM, "probably none of us would have gone to San Mateo."

> It's the only way we got back to school. Otherwise we would have followed the same road we were leading before. Just like people would say, some bums, man, hanging around the streets, going up and down the streets, standing in front of the Doggie Diner, standing in front of a pool hall. And we still do some of that. But most of us have plans to go on to college, and get out of this way of life we had set before us.
>
> *Los Siete* weren't troublemakers. They were out here trying to help their community . . . getting people to school, telling them to get their education, to help themselves, to help our people.

We all became friends, there were social gatherings together, and when the program became big enough to have four or five hundred people it was easy to have several different social groups within that family.

The program was pretty much autonomous from the rest of the college; we pretty much depended on one another and on the program for the survival of our academic careers.

In the summer of 1968, Mario and Tony and Nelson recruited more than thirty young men from the brown community, and in the fall, Tony became chairman of what was then called the Brown Heritage Club.

Thanks to groupings like Brown Heritage, the Readiness Program grew into a community that gave strength and confidence to the Third World students. "The program really reached out and said that you were a member of a family," Aaron Manganiello, a former counselor and tutor for the program, explained.

The program was building a community of Third World students who were determined to serve their people. . . and who were learning about the sources of their peoples' oppression.

"The last time I really felt hungry was the last time my mother was pregnant," one student recalled of his childhood in Latin America.

I remember that we ate only green bananas . . . green bananas, that's how poor our countries are. And this thing is caused by the United States economy: we have such a high standard of living here because they rob the people down there. Our people are always dying . . . three out of five children die before they're five years old, back home . . .

And I started going to college because of Mario.

BeBe Melendez, one of the Seven, didn't think that things were different for brown people in the United States.

The Yanqui imperialist runs everything down there. Like I went back to there in '63. They got the American Fruit Company down there. The people and country don't have the chance to produce their own crops so they could profit off of it. They got all these Rockefellers and all these other people down there, just making profit off the people and land that isn't theirs.

Up here, it's the same way. They give us $1.35 to work at this damn Neighborhood Youth Corps. They tell you to dig a ditch and that ditch might become a reservoir some day and all you got paid for it was $1.35. Our people has more knowledge than that. They tell us "that's all you're good for."

But we need more lawyers, we need more professors and teachers and so forth. The system up here just don't let the brown people have a chance. But the grape boycott and *Los Siete de la Raza* has awakened a lot of people up . . . we tell them, "You're better than the Man tells you. You can do something . . . something for your people."

These weren't the sort of lessons that the Trustees of the College of San Mateo wanted their students to learn.

Aaron Manganiello recalls that when the Administration told Bob Hoover, the director of the program, that he wasn't putting enough students into vocational training, he kind of laughed and said, "I didn't know you had a quota." They said, "You don't, but you still should have put more students into vocational training."

By the fall of 1968, the Readiness Program was in financial crisis. The Financial Aids Office had spent most of the semester budget during the summer of 1968, without telling the Readiness Program director of students.

Aaron Manganiello, the brown tutor in CRP, talked about this "mistake."

One story that particularly sticks in my mind is about a girl in the program—she's 26 years old, and a mother of three children. The college had promised her $140 a month to live on. But after two months, completely without warning, her next check was $12.75. All checks of any size were cut down so that the biggest check that was being given out was $40. When we came on campus at the beginning of the fall semester there was $2500 for 650 students. So between twelve and twenty students were taken care of out of 650.

The Student Council recognized an immediate need and cut back $28,000 from its own budget and put it in the program. There was also $40,000 that Bob Hoover was able to get.

But despite the unity shown by the students, the Trustees' attack was having its effect. According to Mario Martínez,

A lot of students had to drop out because the Administration wasn't giving the bread for the program. They were also trying to pick out counselors. We wanted our own.

Several things happened. Aaron Manganiello was fired. The Third World students asked him to go on tutoring without pay, and he agreed. But when he came on campus, he was arrested for "trespassing."

Third World students were learning fast that in order to survive, they had to learn to struggle together. Under Tony Martínez' leadership, the Brown Heritage Club became COBRA, the Confederation of the Brown Race for Action. Tony explains the importance of the change:

COBRA came about because the struggle was getting pretty heavy over the program. Students were dropping out. The Administration wasn't taking care of the needs of the students.

In the face of these attacks from the Administration and the Trustees, the Third World students struck back. They announced a boycott of classes, and issued a set of demands: new counselors, reorganization of the Financial Aids Office, a separate Third World studies division, more Third World faculty, and rehiring two counselors who had been fired.

Why "demands"? Because the Third World students were through begging and pleading—"no more shufflin' or scratchin'," as Bob Hoover put it. Demands were made, not "requests," because these were the vital needs of the Third World students if they were to survive at CSM.

"One of the things that hangs the Administration up," Aaron Manganiello said, "is the idea of non-negotiable demands. But it's obvious that what we could do is sit down and write another five demands—we want a swimming pool in every classroom, we want grass for our physical education classes—then we could say we were ready to negotiate with them, and throw away those five extra demands after the first fifteen minutes. But we aren't playing those kinds of games. These are our basic needs and we can't play those kinds of games with respect to them."

On Friday, December 13, 1968, Third World students got

together for a rally and to present their demands to the Administration again. The officials answered by closing the Administration Building and sending all office workers home for the day. Third World students had been harassed all day by white students wearing blue armbands, and finally their anger exploded—they marched across the campus smashing windows in three buildings.

The response of the Trustees was predictable. They did not measure the damage to windows against the damage that people of color have been exposed to for centuries in North America. They did not balance the destruction against the patient efforts of the Third World students in building the College Readiness Program over the previous two years. Nor did they recognize their own responsibility.

No. The Trustees responded by turning CSM into a miniature police state. Three hundred cops were called in, and they occupied the campus for the rest of the year. No one could enter the campus without showing identification, and a helicopter was used for surveillance. Many of the protesting students were suspended and expelled. The eruption was blamed on the Readiness Program, which was then brought under Administration control.

The Third World students were not demoralized by these attacks. They got on with the job of building more support and strength to meet the needs of their people. "After the strike," Tony Martínez explained,

COBRA started building its idology toward recruiting more people to be students. So actually, before we all got busted, we were involved in a heavy recruitment program to get brothers from the block to be students. We talked to all the brothers we grew up with and tried to make them see how many lies had been put to them, and that they needed education so they could understand the whole political spectrum of the country. We recruited a lot of people and COBRA grew a lot. Now the organization is doing a lot in our defense. They're doing a lot to get people involved in political activities.

They see that for all these years our people have been denied many things. None of our people have been educated easily. You look up statistics and they will tell you that brown people in this state and in this nation are the ones that are at the bottom of the

scale. Black people have risen up a little, but only because of their
political struggle. So once our people become politically aware,
they can begin to struggle and do something about the things that
are going on.

Our people have been brainwashed for so long that they just
forgot how to act. We were training people to go back into the
community and help our people. We take the program into the
community and talk to the brothers and sisters in the community,
and try to recruit them.

Among the many they recruited were BeBe Melendez, Gio
Lopez, Pinky Lescallet, and José Rios.
BeBe tells his story:

> I've been harassed by the pigs quite a lot. It wasn't till 1967,
> when I was doing a little bit of time for the California Youth
> Authority, that I realized that all these Latin brothers and black
> brothers up there . . . that the system just throws a racket on
> them and says that you did this and you gotta serve so much time,
> even if you're innocent.
> They judge you mostly by your background.
> When I got out in '68, I wanted to be a youth counselor, you
> know. So I got involved with the Mission Rebels, and I was helping
> people go back to high school and so forth.

But BeBe became disgusted with telling people to go back
to high school when he knew what they would have to face
there.

> Like I wasn't doing nothing.
> It was the same thing. The system always tells you, you know,
> you can't make it through school. You're a Latin, you know, you
> gotta drop out, that's the way you can make it.
> So I met brother Roberto Vargas from Horizons Unlimited.
> I rapped to him one day and he was telling me, why don't I go to
> college. Like a lot of brothers, I told him that I couldn't make it
> there. He told me it wouldn't hurt trying. Then I met this sister
> from New York named Sonia Sanchez. She was teaching school
> for the Rebels. I was in her class, she was a Panther and she was
> telling me how the system dominates all brothers.
> Not paying attention to her really hurt me, 'cause I was like
> many other brothers—brainwashed, you know—I didn't right-
> eously realize. That ain't the way to get it. The greener you are,
> the more you accepted. I came to realize that in order for you to
> get someplace, you must help others, you must give a little.
> Then I met brother Gio López (another of *Los Siete*, who was

already into recruiting people for the Readiness Program). And he
was telling me about CSM. I dug what he was telling me. So I was
gonna go . . ."

And he would have gone, if the police hadn't framed him
May 1.

Pinky Lescallet "comes from a long line of 'I ain't taking
nothin',' " as BeBe points out, and came to the struggle after
being battered around by the system of "justice" we have in
this country. Pinky explained:

> When I first got involved in this, Tony told me about San
> Mateo. So I went, but they were having a strike so I couldn't get
> in. So I came back to the city late one night and the pigs stopped
> me. And they told me I committed an armed robbery. So I went to
> jail with them, and they started giving me a five-to-life. And they
> said to cop. So I copped to 160 days.

Pinky pleaded guilty to a lesser charge because he knew he
would be gambling with the rest of his life if he tried to defend
himself on the armed robbery charge. . . It is no surprise that
Pinky decided to plead guilty to the lesser charge. And then,
Pinky said,

> When I got out I went to Tony's house to tell him I wanted to
> get into the program. I had my application all filed and I was going
> to school every day. I started to understand what was really
> happening.

José Rios was also planning to go to the College of San
Mateo at the time of the arrest.

> I was in high school and trying to get out of school. I was
> intending to go to the College of San Mateo when the new
> semester started. I was really looking forward to attending college
> and staying in college—trying to talk to the people while in school,
> rather than just being out in the streets. Because I could see for
> myself that there was a lot of people who were sort of giving up.
> I was sort of giving up myself.
>
> I was going to Balboa High School before I got busted. You
> know, the education in high school is not so good. The classes I
> was taking weren't interesting, so I decided to give it up. Once
> I heard about the program at CSM, I decided to stay in high school
> and try to get along till I could go to CSM.

Partly through the leadership of *Los Siete*, many young

brown people in San Francisco were starting to see that they could develop their skills by going to school, not just to better their own lives, but to strengthen their people as well.

"The most striking thing that I remember," a friend of *Los Siete* observed recently, "was that they were so much in the vanguard already, without going through all the rhetoric, the intellectualizations . . . They had already begun to organize the brothers on the street. The promised land that was supposedly here in California just didn't exist. It was jive, it was another way of shucking the people."

The story of *Los Siete* is the story of official, racist terror. But it is more than that. It is the story of the attack on the Mission by those who measure the worth of a community by the profits they gain from it.

What is their strategy for the Mission? Move the factories, fire the workers and call them bums, lazy and incompetent. Force the kids out of school and into the streets by suffocating their abilities and crippling their initiative. Turn the hospital into a breeding ground for disease rather than a treatment center, by making it an understaffed, bureaucratic dumping ground for sick people without any money. Refuse to build parks, make plans only for more parking lots, forcing the kids to play in the glass-strewn streets. Increase the number of cops to terrorize anyone brown or black who loiters in the streets.

Force them back into their homes, riddled with rats and cockroaches—firetraps with clogged toilets, crumbling walls. Refuse to make repairs, but triple the rents in less than ten years. And always force the cost of food and clothing up, making it impossible to live. Turn the Mission into a jungle. Slander the people and say it's their own fault that they got into such a jam. Punish them for it; force them out with no place to go.

And to justify this, frame seven young Latins. Charge them with killing a cop. Put the Mission district on trial by painting it as a lawless jungle, a den of idlers, hoodlums, and murderous "Latin hippie types." In this way, turn those who might side with the people of the Mission against them. If the white people of San Francisco can be made to believe this false portrait—if the Mission can be isolated in this way—then the last restraints on official violence will be removed.

This is fascism: the use of official terror to enslave all poor and working people, step by step. First black people: isolate them, convince all other workers to fear blacks more than they hate their bosses. Then disarm the black people, destroy their organization, the Black Panther Party, and move the blacks out. Then the rich do the same thing to brown people. Then Chinese, Japanese, Indian, Samoan, and Filipino. Then white workers. This is fascism: the plan of the rich to divide and conquer the poor, by any means necessary.

Nelson, Tony, Mario, BeBe, Pinky, José, and Gio, all have dedicated their lives to serving the people. They know that their people must be educated in order to grow strong—that's why they worked so hard to recruit brothers into the College Readiness Program. That's why they fought alongside the strikers at CSM, San Francisco State College, and Mission High School.

They know that the people must unite and become organized in order to survive. And *Los Siete* know that the people will become organized only by learning to help each other, by working together to solve our needs. Too long we have been like an open hand, separated like fingers. Now we are tightening into a fist.

What *Los Siete* have learned has not been lost. Soon after they were seized in 1969, a group of Latinos came together to mobilize the community to defend *Los Siete*, to work for their freedom, and to serve the people, as *Los Siete* had. This group, itself called *Los Siete de la Raza*, has begun several programs:

Free Breakfast for Children. Five days a week, from 8 a.m. to 10 a.m., the organization is providing a free, balanced breakfast for all children who wish to come, at St. Peter's Hall and at El Basta Ya!

Basta Ya! (Enough!). This newspaper by and for the brown community, in Spanish and English, is the voice of the people. Where the mass media, the *Chronicle* and the *Examiner*, ABC, CBS, and NBC tell lies about the people, *Basta Ya!*

tells the truth. Where the billion-dollar mass media distort the world, *Basta Ya!* lays out the facts and explains them, from the point of view of the oppressed.

Education. As the organization explains, "*Los Siete* were involved in recruiting Third World people for college. We are now continuing this program... If you are interested in getting a college education, come to *Los Siete*. We have information about special programs for Third World people at several colleges." As for those who are still in high school, or thinking about dropping out, a group of high school students in *Los Siete* have begun a group to deal with the problems in the schools: The Mission High Student Union. "Some Mission and other school students have gotten together in trying to liberate the high school students from these prisons... The main idea is to unite all high school students so that they themselves can come to meet their own needs." They have begun two programs: free legal aid to combat the harassment of brothers and sisters, in and out of school; and a newspaper, *Mission Impossible*, to tell of the problems of the students and what can be done to solve them.

Free Medical Clinic. This clinic was started, according to *Los Siete*, because "our people suffer from bad health, poverty, and malnutrition. Our people do not get adequate medical care from the government hospitals." Doctors and nurses have donated some time to this program, but more help—and money for supplies—is needed.

El Basta Ya! People's Restaurant. The organization explains: "All workers in the Basta Ya work on a voluntary basis, and live in the community. We want people to come to the restaurant to see what food really can cost, and what the energy of the people can do... But the Basta Ya is more than just a restaurant. It is a place where people can come and realize what it feels like not to be exploited. It is a place to meet... for group discussions, meetings, films, entertainment... for information to be distributed... to tell people about as an example of what people can do for themselves when they get together, to begin to define and direct our own lives. El Basta Ya! is a community restaurant. It is yours."

These are only some of the programs the organization has begun to continue the work of the seven brothers. They understand that the best way to build the defense of the brothers is to continue to serve the people.

The Mayor and the big corporations have been counting on the brown people remaining passive. "The average business looks for social peace," he told the Chamber of Commerce. "We have it here." But the Mayor and the corporations did not count on *Los Siete* and the growing militant movement of the brown people. They didn't count on the brown people rising up to meet the intensified attacks of the imperialists and their local police.

How long can that "social peace" last—"social peace" that includes the quiet hunger of children who never get three square meals a day, "social peace" that is based on suppressing men's desires for a decent life? How long will "social peace" hold up, when people reply to the contempt that is heaped on them as Pinky Lescallet has replied:

Now brother Pinky, he was pretty hot—BeBe related— because the pigs had just come in our room and they threw his letters all over the floor . . . There was no cause for that. You know, if you're gonna search a man, just search him, but put the things back in their proper place. So brother Pinky said, "Look, man, if you're gonna search me, at least you could have the courtesy to put things back in their proper order." So the pigs tell him to shut up. The pig puts his hand on the oppressor stick and says, "You gonna shut up." And brother Pinky, he comes from a long line of "I ain't taking nothing," you know. So Pinky told him, "You gotta shut me up." So the pig got scared and he went and got three other pigs that all looked like giant polar bears, and Pinky went to the hole.

And how long can that "social peace" hold up when more and more brown people are learning that their oppressor here in North America is the same as the oppressors of their parents in Latin America, as Mario had realized:

We look at this country like an octopus. It's here that the struggle has to be carried out the most. In countries like Vietnam and Bolivia, they're striking at one arm. But here is where the head of the oppression is. Once we cut the head off, the arms won't be doing any harm.

How long will they be able to keep the brown people down, when there are young brothers like BeBe, with faith in the people:

> We tell them, "You're better than the Man tells you. You can do something—something for your people."

How long?
Not much longer, brothers and sisters. Not much longer.

THE TEACHING OF CHICANO HISTORY

By Feliciano Rivera

Because I have been teaching "Chicano" history for the past three years, I would like to share some of my ideas as to *why* this subject should be taught, and to offer some suggestions on *how* it should be taught.

It seems especially fitting at this time that we, as historians and "perpetuators of history," consider the validity and the need for teaching and studying the complete history of our country. To teach the history of a country without giving careful attention to the role and contributions of all its member groups is to present only a part of that history.

Furthermore, in view of the social revolution that is taking place today in our country, it is appropriate that we also consider a new approach in teaching our history and that we re-evaluate basic interpretations.

The current civil rights revolution has raised many fundamental questions involving the essence of quality education and the role of our educational system in preparing young Americans for full, responsible citizenship. In fact, it has forced many schools to reassess their entire educational program. As part of this reassessment, studies have been made of the extent to which history textbooks include adequate treatment of the role of the various ethnic groups in the historical development of our country. These studies have indicated that many textbooks in our schools and colleges either distort or omit important information on the history and achievements of many ethnic groups.

It is a simple matter to check existing history books used in elementary, high school, or college classrooms across the nation to verify this accusation. Where is the Mexican American experience mentioned? Today many schools and colleges, including those in California, are still operating under the assumption that the role of the Mexican in American life is hardly worth considering.

Historically, state and local institutions have insisted that to become "good Americans" all minority and immigrant groups have to abandon their native languages and cultures, give up their group identity, and become absorbed as individuals into the dominant group. If any group has resisted full acculturation in the United States, it has been regarded as uncivilized, un-American, and potentially subversive. Furthermore, it is difficult for many people to accept the idea that a native-born Mexican American who happens to speak Spanish and who retains many of the values of his native culture might well be a loyal American. As a result, social and educational institutions in the Southwest and California have directed their activities toward the elimination of both the Spanish language and Mexican culture.

This is why today Chicano student organizations and Chicano community organizations are questioning the ability of the present school system, under its present structure, to give instruction about the contributions of the Mexican American to American life. They point out that schools and colleges are too conservative and unresponsive to new techniques and suggestions for the formulation of a more relevant curriculum. And because they are afraid of public controversy and debate, institutions of learning "drag their feet" in implementing their demands.

How valid are these accusations? Are our schools, colleges, and universities guilty of these charges?

In searching for an answer, many other questions must be asked: How many Americans, including college administrators, teachers, and counselors, understand the Mexican American community? How many understand the views of its leaders, the feelings, attitudes, and history of its people? As a matter of fact, few Americans have any knowledge about the Mexican American. Many do not even know he exists. Easterners, especially, seem to have a mental block in regard to the Mexican American. If they have any knowledge at all, it is usually negative.

The reasons for this lack of knowledge about the second largest minority in our country can be traced to our school system. In analyzing the structure of our school system one finds that the majority of our schools and colleges are too traditional in cirriculum. In history, geography, and the social sciences they are oriented to Anglo-America and to Europe and contain little material and few courses on Latin America, Asia, and Africa. Furthermore, they practically ignore the languages and cultures of minority groups and do little to promote a better understanding of America's past.

There are many reasons why the Mexican American has been denied his right to enter the mainstream of American life. At the top of the list is the fact that an understanding of the Mexican American has been almost entirely lacking in our school system. In addition, many persons have tried to understand the Mexican American experience in terms of other ethnic groups. These misguided souls assume that the problems of disadvantaged people are all caused by the same reason, that is to say that all poor people are poor because of the same factors, that all uneducated people are uneducated because of the same reasons.

In short, total society has never viewed the Mexican American community in a true perspective. For this reason, when the Mexican American "problem" is discussed or mentioned, there are many who do not understand that we are faced with a problem of long standing. When two people do not get along together, it is not something that happened overnight. Its framework is *history*. And if we are sincerely concerned about finding solutions to this conflict of cultures, then a clearer and more honest understanding of our historical development must be achieved.

Few Americans are familiar with the legal status of the Mexican American and fewer with the date and the documents that made him part of the United States. Many consider him a foreigner because his culture and language are distinctly different from the majority. How many stop to realize that Juan de Oñate, the founder of Santa Fe, New Mexico, and Ponce de León, the explorer of Florida, are just as important as Roger Williams of Rhode Island or William Penn of Pennsylvania? Or that Juan de Oñate and Ponce de León spoke Spanish and Roger Williams and William Penn, English; that the Spaniards were Catholics and the Englishmen Protestants? Many Americans do not think of Spanish as an American language and the people who speak it as loyal citizens of the United States. In fact, there has been an attempt by state and local institutions to remake every Mexican American in the image of his Anglo-American counterparts. Spanish has been banned from the playgrounds and classrooms, Mexican customs and traditions discouraged in the community, and Mexican habit and culture ridiculed in public. Time and again we have witnessed, especially in the Southwest and California, a society that has commercialized the Mexican American past while, at the same time, it has ignored the living representatives of this past who reside in its midst.

Again today, a majority of Anglo-Americans find it difficult to understand the prevailing attitudes of the Chicanos toward Anglo-American culture and society. And because they are unfamiliar with Chicano history all they can do is ask, what is wrong with these people? What do they want? Why are they so upset?

What can be done? It seems to me that by developing increased awareness of the history of the second largest ethnic group in our country, numbering over seven million today, and their role and their accomplishments in our total history, a great amount of this ignorance would be eliminated.

It is within the framework of the past that we will discover the foundation for the exclusion of Mexican Americans from housing, restaurants, schools, employment, and hospitals. It is in the past that we find the roots of discrimination. It is in the past that we find that the laws, the courts, the constitutional guarantees, and the government did not function for the Mexican American as it did for others. It is in the past that we find the answers to the questions, frequently asked by Anglo-Americans: What is wrong with these Mexican Americans? What do they want? Why are they so upset? And this brings me to several important principles that should underlie the teaching of Chicano history.

WHAT AND FOR WHOM?

(1) First of all, we must understand that we are dealing with a truly bilingual, bicultural group, and that the Spanish language and Mexican cultural patterns are a real part of their way of life.

(2) The major historical forces which have influenced the Mexican American community are deeply rooted in regional and national developments. At the same time, regional, national, and even international developments have been affected by the events and movements associated with Mexican history.

(3) Chicano history should be presented and taught to the majority. The reason for this is obvious: First, the Mexican American students will discover and learn about their part in the American heritage and will thus gain a source of motivation as well as an elevation of their own self-esteem. Secondly, such a program would help other Americans better understand the Mexican American experience and, hopefully, enable them to form more accurate notions about the Mexican American.

(4) Chicano history should be presented as part of the greater history of the American past. Every effort should be made to concentrate attention on those historical events and movements which, for good or evil, affected the Mexican American population as a whole.

(5) No attempt should be made to hide the fact that Mexican Americans have been exploited, discriminated, segregated, and considered inferior in our country.

(6) Chicano history should not be merely a record of contributions and achievements. It should concern itself with what happened to the vast majority of Mexican Americans within a given era as well as with the achievements of the few.

(7) Individual or group achievements should neither be deprecated nor exaggerated. All facts and information must be put in honest perspective. Only the truth will do!

(8) Finally, and most important, the instructor must have the courage to reconstruct history if he feels that part of the

people who were participants in what took place have been neglected or given subordinate roles because of biased interpretation or biased material.

It is obvious that ethnic studies programs and courses are definitely valid and needed. They not only enable people who have been the victims of discrimination and bigotry gain self-respect, but they also help them to face the world with feelings of self-assurance and dignity. This can only be accomplished, however, if these programs and courses are made academically respectable and self-sustaining. Further, the success of these programs and courses will depend on the support they receive from administrative bodies, faculty organizations, community organizations and agencies, and student organizations. Ultimately the success of ethnic studies programs will depend on faculty commitment and participation. It is with faculty commitment, comprehension, and creativity that it will be possible to adjust our curriculum to the demands and requests of our students without, as many believe, bringing about an academic catastrophe.

Finally, I realize that history is not a panacea for our problems, but I am sure that many of you will agree with me that it is a step toward understanding.

CHICANO STUDIES: SENSITIVITY FOR TWO CULTURES

By Richard Vásquez

Ramon Garza and Jim Hansen, junior college classmates, had been friends for years. Ramon looked very Mexican. Jim, of Scandinavian descent, was fair-skinned and blue-eyed.

One day, Ramon, a student in one of the newly instituted courses in Chicano studies, opened this conversation:

Ramon: Tell me, Jim, just what do you think of me as a Mexican?

Jim: What do you mean?

Ramon: Just what I said. What do you think of me as a Mexican?

Jim: You're not a Mexican. You're as American as I am.

Chicano studies had prepared Ramon for this reply. After they talked some more, it was established Ramon was Mexican—in the same sense John Kennedy was Irish, Alioto is Italian and Goldberg is a Jew.

Then their talk proceeded to the next logical and predictable (for Ramon) stage:

Jim: Ray, I don't really think of you as a Mexican. I think of you as one of us.

Ramon: One of who?

Jim: Well, you know, you're not like ... well, like the others.

Ramon: You mean I'm not like Roberto (a Chicano acquaintance)?

Jim: No, he's OK too ... I mean, I didn't mean that.

Ramon: OK. You said I'm not like the others. What others?

At this point both boys were feeling more uncomfortable with one another than ever before, but Ramon was following a course set down by his Chicano studies teacher.

Jim: Well, you're not like other Mexicans I've known. Are you? You've got to admit you're different. You've tried.

Ramon: What others? You said I was about the first Chicano you ever got to know real well.

Jim: That's not true! I know your family.

Ramon: And you're my friend because I'm not like my family?

Jim: I didn't say that.

Ramon: Yes, you did.

Jim: Well, what I meant was—well, all right. You're not like your family. You're different from your parents.

Ramon: So if I was like my folks, I wouldn't be your friend.

Jim: Now, Ray, don't put words in my mouth . . .

So the conversation went careening out of control. Jim was surprised to suddenly hear himself saying he didn't like the smell of strong food in Ramon's home and that was one reason he didn't like to go there.

And he was surprised to find that Ramon was keenly aware of a different kind of smell in Jim's home. Jim insisted that his and other Anglo homes had no odor, but that he'd noticed in "foreigners' houses" there was always a strong smell. And Ramon was quick to seize on the slip "foreigner."

"I thought you said I was as American as you," he accused.

This friendship and perhaps hundreds like it—there's no way to tell how many—was dissolved. And, according to many who are involved in the newest addition to high school and college curricula, it really never was a friendship.

Many persons today are angered by such deliberate confrontations, which seemingly create antagonism. But a great number of Chicano faculty members and administrators agree such a confrontation is a fundamental step in the studies.

Students in Chicano studies are taught that reactions like those of Ramon and Jim are the result of a lifetime of living in an insensitive—if not racist—host society.

Without his realizing it, ever since Jim had been old enough to watch movies and television, the image of a Mexican as either a buffoon or merciless cutthroat had been thrust upon him.

In Chicano studies sensitivity sessions, Anglo students frequently say they can't recall seeing a Mexican portrayed on the screen as a responsible, sober person capable of doing competent, technical work.

Chicano studies teach that it is impossible not to respond to this stereotyping, and that the only "cure" is re-education —which is one reason why in some Chicano studies programs as many as one-third of the students are Anglo or black.

Conversely, it is impossible for a Chicano not to react to a lifetime of ridicule and maligning. Inasmuch as he cannot escape the accusing finger, he gets into all kinds of psychological trouble.

Raoul Guzman, dean of community services and adviser to MECHA, a student group, at Pasadena City College, points out that a double consciousness exists for many Chicanos.

"This double image is caused by constantly being forced to look at one's self through the eyes of others," Guzman explains. "This distorted image exists because the dominant society works against a Mexican being a Mexican."

According to Guzman, the Mexican, or Chicano, must become an American before the Anglo can be comfortable with himself and accept the Chicano as a friend and still condemn Mexicans through stereotypes.

"This wholesale generalization of the Mexican and his way of life simplifies the resolution of many Anglo problems," Guzman said.

"For example, the sick scapegoating—ascribing one's own hangups and unacceptable characteristics to Mexicans— allows the Anglo to feel superior while at the same time inferiorizing the Mexican."

The other side of this double image, Chicano studies experts agree, is how the Mexican American feels about himself.

"To be a Mexican is to enjoy and accept himself as he is, rather than how others, such as Jim, would like him to be," Guzman says.

This is what Chicano studies is all about: getting the Mexican American, or Spanish American, or Chicano—whichever word is preferred—to understand himself and his people, his history and his culture, his heritage and his destiny.

But how can this be accomplished with a race—*la Raza*—a people who until very recently had never had a novel published by one of their own about themselves, never had a history book written by one of them about them, never had a single course offered about themselves in all the universities and colleges across the nation?

"You do it through Chicano studies," answers Francisco Sandoval, chairman of Chicano studies at Cal State Long Beach.

Sandoval believes the reason so many Chicanos drop out of school (a 90 percent high school dropout rate in some parts of the nation) is their lack of identity, caused by having been left out of history, literature and society, except in negative respects.

"It's heartbreaking, but it's not hard to figure why so many Chicanos are on 'red,' over-dosing, dropping out and in jail," he says. "It's part of my job here to make 400 Chicano students aware of what this society has done to them."

He continues: "When I came to Cal State, I did the white thing in the white establishment, but I kept thinking about how most of my people are working in the fields, parks and factories. There was just a handful of Chicanos here.

"Most never get a chance because they're born into disadvantaged families, subjected to inferior schooling, which conditions them to failure because of teacher attitudes. And in high school they get counseled away from college prep courses."

Most Chicano studies programs throughout the Southwest have been in operation less than two years. Many California colleges with relatively high Mexican American enrollments are just beginning to offer such courses.

Sandoval's department has been in operation only since the fall of 1969, but it is one of the most comprehensive and advanced in the region.

The seven-instructor department offers 27 courses and a B.A. in Chicano studies, as do most programs elsewhere, and Sandoval says his staff will be expanded.

The courses range from Mexican American Heritage and

Identity to Pre-Columbian Meso-American Civilization, which covers the various societies in middle America from prehistoric times to the Spanish conquest of the Aztecs.

Sandoval realizes that not only must the Chicano be re-educated about his potential but that the host society also must learn. Sandoval, thus, is encouraged to see that about one-third of the students in his department are Anglo or black.

"We're making up for defects that kids began picking up in elementary school," he said. "We hope that prospective teachers who take our courses—white, black or brown—will begin to make changes when they start teaching in the barrios."

Gil Garcia is an East Los Angeles barrio product. Years ago he was kicked out of Hollenbeck High School, and he spent three years in Jackson Correctional Institute. Now, at 40, he is the director of the UCLA Mexican American Cultural Affairs Center.

He thinks the problem of that giant university relating to Chicano students is immense but not insurmountable.

"Out of 31,000 students here," he laments, "we have about 600 Chicanos. We have more foreign students—and their needs are better met—than Chicano students. Of 1,800 faculty members, at present five are Chicanos. This must change.

"We have practically no Chicano studies program here now, but we plan to launch a big program by fall. We're desperately recruiting Mexican American teachers. If we have to, we'll accept white or black teachers who are sympathetic to our cause.

"But we can't have the middle-class teachers from middle-class colleges who have the Mexican stereotype in mind—the kind who urge girls to take home economics and boys to take auto shop."

It is generally agreed that sympathetic Anglo instructors of Chicano studies can fill the needs of students when Mexican American teachers cannot be found.

One such pioneer in the field is John Reib in Pasadena, instructor of English literature and president of the Southern California alumni of Kappa Delta Pi, an honorary educational society.

Reib, who teaches Mexican American literature to Chicano students, has seen dramatic changes in individual students who became aware of their identity and heritage.

"I could cite several examples that old-time educators wouldn't believe," he claims. "One man came into the program with the traditional street-gang tattoos on his arms. He was older than I. And then he started learning about himself and his people, and the accomplishments of heretofore obscure Chicanos.

"In a single semester he became an outstanding scholar. He reads everything he can get his hands on, and does independent research. He brought to our attention literature we were unable to find for our studies."

But brown studies boosters run into heavy opposition. The encouragement of such confrontations as that of Jim and Ramon is greatly criticized by well-meaning white liberals who spend considerable time and effort bringing about racial "harmony."

One activist coed bitterly denounced a Chicano studies program for recruiting nonmilitant Chicanos and turning them into what she calls "raving radicals."

"There was this group of Spanish girls in our organization," she said. "They were happy. We went places and did things together. Then these Chicano studies guys talked them into attending some sessions. Before long they came back, challenged everything we did for them, and left."

Guzman agrees the problem ostensibly exists.

"We have a lot of Chicano students who come on campus disagreeing with what we're trying to do," he explains. "These kids hear about injustices and prejudice and they say, 'But nothing like that ever happened to me,' or 'My best friends are Anglo.'

"We ask them to put the question to their Anglo friends: 'What do you think of me as a Mexican?'

"The inevitable confrontation arises. What was seemingly

a good friendship begins to come apart. That isn't good: what's good is that then—at that point—both Chicano and Anglo are ready to start learning what each other's culture and dignity is all about.

"The ones who said at first, 'That never happened to me,' their memory isn't too hard to jog. In the rap sessions you can hear them tell how an Anglo friend explained there wasn't enough room in the car going to the beach, or that some one else sent the invitations to a party the Chicano was left out of.

"They begin remembering, but what's important is they learn to cope with reality, instead of forming mental blocks in their memories."

And what is the reaction of the students who were at first reluctant to face reality?

Guzman says they usually react in one of two ways: they become extremely militant and join every group that is trying to break down social barriers—or they become tremendous academic achievers, as did John Reib's students.

And what about the Anglo who feels he lost a friend because of Chicano studies?

Instructors agree this can be the most gratifying experience in the field. Sometimes the Anglo student realizes he has been a victim of a system he didn't understand. More and more of these Anglo students show up at the Chicano studies registration desk. And this time they are ready to really learn what their former brown friend was all about.

Facing Anglo Society

FROM PRISON: REIES LÓPEZ TIJERINA

By Reies López Tijerina

I, Reies López Tijerina, consent to write the following for the information of the public.

For 40 days, since my arrest and incarceration in the New Mexico State Penitentiary, Cell #49, Block 3, I have been without communication with the offices of the Alianza (Confederation of Free City States) or with its officials. Because of this fact, I have been unable to proceed effectively with the programs and projects pertaining to the claims about the land, culture, and hereditary rights of my people.

But for the first time in all my life, I feel a deep satisfaction and conviction that I am serving my people with all my energy and strength of my heart. For the rights of my people, I am held captive. Because of the rights of my blood brothers to their property, their culture, and their inheritance, I suffer imprisonment. And I shall suffer it again if necessary. In the future, people will not underestimate the Hispaño community.

Here in my prison I feel very content—I repeat, very content and very happy because I know and understand well the cause I defend. My conscience has never been as tranquil as it has during these days in prison because, as I have said before and now repeat from prison: For the land, culture, and inheritance of my people I am ready not only to suffer imprisonment, but I would, with pleasure and pride, sacrifice my life to bring about the justice which is so much deserved by my people—the Spanish American people.

Every day the daily news in *The New Mexican* gives me encouragement, as does the news coming over the radio and the television which is told to me by other prisoners. I am little perturbed by what my critics say against me, because I know that I defend a just cause and that they are ignorant of the documents, accumulated with great expenditure of time and money, to prove my people's claims to their land grants. I am convinced that those who now oppose what I do will someday also come to support the cause of my people, a cause which now cries out for justice—as well as for personal and cultural dignity—in the desert of darkness.

In prison, my health has been excellent. My doctor, Robert Castillo of Albuquerque, is always advising me to take care of my throat by not talking so much, so I enjoy this kind of rest.

The prisoners treat me as a brother and with much respect, for which I am grateful because I know that they sympathize with my struggle for justice.

My days in prison have gone by rapidly, and I believe this is due to the sympathy of the public and to the good news that is constantly being brought to me by those who surround me in prison. It is also due, I believe, to the preparation that I have undergone since the days of my youth for the sacrifices demanded of a man dedicated to the salvation and culture of a people.

In spite of my imprisonment, I am very pleased that my blood brothers and the officials of the Alianza are carrying on, holding meetings with much success. Also we appreciate very much the many things done by the non-Hispaño people on our behalf. In spite of the fact that in New Mexico it is the Latin and the Indian who have suffered injustice and wrong, I must say that the desire for justice knows no boundaries of race or culture.

I think that if another race were the victim of oppression, I would defend it as I now defend my people.

Some of those who sympathize with the just cause of my people will say that I am suffering bitterness in prison, but this is not the case. In my reflections during these last 40 days, I see that the whole world now recognizes the problems in New Mexico and those of my people. This thought is sufficient to keep me content and tranquil. Certainly in the silence of my cell I have thought about the thousands of people who know nothing of the afflictions of my people and of their lost inheritance. I welcome this opportunity to explain to the public our rights and obligations to ask for justice and the restitution of our inheritance, our property, our culture . . . I shall do the best I can with the knowledge I have relative to the land grants and the sovereign city states which our fathers founded here in New Mexico, Texas, California, and other parts of the Southwest.

The question of the land grants is of tremendous social and economic importance to the Southwest. To ignore their importance and what they represent is to ignore the history of the entire Spanish American culture in the Southwest. This would be a political and economic error of the first magnitude.

There are persons who have full stomachs and contented hearts, but very little knowledge about the situation of the Spanish Americans and the facts and laws concerning the land grants. They say that in New Mexico there is no discrimination against the Spanish Americans, that there is no poverty, and that the land grants have already been decided by the Congress, the Court of Private Claims, and the courts of New Mexico. But those who had thought that the Hispaños were content with the arrangements of the land grants are now discovering that the Spanish American people are uniting to struggle against the fraud and corruption of the famous "Sante Fe Ring" and its present representatives.

I have tried to explain the rights, the evidence, and the laws which support the claims of the Hispaños over the land grants. Thus the Hispaños may be able to solve the problems resulting from them.

An *ejido* is common land or pasturage that the Kings of the West Indies donated, in the form of land grants, to towns and villages already settled.* *Ejidos* were common properties of those people who used them in earning their livings. These *ejidos* cannot be sold nor taxed, nor can they be lost during the passage of time.

All nations and governments of the world have respected the concept of the *ejidos* which belong to villages and towns. Even in Russia, the *ejidos* are respected, as the history of laws of property will confirm.

*He means here that, except for the original thirteen colonies, America is still the sovereign land, legally, of the King of the West Indies, as it was during and after the time of Queen Isabella of Castille. Ed.

In the year 1947 the United States, during the administration of Harry S. Truman, aided the Jews in their claim to Palestine. The towns and villages of the Jews, according to the Bible, received *ejidos* which have always been respected. Law 7, Title 20, Section 3 of the Law of the Indies reads, "Neither plaza nor street nor road nor pasture nor *ejido* nor any other land similar to these which is in use *for the communal benefit* of the people of a city or village or castle or other place can be gained by any man through time."

The land grants or free cities which we are claiming can never be lost because of the passage of time nor through taxes nor by presidential decree. Each community land grant had and has an *ejido*, and the size of an *ejido* has no limitation. It can contain up to several million acres of pasture. The *ejidos* cannot be closed in, or fenced in, at any time.

The Spanish American people and the American Indian have been basely betrayed by the Federal Government of the United States, and the State of New Mexico is also involved in this gigantic injustice. The politicans, especially those of the "Santa Fe Ring," know the truth. The self-centered politicians of New Mexico do not want the truth revealed. They do not want the Hispaño to become aware of such a monstrous theft. But if all we poor inheritors unite, we shall see justice. The land, the *ejidos*, will return to their true owners.

The Federal Alliance (Alianza) provides our response and our remedy for all the wrongs we have endured. All Hispaños must unite. The conscience of New Mexico lies within the Federal Alliance. The criminals hide behind those who control the government of New Mexico.

Without our *ejidos*, there can be no justice. And without justice in New Mexico, our culture and our language will never be respected. Progress in New Mexico depends upon the solving of the problem of the land grants; thus, progress depends upon the rights allowed the Spanish American.

We want to see schools and high schools in New Mexico where the Hispanic, the Anglo-Saxon, and the Indian cultures are equally studied. Only thus shall we have future harmony and friendship between the United States and South America.

We should prepare ourselves for the year 2000 when there will be 600 million Hispaños south of the Rio Grande, when all the world will reject the imperialist doctrines of the United States, when only South America will remain as the last friend of the United States. In New Mexico lies the last hope of the United States, and we, the Hispaños, will be the salvation of the Anglo-Saxon. If the Federal Government of the United States denies us justice now, ten years from now it will regret it. This is the future I see, and we shall see it with our own eyes.

We are determined to ask for, to demand, and to struggle for justice until the world gives it to us. There are a thousand ways to seek and to find justice. Thus, as the cricket in the fable defeated the lion, the king of beasts, by climbing into his ear and tickling him, we shall do the same even if we have to form a car caravan to the Capitol in Mexico City to ask that Mexico take our case to the United Nations. If the United Nations investigated our complaint, it would be easy to prove our rights, for we have all the necessary documents.

We do not want to destroy the culture of the Anglo; we only ask that our culture also be protected by the law, just as the law reads.

We have not robbed the Indian, as some accuse us, nor do we seek harm for the Indian. The Indian is our brother, and that same law of the Indies commands us to live as brothers with the Indians. Law 7, Title 17 of Book 4 reads thus:

> The mountains, pastures and waters of the places and the mountains contained within the grants which may be made or that we may make of dominions in the Indies should be common to the Spaniards and the *Indians*, and thus we command the Viceroys and Audiencias to protect them and to comply.

The *ejido* or pasturage of the land grants is for the Indian and for the Hispaño.

One of the future objectives of the Alianza is to end the poverty and misery which exist among the Hispaños, to end discrimination, bad judges, and the criminal "politics" which are practiced in New Mexico; to end all thefts of land, and everything which obstructs progress.

The Hispaño, the Indian, and the Anglo people should insist that the governor and the legislature of New Mexico appoint a committee or commission to investigate all the fraudulent acts of the Federal Government committed in opposition of the purpose of the land grants. This is the greatest emergency in all the State of New Mexico. I hope that this article will help to clear the minds of some whose information has come from false rumors.

I have at no time said or claimed that which cannot be proven with documents. I am positive of everything I tell to my people, and I am ready to prove it in public if I am given the opportunity.

In the future the Alliance will attempt to help the Spanish people clean up politics in the state, to use the vote wisely and elect good candidates to government positions in New Mexico—candidates who will see that the Spanish culture, history, and language are studied in the schools.

For example, Article 12, Section 8 of the Constitution of New Mexico establishes that the Legislature of New Mexico shall provide for the preparation of teachers of normal and other schools so that they are proficient in both Spanish and English in order to qualify to teach Spanish American students in the public schools and in state educational institutions and, also, to provide a proper means of teaching English and other subjects to such students. This article has been violated; also, Article 2, Section 5 of the New Mexican Constitution, which reads as follows: "The rights, privileges and immunities, political, civil and religious, guaranteed to the people of New Mexico by the Treaty of Guadalupe Hildalgo will be preserved inviolable." Article 2, Section 3, reads, "The people of the State of New Mexico have a sole and exclusive right to govern themselves as a free, sovereign and independent state."

The flagrant violation of these constitutional guarantees has caused continual chaos in the Hispaño communities and has created the greatest resentment by the Hispaños against the Anglo and his culture.

So we will have meetings in all of New Mexico; we shall

have marches and establish contact and union with all the Spanish American groups throughout the United States. We shall struggle so that the Hispano will have a part in the control of education in the State of New Mexico, in work projects, and in politics. We shall also struggle for peace and harmony among the different races here in New Mexico.

I do not feel like a prisoner here in my cell. I am not sad, like a defeated criminal—on the contrary, I see and feel that the one being judged by the whole world is the Federal Government of the United States which has failed to respect its obligations and has robbed the Indian and the Hispano of their lands.

Here in my cell, I have a book from the prison library called *The Spanish Empire in America*, by C. H. Haring. Upon reading this book, I discovered that the present attempt of the Anglo to destroy our free cities is not the first time that Hispanic cities (grants) have suffered such injustice and aggression. The Arabs who invaded Spain in the eighth century and who dominated her for 700 years, also tried to destroy the free cities which existed in Spain. But they did not succeed, because the neighbors of those free cities resisted, defending their rights. Finally the Arabs respected those cities and realized that is was wise to incorporate them in the Arabic political structure.

It is sad to see that Anglos do not have the wisdom to comprehend the advantages that would result from allowing these free Hispano cities to govern themselves. The Anglo in New Mexico should know that even after a century of efforts to destroy these cities, the Hispano has resisted those efforts. The Anglo should realize that the resistance of the Hispano will grow stronger each day.

During these days during which the criticism from my adversaries has multiplied, many valiant friends have distinguished themselves by speaking on my behalf and in support of the case for my people. My imprisonment has also resolved what to me has been an enigma—the fact that many of my adversaries continually accused me of robbing my people and working for my own interests . . . But now that my people see me imprisoned and at one time on the point of dying in the gas chamber, they are convinced more than ever that I was not and am not a fraud, that I work with goodwill and an honest heart for their benefit.

Prison has made me feel more worthy of my people and much stronger than before in offering my life for the protection and advancement of their rights.

THE GORKASE MIRROR

By Eliu Carranza

Suppose a modern day Sophist named Gorkase upon being asked, "What are Chicanos?" were to respond that the answer although brief would nevertheless be worth a certain sum of money. The sum having been agreed upon, he directs his questioners "to seek out and ask a Chicano" whereupon he is informed that the questioners *are* Chicanos and that they ask the question of themselves.

To this, Gorkase expresses some distress in his characteristic way, for he recognizes immediately another case of "identity crisis," a slight variation of an ancient preoccupation of the Greeks, who, as Greeks, asked themselves, "What is man?"

And even the Greeks, he reminisces, had not settled the question. Some Greeks had reasoned that man was a rational animal; others that man was the measure of all things—a perspective he was not only personally inclined to argue for, but a perspective admirably suited to the increasingly rapid changes taking place in the world of men and machines. Some persons experience rapid change as "future shock"; others experience change as "cultural shock." Both, of course, are the result of too sudden change in an environment wherein novelty and diversity rule and the familiar disappears.[1] The questions arising from future or cultural shock, however, do not usually begin with, "What am I?"

The latter question signals for Gorkase a dialectically related shock, namely, "identity shock," a concomitant effect, Gorkase reasons, of emphasizing the "rational" at the expense of the "animal" or vice versa, causing the one to become two and each a stranger to the other. The unhappiness is inevitable: despair at stage one (despair improperly so-called, according to one writer).[2]

[1] See Alvin Toffler's *Future Shock*, Random House, New York.
[2] See Søren Kierkegaard's *The Sickness Unto Death*, Doubleday & Company, Inc., Garden City, New York.

Gorkase has had similar encounters. Some of these have been disastrous, forcing him to reconsider at length the Aristotelian definition of man, for the "animal" in some of his dissatisfied questioners has emerged victorious over the "rational" and his body bears the evidence. He feels inclined to demur the invitation of the Chicanos, except that he is intrigued by their brown faces and the almost passive look about their eyes. He has read that they are relatively harmless, inclined to *viejas*, *pisto* and *songas* in that order, that is, until lately.

Not that such had changed. According to his research, however, a small minority within the minority (while still keeping to women, wine and song) had apparently shed their passivity and assumed a more aggressive stance toward friend and foe alike: *militancy*. No question about it, Gorkase recognizes the mood. He has experienced the impact of that mood with the blacks who, without his consent although based on his refusal to become part of the solution, made him *ipso facto* part of the problem—a problem most of the blacks wanted to eliminate.

Of course, he did injury to his case at the time by insisting that his choice, if forced, was vulnerable to the error of the Black-or-White Fallacy (False Dilemma).[3] In retrospect, Gorkase felt he had made an unfortunate choice of words, considering the occasion. It is truly a lonely feeling to be the only white in a sea of black hostiles, which Gorkase distinguished from hostile blacks. His reaction to the former was fear; to the latter a guilty conscience. He had come off badly on that occasion.

This occasion, however, promised to be less threatening. In the first place, consider the question: "What are Chicanos?" That non-Chicanos should ask, "What are Chicanos?" is understandable. The question could be interpreted as a request for information to which one produces a batch of statistics dealing with their economic, educational, or social

---

[3] We are guilty of the Black-or-White Fallacy (False Dilemma) if we fail to admit the possibility of more than two alternatives.

plight. Or, the question could be an expression of puzzlement, as one who comes upon a strange phenomenon and asks: "What is it?" "What are Chicanos?" is really "Who are Chicanos?"

In truth, thinks Gorkase, all that non-Chicanos ask by such questions is "minimally identifiable characteristics" used as an easy standard to distinguish one group from another: stereotyping. No doubt about it, thinks Gorkase. Most certainly the Chicano question is not of that sort—in which case, no need for additional research!

In the second place, the question can be interpreted as a request for a difference which admits of articulation and beauty. Such a question, thinks Gorkase, could reasonably be asked by Chicanos. If such was the case, all of his art at making the worse better and the better worse would be needed. Perhaps this is all that is meant by Chicanismo: a difference in search of the beautiful. Such requires a different perspective, however—a difficult task which requires full cooperation and "learners." Gorkase is unsure of both. Of course, it was possible that Chicanos had already achieved that perspective, in which case his task would be to work from "a difference" to a "beautiful difference." That would require the skillful use of rhetoric and a straw man. Or, the strategy of the "via negativa" suggests itself, a strategy which reinforces the difference and taxes human endurance toward termination, if not the cessation of thought.

Or, why not a rare combination of all three. What a brilliant thought! It came to him all in one flash, a beautiful sign to commit his talents. The strategy of thought: the "via negativa," namely to show a difference which at the same time is a beautiful difference. An assumption for which Chicanos experience a definite aversion will permit thought to glide more quickly toward the beautiful difference: two straw men, one for the assumption and one for the conclusion.

We need not return to the assumption; we shall not require the troublesome business of a different perspective with all of its attendant dialectical twists and turns. Of course, all of the key terms must appear if the scheme is to attract credibility.

An afternoon's work, he thinks. Besides, he sighs, there was the grumbling in his stomach. He needs the money! And all that Chicanos are asking for is reassurance.

There was one last consideration. Suppose the question "What are Chicanos?" is asked in despair at not being conscious of having a self? The possiblity had occurred to Gorkase before. The job of tracking down that philosophical bug could have disastrous consequences, especially for himself: a Pandora's box. No question about it. Such could very well be the case. If so, the question could serve as a key to a host of difficult problems.

Could it be a case of a self in search of an undiscovered self? He never ceased to marvel at examples of "identity shock." Here was the possibility of another: a Chicano in asking not another Chicano, but himself, "What is a Chicano?" is asking, nevertheless, a Chicano (himself) what he is. Surely, he thinks, such is a most beautiful example of thought on a holiday. It would take a month of Sundays to unravel that one, more like unscrambling a scrambled egg. But if the Chicano question led to paradox, he would slip away.

He turns to meet his questioners.

Wherein a Difference is Established

Gorkase: I am happy to have been introduced to each and every one of you. It is good that you have spokesmen. If I become carried away in thought and do not notice or hear you, please forgive me and bear with me. Such is the product of long years of training in such matters. Now, to the point. I have done some research on the matter before us. For example, an etymological analysis of the word "Chicano" reveals it to be composed of the morpheme "chi" and the morpheme "cano." "Chi" is the consonant sound of the twenty-second letter of the Greek alphabet X; "cano" as far as I am able to determine is the Spanish adjective for grey-haired. A grey-haired twenty-second letter of the Greek alphabet has obviously no relation to the Chicano.

Other accounts appear to be relevant. One account holds that the word is a combination of the words *Chihuahua* and *Texano;* another that the word is a corruption of *Meshicano* from the Nahau language; still another suggests it to be a corruption of the word *Chinaco,* a word applied by the French to Mexicans; another concludes that the word Chicano comes from the Chichimeca, an Indian tribe.

My research has revealed not only etymological differences of opinion concerning the word "Chicano," but also certain questions concerning the characteristics or attributes of the Mexican American. One writer, for example, distinguishes the attributes of the culture of poverty from the attributes of Chicanos.[4] Essentially his analysis reveals that (1) Chicano's parents or grandparents came from Mexico or he himself was born there, (2) his language is usually Spanish, (3) his religion is usually Catholic, and (4) his skin is usually brown, his hair black and his eyes brown.

What are we to do with Carlos here, a black from Yucatán who fits all of the requirements but who calls himself, nevertheless, a black? Or his brother, who calls himself a Chicano? Or Jane who fulfills all of the requirements but refuses to yield to the label? Or, Carlos Montgomery who fits none but who insists that he is a Chicano? I do not wonder that you ask, "What are Chicanos?"

Before we proceed, allow me to make a special request. Will the spokesmen for the Chicanos please come forward? In this way, when you speak all of the members of our audience will benefit. At the same time, and as quickly as possible so that we may proceed, will all Chicanos be seated to my left? Excellent! Now will all non-Chicanos be seated to my right? Thank you, gentlemen.

---

[4] Edward J. Casavantes, *A New Look at the Attributes of the Mexican American.* Southwestern Cooperative Educational Laboratory, Inc., Albuquerque, New Mexico, 1969. (Gorkase hardly does justice to Casavantes' excellent work.)

Please observe that by this division we have at least established *who* Chicanos are. They have made themselves visible to us as the group to my left. By the same token, we know also who the non-Chicanos are; they have made themselves visible as the group to my right. Henceforth shall I be your "divider" or your "mediator"? Should you again become confused as to who you are, I shall remind you.

José: We were one group until you chose to divide us! You have cleverly separated us and now we must recognize the difference. But the difference was there before the separation, else you would not have separated us, even cleverly.

Gorkase: Good Heavens, José! I merely sought to address my remarks to the proper persons. I do not want to be like the cross-eyed man who looks in the direction of the far corner when he speaks to you at arm's length. But you do admit a difference, do you not? That is to say, José, Chicanos are different and their difference does not consist in merely *choosing* to be different; rather, in *choosing* as you all have done, you announce a prior difference?

José: We knew we were different before the choice to take a seat to your left, yes!

Wherein a Difference-From _____ is Established

Gorkase: I did not ask that, José. Let me put it in another way. Let us look at the difference you speak of in terms of what Chicanos are not. After all, a difference is a difference to someone. It is nonsensical to talk of a difference that is not a difference to someone. It follows, then, that a difference to someone is also a *difference-from* something. Do you follow? For example, you claim that Chicanos are different and that you were in possession of that difference *prior to choice*. Hence, Chicanos separated themselves to the left *from* the non-Chicanos to the right. Choice does not determine the Chicano difference-from_____; choice expresses it. The Chicano difference-from_____ determines choice. Isn't that what you meant when you accused me of cleverness, José?

José: I . . .

Gorkase: No matter! Will you admit that a difference in search of a "differer" is not our topic for discussion and that a difference is a difference to someone and from something?

José: I suppose . . .

Gorkase: All I am asking, José, is for you to consent to facts. For example, Chicanos are different from Japanese, Chinese, Russians, etc. Would you agree?

José: Of course, but . . .

Gorkase: And are Chicanos also different from the Mexican Americans to my right? I did not make you different from them, did I, José? As if I could, clever though I may be!

José: Very well, yes! As a group, Chicanos are different from those Mexican Americans who choose not to join us!

Gorkase: But, José, you agreed a moment ago that to be a Chicano had nothing to do with choice. Have you now changed? Do you recognize what power I exercise over you that I do make the better appear worse and the worse appear better, for insofar as you are a Chicano not by choice but by virtue of a difference-from _____, I have made you into a Chicano not by virtue of a difference-from _____ but by choice. Am I really that clever, José? Or, shall we remain with our former thesis?

José: I meant . . .

Gorkase: Yes, yes, yes, José. Allow me to ask you a most crucial question: Are Chicanos different from not only Anglo-Saxons, Chinese, Russians and some Mexican Americans, but also Mexicans?

José: We come from Mexicans!

Gorkase: I did not ask that, José. Allow me to rephrase the question and at the same time introduce you to a people whose "suspicion, dissimulation, irony, the courtesy that shuts [them] away from the stranger . . . are traits of a subjected people who tremble and disguise themselves in the presence of the master." Their ". . . intimacy never flowers in a natural way, only when incited by fiestas, alcohol or death." José, what do you conceive to yourself of a people who like "slaves, servants and submerged races always wear a mask, whether smiling or sullen," who "only when they are alone, during the great moments of life, do they dare to show themselves as they really are? All their relationships are poisoned by fear and suspicion: fear of the master and suspicion of their equals. Each keeps watch over the other because every companion could also be a traitor. To escape from himself the servant must leap walls, get drunk, forget his condition. He must live alone, without witnesses. He dares to be himself only in solitude." [5]

Wherein a Difference-Toward _____ *is Established* (a Difference-Toward Improperly So-Called)

Gorkase: José, are Chicanos different from the people I have described? . . . José, you have grown into silence! . . . Alex, will you assist me to help you? Whoever the people described may be, are Chicanos different from them? Or, have I by a divine stroke hit upon the exact description of Chicanos?

Alex: What you have said appears to be Paz's description of the Mexican; if it is, it is not true of the Chicano. The Chicano no longer shuts himself away from the stranger. His intimacy reveals itself no longer exclusively in fiestas, alcohol or death, but in *confrontation* with the *oppressor*. He has removed the mask and seen himself for what he is, a human being!

Gorkase: The Chicano then, although he comes from the Mexican, is different from the Mexican in that he has removed the mask and reveals himself face to face to his oppressor in confrontation. The relation he exists in is one of *confrontation with the oppressor*. Shall we label such a relation the relation of *militancy* and those participating in it *Chicano Militants?*

Alex: Certainly; and *Chicano Militants* are the embodiment of a *Cultural Revolution*, a change which stands forth as

[5] Octavio Paz, *The Labyrinth of Solitude—Life and Thought in Mexico*, Grove Press, New York pp. 70-71.

an honest difference. From the point of view of the Chicano Militants what has occurred is a Cultural Revolution; from the point of view of the Mexican American what has transpired is the *Chicano Movement*.

Gorkase: How beautiful thought is, Alex. I would that I had discovered you earlier, for you truly are a fountain of knowledge. I must congratulate you for a remarkable exercise of . . . thought. Observe carefully, Alex, for we are about to achieve our goal. With your help, we shall catch it by the neck and pin it down. Does a Mexican American who participates in the Chicano Movement become a Chicano by so doing?

Alex: If his participation is the result of the awareness of a difference-from _____, yes! He passes from a kind of nonbeing to being . . .

Gorkase: Alex, I was just about to congratulate you again, but obviously I shall not be able to do so if you persist in using the words "being" and "nonbeing"—both representative of muddled thought.

Alex: Let me answer your question in this way: Paz states that the Mexican neither wants nor dares to be himself. The Chicano not only wants but has dared and will continue to dare to be himself because he cares, where no one else has cared; he demands, when others plead; he reaches out, while others shrink inwardly; he dares to look up, while others bend their necks; and he speaks out, when others remain silent. In short, he dares to be a human being in an age of robots. He will not tolerate dehumanization by anyone or anything. Now, if a Mexican American has joined the Chicano Movement as a result of an inward change, then he is a Chicano!

Gorkase: Beautiful, Alex, although I would prefer the words "different perceptions of himself" to "an inward change." Would that be agreeable? Very well! Chicanos then are Mexican Americans who, unlike their ancestors, have removed their masks revealing themselves in confrontation against their oppressors and who, unlike other Mexican Americans, have acquired different perceptions

of themselves concerning their role, purposes and goals.
We have already explained the *Chicano role* in that they
confront the oppressor. What guides or *determines* their
roles beyond their commitment, dedication and devotion?

Alex: I would say that the Chicano role is guided by the
principle of self-determination; that is, Chicanos determine their role.

Gorkase: Each by himself or each by the group?

Alex: The latter! A movement cannot put the individual
above the group interests, for Chicanos seek to free others
to a new awareness of themselves.

Gorkase: And understandably so. I perceive that you call
such the *liberation* of the Mexican Americans. Does such
constitute the purpose of Chicanos?

Alex: Yes; however, it is more than our purpose. It is our
obligation which, as such, becomes *La Causa*. We strive to
include others also. We are not separatists! Ultimately,
the Chicano seeks the unity of all in *La Raza Unida*. Such
is the goal . . . where we are all together again, where
"difference that separates" becomes "difference that
unites in respect."

Gorkase: And what of those who refuse your Utopia, Alex?

Alex: We have a strategem for such. It is called "a return
to one's Cultural Heritage," and for those who need a
religion we have another. We call it "toward a New
Humanism."

Gorkase: Is *La Raza Unida* concept a device also?

Alex: Of course; it is a goal, is it not? Goals are things we
strive for and may not reach. We set goals for the same
reason you introduce assumptions in thought, namely, to
create movement, to give purpose and direction. This is
what is done when a minority seeks to survive as a minority in the face of a powerful racist majority. You create an
awareness based on a difference-from _____ concept.
Thought, in order to gaze at the relation, separates itself
from itself and constitutes a different relation, and . . .

Gorkase: Stop! I implore you! I must warn you that such
language will only create difficulties for us. It is language

on a holiday and I prefer to spend my holidays elsewhere. I have completed my assigned task. Let me render an account and be gone.

Your thought about yourselves deserves a name. Allow me to call it by one which I consider truly appropriate: "Chicanismo: the Dialectics of Survival," or "Chicanismo: Coping Strategies of a Minority in a Racist Society." That shall be my contribution. To the thought, "What are Chicanos?" we respond: Chicanos, a minority within a minority who, seeking survival as a minority in a powerfully racist society and who, unlike other Mexican Americans, have acquired different perceptions of themselves, perceptions that raise up their humanity, *represent* an honest difference-from the perceptions of the slave and servant and an honest difference-toward the liberation and reunification of all Mexican Americans and others in *La Raza Unida* wherein difference will equal respect.

Finally, Chicanos and Mexican Americans, I have learned much from you. *You* . . . have come to a newer realization of yourselves. *I* . . . have been instrumental in bringing you to a newer awareness of your role, purposes, and goals. *I* . . . feel honored and humbled at the same time, for one must be both honored and humbled at the perception of beauty in a wilderness of ugliness and disenchantment. And what reasonable person would deny that you are engaged in a task worthy of admiration as well as commitment and devotion? We realize that not everything that stands opposed to Racism is necessarily beautiful, for the confrontations of others against Racism have been violently bloody and unbeautiful.

Your confrontation, however, commends itself, for on the whole it has been a "psychological" confrontation of bloodless beauty that has made giant strides. The absence of terror among yourselves is further evidence of the humanitarian relation which you share among yourselves: *carnalismo*. To those who seek to impute to you a carelessness of thought, a passivity of action, and an ignorance of human relations, let them but meet you and they will discover, as I have, the truth. And the truth about your-selves is that you constitute a beautiful difference which became beautiful not merely in casting off old slave-ser-vant perceptions about yourselves, but in the liberation of the mind from the old toward a reunification with all Mexican Americans in your *Raza Unida*. Your libera-tion houses your beauty; your perceptions of yourselves heretofore distorted by difference as separation are tran-scended in and through perceptions henceforth made beautiful by difference-toward unification. Man is, after all, the measure of all things—of the things that are that they are and of the things that are not that they are not. Chicanos are men: therefore, Chicanos are the measure of the things that are. You are beautiful.

Leonardo da Vinci once wrote: "Seek what you are capable of, and be capable of what you seek." You are the seekers who have found your humanity; therefore, you are also capable of what you seek. I congratulate you.

Somewhere, I have also read that the Mexican has shown us all how to die; the Chicano, I now believe, will show us how to live.

As you say, *Vayan con Dios!*

THE NATIONAL CHICANO MORATORIUM
and
THE DEATH OF RUBEN SALAZAR

By Albert Herrera

For a hundred years or more the Eastside of Los Angeles has been a third-class community inhabited by poor Mexicans, Jews, blacks, Orientals, and their descendants. Today, the minority-group dwellers live in the smoggy midst of foundries, soap factories, chemical plants, railroad switching yards, gas works, sausage factories, warehouses, stockyards, tallow-rendering plants, and junk yards. Up to about fifty years ago, very few members of minority groups lived outside the barrio or ghetto, even if they could afford to.

Beginning with the close of the United States war with Mexico, European Americans (with the possible exception of Spaniards) have had a very low opinion of minority groups in California, and especially of the Mexicans. In 1859 the San Francisco *Herald* referred to the Mexicans of Los Angeles as a degraded race, "many of them exceedingly dark-complexioned, who could not be distinguished from Indians and Negroes."

The despoliation and exploitation of the Mexicans began primarily in 1851 with the passing by Congress of a bill to settle private land claims in California. The act gave the newly arrived "Americanos" free rein in despoiling the new Mexican Americans of their lands. The law resulted in the Mexican being left landless and penniless, including the last Mexican governor of California, Pio Pico, who had to pawn nearly everything he owned to prevent starvation.

The Mexican suffered physical abuse too. If he reacted normally and did not meekly accept mistreatment, he was likely to be maimed or killed, with almost complete immunity for the wrongdoer. If he retaliated and escaped, he was labeled a bandit and outlaw.

Great celebrations would be held whenever one of the

"bandits" was caught and executed. In 1875, for example, when the much-sought "bandit" Tiburcio Vásquez was apprehended, public schools in Los Angeles closed so that children could go to see Tiburcio in his cell the day before he was hanged.

This early conditioning of children of European Americans in psychological and overt sadism has had lasting effects clearly visible to this day.

The National Chicano Moratorium was held in East Los Angeles on August 29, 1970, to protest the Vietnam war. Of 27,000 Chicanos shipped to Southeast Asia to fight in this war, more than 8,000, or about one-third, have been killed in action or died of wounds. The moratorium was planned as a peaceful protest. About 25,000 people participated in the parade, many of them women and children.

The march began at 11:30 a. m. at Belvedere Park, on Third and Mednik, with Laguna Park as its terminal point. It was a hot day, but the people were in a cheerful mood. The first untoward incident occurred on Whittier Boulevard near Eastern Avenue, where some hooligans standing on an overpass threw bottles down at the paraders. A number of marchers were cut on the head and shoulders. And about two blocks before the parade reached Laguna Park, there was a brief scuffle between some of the deputies and the marchers. The moratorium monitors soon quieted things down.

There were to be speeches and music at the park, and the adults, with their children, found places to sit on the grass. It was a warm day, and some of the people walked to a nearby store to buy cold drinks. In fact, there was such a run on business that the proprietor of the store closed the doors in order to take care of the customers already inside.

It was at this point that the sheriff's deputies began to concentrate their forces around the park. They alleged to have responded to a call from the proprietor of the store, but the owner denied ever having placed such a call. At any rate, deputies already on the scene received reinforcements, and they began to prepare for an attack. According to witnesses, no warning or notice to disperse was ever given. The deputies moved forward in an all-embracing formation, billy clubs in hand, and were met by peace rally monitors who tried to persuade the deputies to let them handle the people in the event of trouble.

But the sheriff's deputies, also according to eyewitnesses, swept the monitors aside and began to throw tear gas cannisters at the unsuspecting crowd. Many of the people were lying on the grass, listening to speeches. Fright and consternation seized them, and most took flight. Tear-gassed children were separated from their parents; many became lost. Shoes, purses, and food baskets were left behind.

Indiscriminately the deputies struck men and women on the head, shoulders, and stomach. Some of the injured were dragged, semiconscious, to waiting buses. At this point, some of the younger and more militant of the people began to throw rocks and bottles at the deputies. The Los Angeles Metropolitan Police sent reinforcements. More tear gas was used. By now, there was a full-scale melee with fighting spilling over onto Whittier Boulevard. Store windows were broken, some buildings set on fire, and cars overturned. The militants were reacting to the animalistic violence triggered by officers of the law. Sporadic fighting and destruction continued until the early hours of Sunday.

Although Sheriff Peter Pitchess claims that the confrontation was caused by outside agitators, Chicano leaders say that outsiders are unnecessary to arouse people who have been gassed, kicked, and clubbed.

The Reverend Antonio Hernández, director of the Mexican-American Community Programs Foundation, told Octavio Costa, columnist for *La Opinion* of Los Angeles, that the Mexican American community and its leaders have no confidence in the police. He also stated that in 1969 the leaders of the Eastside began talks with the police with a view to avoiding just such confrontations as occurred on August 29 at Laguna Park, but with no results. The Reverend Hernández complains that the Federal Government is helpful and even liberal with other minorities. "But for our people, only crumbs!"

There has been one disastrous confrontation; until the American citizen of Mexican descent is given fair treatment in schools, housing, jobs, and in the local community, Antonio Hernández feels that there will be others in the future— possibly of greater magnitude.

Ruben Salazar, a Mexican American newsman, was covering the National Chicano Moratorium parade with its 20,000 marchers on that hot Saturday of August 29, 1970. Salazar was news director for the Spanish language television station KMEX in Los Angeles and a writer for the Los Angeles *Times*. He had covered the war in Vietnam for the *Times* and was no stranger to front-line hostilities. Often his cables from Saigon had reflected his growing distate of the war. Enrique Hank López describes him as "our only established newspaper columnist, the most experienced and articulate Chicano writer in this whole country."

At the time of his death, Salazar was sitting on a stool in the Silver Dollar Bar, which is at 4945 Whittier Boulevard, in East Los Angeles. The Silver Dollar is an ordinary tavern, with an interior measuring about twelve by twenty-four feet, and a counter running the length of the center. There are two billiard tables, a jukebox, and paintings on the walls depicting nude ladies in varying poses. A genial, bright-eyed barmaid tends to the requests of customers. Immediately west of the Silver Dollar is a bridal shop, and to the east there is a furniture outlet store. It was in these surroundings that deputy sheriffs of Los Angeles County caused the death of Ruben Salazar. Partisan East Los Angeles newspapers claim openly that Salazar was murdered.

The riot at Laguna Park, which Chicano leaders say was provoked by police, had begun about 3:00 the afternoon Salazar was killed. But even before 11:30 that morning a radio announcer was already broadcasting rumors about a riot. Those in the park had been listening for about an hour and a half to music and speeches. The scene was a peaceful one—like that you might see on a Sunday afternoon in Chapultepec Park in Mexico City: children playing, young lovers walking around in pairs, men exchanging views, mothers talking about their children and houses. It was a scene that inspired Ruben Salazar, in the park at that time, to remark to a friend, "Isn't this just beautiful?"

Eyewitnesses say there were no disturbances in the park until the deputies charged with sticks, gas guns, and other battle gear. Delfino Varela in *Regeneración* writes, "I was on the immediate scene, and there was *absolutely no warning*, nor any audible call to disperse. The crowd was first contained within the park, and the police then came in from the back and started swinging . . ."

Once the melee got underway, it spread rapidly into adjoining streets, although never reaching the vicinity of the Silver Dollar, at least a mile away, until after the death of Salazar.

The Silver Dollar was not closed or locked. Only a curtain prevented passersby from looking inside the bar. With Salazar were Guillermo Restrepo, a reporter for television station KMEX, Hector Franco, and Gustavo Garcia, friends of Restrepo. These witnesses say that they saw no one enter the tavern with a gun and that they heard no warning to clear the tavern before the gas-shelling.

The 10-inch missile that killed Salazar was a high-velocity tear-gas projectile fired through the flimsy curtain covering the *open* doorway. Gene Pember, consultant for the Peace Officers Standards and Training Commission, stated that the missile—fired at a point-blank range of 15 feet—could easily penetrate a thick stucco wall. Its purpose, in fact, was "to penetrate a house or an object behind which a dangerous suspect has barricaded himself. But even then they should never be fired at a person."

In addition to Restrepo and his two friends, about nine other persons are reported to have been in the tavern at the time of the first gas-shelling. All occupants of the bar testified that there was no warning of any kind from the deputies before Deputy Wilson fired. Wilson testified at the inquest hearing that he had been informed by another deputy that three armed men were inside the bar. He also said that he had heard deputies shout repeated orders at the bar, asking the occupants to come out unarmed. Since no one emerged, Wilson regarded the tavern as a "barricaded situation." At least two persons outside the bar, as well as the owner of the bridal shop next door, testified that they had not heard the deputies give any warning to the occupants of the Silver Dollar. And no armed persons, according to the testimony of a sheriff's homicide detective, were removed from the bar.

The tear-gas shells were fired into the tavern sometime between 5:15 and 5:30 p. m. on August 29. All occupants fled through the rear door, except Salazar, who lay dead on the floor with a shattered skull.

Meanwhile, Joe Razo and Raul Ruiz, co-editors of La Raza, an East Los Angeles community newspaper, were watching the activities of the deputy sheriffs from a spot directly across the street from the Silver Dollar. Razo is a law student, Ruiz a college instructor. They took numerous photographs of the movements of the deputies which were printed in La Raza and later reproduced on the front page of the Times.

Both Razo and Ruiz testified that they saw the deputies point guns at chest level at a number of tavern patrons who were standing in front of the curtained entrance, forcing them back into the tavern. It was soon afterward that the deputies fired the first tear-gas shell. Five shells were fired, four of them entering the bar.

At a news conference held by Razo and Ruiz in Los Angeles on the following Thursday, September 3, during which they displayed their many photographs of the incident at the Silver Dollar, Attorney Oscar Acosta charged that the deputies, knowing Ruben Salazar to be inside the tavern and fearing him as a spokesman for the Mexican American community, committed "political murder, plain and simple."

Salazar's family was not notified of his death until about five hours after he had been fatally shot, although officials of KMEX-TV had frantically notified the sheriff's office of the incident soon after they received the first report about it from witness Guillermo Restrepo. In fact, for reasons still apparently unexplained, the deputies *did not enter the tavern* until several hours after the killing.

The Los Angeles *Times* wrote, "The unanswered questions are obvious: Was sufficient warning given before those shells were fired? Why didn't deputies enter the bar afterwards to see if anyone was left there? Why the delay in entering the bar and the delay in reporting Mr. Salazar's death?

"Why, above all, were those deadly wall-piercing cannon shells used in a situation they were not designed for, a situation they are never supposed to be used in? Who authorized their use? Have those responsible been relieved of field duty? What are the sheriff's rules about the use of the weapons?"

There was a 16-day coroner's inquiry into the death of Ruben Salazar. Sixty-one witnesses testified; over 200 exhibits and some 2,000 pages of testimony were received in evidence. Perhaps 90 percent of the testimony was irrelevant. The hearing often went far afield in attempting to prove that the riot of August 29 was the real cause of Salazar's death; that it was the Mexican Americans who provoked the disturbance at Laguna Park; that the deputies acted within "established procedures"; that outside agitators were responsible for the violence.

The coroner's jury voted for two verdicts, four jurors deciding that Salazar's death had been caused "by the hands of another person," and three voting that it had occurred "by accident."

District Attorney Evelle Younger, after studying the two verdicts, announced that "no criminal charge is justified." And he added, "In the absence of any additional evidence, this case is considered closed."

Apparently 2,000 pages of testimony, some Chicano leaders remarked, was not enough.

And Sheriff Peter Pitchess commented, "There was absolutely no misconduct on the part of the deputies involved or in the procedures they followed."

A CHICANO VOTING RIGHTS ACT

By Roberto and José Aragon

The unfair requirement that candidates for U. S. citizenship be able to pass their test in English is preventing one million of our Chicano brothers from full participation in the political life of this country. It also deprives them of certain basic economic rights which they have earned as workers and tax-payers in the American economy. The future of the entire Chicano community in this country will be greatly hampered if we are unable to solve this problem NOW.

The McCarren-Walter Amendment to the Immigration and Naturalization Act requires that the U. S. citizenship test should be given in English. This requirement has proved to be a total roadblock for literally hundreds of thousands of non-English-speaking permanent residents and especially for Spanish-speaking people in the southwestern United States. It is a roadblock because it has not been accompanied by a massive outlay of public resources needed to teach English to those who don't know English but who have been here long enough to be eligible for full citizenship. The time is right for a legislative initiative to remove the English language requirement from the immigration law and/or to question its constitutionality through the courts.

The National Action Council, which is the lobby arm of the National Urban Coalition, recently endorsed this legislative change and voted to make it one of its national priorities. Efforts are just now getting underway to build the national organizational support needed for the passage of this amendment.

On the legal front, the Western Center on Law and Poverty, on the prodding of Chicanos from the Mexican American Political Association (MAPA), the Congress of Mexican American Unity (CMAU) and the Chicano Law Students' Association (CLSA), has undertaken a class action suit to challenge the constitutionality of the English-speaking requirement for citizenship. It believes that there are certain equal protection questions involved here, and that there may be grounds for challenging the proposition implied in this, namely, that English is the national language.

Both the legislative and legal initiatives will find strong support in a recent decision of the State Supreme Court of California which knocked down an English-speaking requirement for voter registration. The reasoning of the court was that *there are sufficient sources of information available in languages other than English to assure the intelligent and informed participation of non-English-speaking people in the political process.* That reasoning is absolutely and directly applicable to the proposed amendment.

Even the most superficial review of activity in the area of citizenship training indicates that nothing less than the elimination of English-speaking requirements for citizenship will allow substantial numbers of disfranchised and marginal people to become full participants in our society.

Let us review the current statistics. Official figures obtained from the Immigration and Naturalization Service indicate that there are nearly 230,000 Mexican nationals who are permanent residents, who are adults, who are not citizens, in the three County areas of Los Angeles, Orange and Riverside. Of course, not all of the permanent residents have been here long enough to be eligible for citizenship, but substantial numbers of them have. *In each of the last three years, less than 500 Mexican nationals became citizens in this three-county area.* The need for immediate remedy should not require more extensive comment.

Why has there been so little activity in this area? The answer is that the resources needed to support a massive program of language training have not been made available. And even if they were, the technology of language training being what it is, the program would cost an astronomical amount of money. The public institution which has been charged with the responsibility for providing language training leading to citizenship is the adult division of the secondary schools. But that institution has been demonstratively and dramatically ineffective. Its results, namely, about 400 citizenships last year out of an *eligible* group that may be over 300 times that size, are totally unacceptable. Putting it simply, the two-nights-a-week, two-year courses are not going to do the job.

Other efforts by groups such as the Community Service Organization (CSO) and the International Institute are also inadequate to the size of the problem due to insufficient funding. A third resource is in the basic education training slots in the concentrated employment program, some of which have been used to provide language training. But even here the activity is minimal. In recent years, for example, East Los Angeles has received something like 150 of these positions. Thus, short of an amendment to this Act or a successful legal challenge, nothing less than massive investments in language training will overcome these deficits.

We feel strongly, based on our research, that the elimination of the English language requirement would do for the Chicano community throughout the entire Southwest what the Voting Rights Act of 1965 did for black people in the South. Such a change would amount to nothing less than a "Chicano Voting Rights Act." Should the Chicano community be able to overcome its voter registration problems which are rooted in noncitizenship, its political strength could be increased substantially. In Los Angeles County, it could make voters of perhaps as many as 200,000 Spanish-speaking people. Throughout the Southwest that figure could perhaps ultimately approach 1,000,000—enough to make the Chicano community the decisive force in states like California and Texas, which themselves are destined to be decisive in national politics.

There are some myths that surround this entire issue and these should be discussed briefly. The state of New York did away with the language requirement for voter registration and voting just a short time ago. This proved to be of great consequence for Puerto Ricans and prompted similar proposals in California. But for some reason people do not seem to realize that Puerto Ricans are United States citizens by birth. The problem of hundreds of thousands of Chicanos is not that they have not reigstered or do not vote. The problem is that they are ineligible to do either because they are not citizens.

It should be made clear that we believe that a citizenship test which measures the candidates' knowledge of United States History and United States Government is valid. We do not propose that it be eliminated, but that the test should be given in the native tongue. Our analysis of that test is that a non-English speaker could be prepared to pass that test with 50 to 60 hours of instruction.

Between Two Worlds

THE MEXICAN AMERICAN IN TWO CULTURES

By Albert S. Herrera

Mexican Americans in the United States, in varying degrees, live in two cultures: that which they or their parents brought from Mexico and the Anglo culture which predominates in the United States.

A person of Mexican parentage becomes a "Mexican American" by being born in this country or by obtaining a certificate of citizenship. Most children born in the United States of Mexican parents live more in the culture of this country than they do in the culture of Mexico.

There are families, however, whose members were all born in the border states of Texas, Arizona, New Mexico, and California, who speak only Spanish and who live almost totally in the culture of Mexico. By contrast, there are other families living in the same border states whose members, from grandparents to the youngest children, speak English almost exclusively, prepare their food in American style, read newspapers and books in English, and never watch or listen to Spanish radio or TV programs. Children of these families sometimes say that they "hate" Spanish. And they take little or no interest in what occurs in Mexico or in other Spanish-language countries. These are the so-called "assimilated" or "acculturated."

The first class of Mexican Americans described, those who live almost wholly within a Mexican culture, refers to the second class as the *agringados* or the *presumidos*, Mexicans who act like Anglo Americans or who are presumptuous. The second class, on the other hand, calls the first class the *atrasados* or the *pelados*, backward or penniless nobodies.

There has been little unity in the Mexican American community in the United States, due largely to class differences and attitudes. This lack of unity has resulted in little or no representation for the Mexican American on the political and economic levels. Though there are over one million Mexican

Americans in southern California alone, there are but a miniscule number of political and trade union representatives of their own national origin. Up to now there has been little collective and effective organization among people of Mexican ancestry. They are reserved by nature, and it is sometimes difficult to persuade them to join groups. In Mexico, they or their parents had homes which were often protected by high walls or by fences made of spiny cactus plants. In this country they still hold fast to their reserve, their individuality.

But things are changing. The Mexican American is beginning to realize that effective organization is essential to promote and protect his interests. Thirty years ago there were few Mexican American clubs or associations, and those which existed were largely of the mutual aid type, such as the *Beneficencia Mexicana*. Today there are literally hundreds of Mexican American groups of varying degrees of effectiveness.

These groups are needed. There is discrimination against the Mexican American, of the subtle as well as the not-so-subtle type. There is discrimination in employment, in education, in relations with the police, in performing jury service, and even in buying a cemetery lot.

In California and other western states, at least one half of all Mexican American men of working age are employed as farmhands, factory workers, or railroad laborers. As for discrimination in education, there has been segregation of Mexican American school children in separate buildings, classrooms, and classes. The "acculturation" process of the school system has had as its alleged objective the eradication of the language and culture of the Mexican American child. This apparent objective reflects the thinking and feeling of the dominant Anglo majority that the English language and Anglo American ways are superior to those of the Mexican American.

Many police, especially in the Southwest, are biased against the Mexican American and agree with former Chief Parker of Los Angeles, who said, "I don't think you can throw the genes out of the question when you discuss behavior patterns of the people."

Mexican Americans are almost systematically excluded from serving on juries, especially those involving minority-group defendants. If a court clerk does not eliminate a Spanish-surnamed citizen from a list of prospective jurors, the Deputy District Attorney will exercise his right of peremptory challenge and excuse the Spanish-surnamed taxpayer and prospective juror in quick order.

And it seems that even after death the corpse of a Mexican American is subject to discrimination. In many small-town cemeteries of the Southwest, there are obscure and neglected little corners set aside for those who in life bore Spanish surnames.

In the spring of 1969, police swept through the East Los Angeles area and arrested a number of Mexican American leaders, including Moctezuma Esparza, Eliezer Risco, Sal Castro, and José Angel Razo. The homes and offices of some of these young leaders were searched and ransacked, all without search warrants. The charge against them was "conspiracy to disturb the peace," a felony. Bail was fixed at $12,500, although later reduced to $250. The Chicano leaders said that they were arrested merely for "carrying on activities in pursuance of their efforts to change a racist system that had kept them down educationally, economically, politically, and socially."

Some citizens of Mexican descent regard the label "Mexican-American" as an effrontery. They say that it is discriminatory and segregating. They point out that naturalized American citizens born in the various European countries are not referred to as English-Americans, German-Americans, French-Americans, or Danish-Americans.

So the Mexican American has seen the need for effective organization and is doing something about it. The Southwest Council of La Raza, the Congress of Mexican American Unity, and the Confederacion De La Raza Unida are doing creditable spade work in welding together the many diverse Mexican American groups.

The Mexican American wants to be himself. Why should he apologize to anyone for the color of his face or the shape of his nose? Why should he hesitate to speak Spanish among other members of La Raza, or to eat boiled beans and tortillas, or to listen to or watch Mexican radio and TV programs, or to sprinkle chili powder on his food, or to read Spanish language books and newspapers, or to take pride in his Indian-Spanish culture? These acts can be of great value to the Mexican American, and he is a fool to be "assimilated" or "acculturated" away from them. Sincere and alert Mexican Americans, especially the young, aspire for a dual culture, an amalgam of the Indo-Hispanic and Anglo American cultures. They want to retain and enjoy their Mexican ways and values, and at the same time acquire and enjoy the Anglo American culture.

Some Mexican Americans are ashamed of their Mexican ancestry. They feel that having a Mexican origin holds them back in achieving full Anglo American success and recognition. The anthropologist William Madsen, in his book *The Mexican Americans of South Texas*, reports on one young Mexican American who bitterly complained about his lot:

> "When Paul came home from college on a vacation one time, he told his mother about a real or sensed insult he had received from a professor about being a Mexican American. 'I wish I could get every drop of Mexican blood out of my veins and change it for something else,' said Paul to his mother. 'I'd take any blood in the world. Anything except Mexican!'"

These feelings of inferiority on the part of some Mexican Americans have their origin in discrimination and in an inadequate knowledge of their own virile and rich Indian-Spanish culture. They know little or no Spanish, the key to the world of their ancestors. So they feel frustrated because their assimilation or acculturation has not brought them joy or full material success. They are uneasy in both cultures.

As a group, Mexican Americans have no feelings of inferiority. They don't aspire to ownership of many material possessions. And they are rather contemptuous of too much law and too much order. Like the Greeks, they believe that more human waywardness should be considered as mistakes rather than as crimes; that there should be fewer policemen and more philosophers. They are not too interested in saving the entire world, but they would like to save themselves, if possible. Yes, some of the younger Mexican American militants, in asking for recognition of their privileges and rights, are boisterous and aggressive and sometimes even destructive. But this is a trick they have partly learned from their black and Anglo brothers. They ask for the unattainable in order to secure the attainable.

The Mexican American realizes that the Anglo Americans have money to burn (as in Vietnam) and talent to spare (as in reaching the moon), but he scratches his head and wonders why they can't resolve or even minimize their cultural, human-to-human problems: poverty, juvenile delinquency, drug abuse, obsession for sex, crime, and their bloated ego, among others. This points, in his mind, to a jumbo-sized insecurity complex. Something must be wrong, he feels, with the national nervous system. The citizen of Mexican ancestry would like to be given the chance to resolve some of his own human-to-human problems, those which affect him directly as well as those which affect the whole society. In the past, the European-American majority has used and exploited the overworked muscle and enduring back of the Mexican American in field, in factory, and on railroad track. Seldom has he been given the chance to contribute his initiative, his creativity, or his philosophical viewpoint.

So the Mexican American wants to change this, and he is going to change it, for his benefit as well as for that of the European American majority. He knows that rather than being a detriment, it is a great benefit to man to accept diversity in human beings. He believes that from an esthetic and psychological viewpoint, man needs and must have diversity in human beings—in color, in shape, in thought, and in culture. Complete uniformity in man—in appearance, color, cultural patterns, religion, and thought—would make this a pretty dull world and hardly an enjoyable place in which to live.

And so Mexican Americans and black Americans and Chinese Americans and Indian Americans who are seeking a dual culture—their own and that of the European American—are in pursuit of a wider and fuller life. They don't want to be assimilated or acculturated. They want to be themselves, to enjoy the good and help eliminate the bad that is in this country, the country where they were born, where they live, and where they expect to die.

THOUGHTS ON A SUNDAY AFTERNOON

By Joan Baez Harris

This article was written following our visit to her home near California's Palo Alto. It was a quiet, warm Sunday afternoon in Spring, and her small house lay a distance from a narrow mountain road, concealed by oak and eucalyptus.

Joan met us outside her door, smiling, almost as if she were coming to see us, not we to see her, and with the expression of one who likes people and enjoys meeting them.

Inside the comfortable house was an aura of peace and simplicity and, strongest of all, of life. Her small baby lay asleep on a bed throughout our visit; a half dozen or so tiny newborn kittens were on a pillow in a corner. It was the kind of house where you are free to live as you wish, not the kind that determines how you live.

But the aura was touched with loneliness, and the photos of David Harris on the walls reminded us that he was still imprisoned for the crime of expressing dissent.

I have been asked if I think of myself as a Mexican or a Chicano or as being dark-skinned.

This is a difficult question for me to answer, since for the past ten years of my life I have made a point of not categorizing myself. I have refused to accept the title of singer, for instance. I have not particularly identified myself with any special group, but more with humanity as a whole.

I've always thought brown is beautiful, and every chance I've had to get into the sun I've done so, because I like being brown.

When I entered junior high school there was prejudice against brown people. It took me a couple of years to realize that my being brown was why I did not make friends easily.

I have never really regarded myself as Mexican or English. My father was Mexican and was born in Pueblo, Mexico. On my mother's side there was English and a dash of Irish. I never thought of myself as an English girl, and not too much as a Mexican. I feel distant from the cause of any particular minority group in the sense that when I throw myself into "the cause," it is that of mankind. I have never felt I should work just with browns or just with blacks or just with whites.

In the same way, my husband David, who is in prison, has not wanted to involve himself only with political prisoners. When he was in Safford, a federal prison, about half of the prisoners were Mexicans. After he had finally got them involved in "the cause," they reached a point where they too felt that they were participating in the struggle of all persecuted people.

I know that color made a difference in junior high school. I think I find difficulty talking about this because I never felt I personally was badly discriminated against. When I was in junior high my father was a professor at a university, and although I looked very Mexican I did not speak Spanish. I felt that Mexican kids were getting a dirty deal, but I did not feel that I was. When my father first came to Stanford University, one of the top professors there would hardly speak to him. My father really had to struggle to break through that barrier.

I remember a story my parents told me. In a little town in New York State somebody called me "nigger" because they had never seen anyone as dark as I was. I said, "You ought to see me in the summertime." I loved dark-colored skin.

Once somebody called me a dirty Mexican, and a student asked my teacher, "Is she a Mexican?"

My teacher, attempting to defend me, said, "Joan is the very highest breed of Spanish."

I said, "What do you mean, the very highest breed of Spanish? I'm a Mexican." I made a big point of saying I was a Mexican.

Probably the worst place in my childhood, so far as prejudice is concerned, was southern California. For about a year my younger sister did not want to play with me or be seen with me. She tagged after my older sister, who was fair.

But I've put that thought out of my mind—perhaps because it's unpleasant, but also because I have now done all right for myself. Maybe I feel guilty about my success and don't like to harp on the times I have sensed prejudice in people.

There's a theory that people who have known struggle—minority-group people—may have become more sensitive, especially in their music or writing, than most white middle-class Americans.

I have a feeling that probably this isn't true. Ira Sandperl, my friend and co-worker, is a Jew. At times some other people get very righteous about how much their group has suffered. But Ira said, for example, "Four thousand years we have suffered, and look what we are doing in Israel now—bombing Arabs."

I don't know what creates sensitivity in people, but it pops up in very odd places.

Is it possible for us to be nonviolent in a violent world?

Yes, I think it is possible and necessary for us to be nonviolently active everywhere. Of course, nonviolence offers no guarantees. But the curious thing is that people who do violence don't receive any guarantees either. Statistics show that you have a much better chance of coming out alive in a nonviolent battle.

Too many people are hanging onto the old idea of violence. All that violence has done is to destroy people, but we are too terrified to try something different.

Cesar Chavez may provide the best example of strong nonviolent action, and I am sure he does not offer any guarantees.

In the Institute for the Study of Nonviolence, we do not have any special training for the practice of nonviolence. We do not have a tactical approach. To root yourself in nonviolence and to be a nonviolent soldier means that you make a decision to go out into the world to confront evil and organize against it, and at the same time make the decision not to do harm to people.

Our approach at the Institute is more on a level of what you and I are going to do to make a change in our lives. Basically, how do we break down the nation-state—which also means breaking down smaller nationalistic groups?

It is assumed that deprived groups should have what everybody else has. But in this society if all the browns and blacks had what the whites have, we would be in an even more hideous situation than we are in now. If they got into the stream of what is now America, then they, too, would be exploiting others, say, in Latin America, Vietnam, Africa. America as a nation is the most destructive force in the world today. In the search for equality our vision must go farther than just wanting what other people have and what we have been deprived of.

In short, I would never want to see a good Mexican become a good American. I would rather that he become a brother in the brotherhood of man.

Browns and blacks are the targets of the most vicious attacks by the state because minorities are the easiest to manipulate. They are the brunt because America needs them. America needs a brunt to go on doing what she does in the world and at home. One of the tragedies of war is that the poor people of every nationality are the ones who carry most of the guns, fight, suffer, and die.

These people who are kept in ignorance and poverty will grab anything that comes to them. If they are educated as to what the nation is really like, it will be easier for them to resist what is offered. But we have to offer them alternatives that do not yet exist. Until we can offer them something that looks like a real alternative as a way of life, we can do little, and they, less. In a sense, you can say that this is what our work is all about—trying to create that alternative.

It is very difficult to live in a society like this. I think it is up to everyone to help find this alternative. The beautiful thing about Chavez is that he is working with poor people and together they are trying to make something out of nothing. He is building something in spite of America.

I feel that the sooner we become color-blind the better it is going to be. And while we attempt to become color-blind, white people should stop destroying brown and black people.

I don't think that an alternative can be found within the governmental institutions we have now, because when a person enters the system he has to pledge himself to the nation-state. In the nation-state when we talk about defense we are talking *not about defense of people but about defense of land*. Because the nation-state emphasizes the importance of land, people have to die to protect land. The most expendable thing turns out to be human life.

Obviously, it is not possible to find human alternatives within the existing judicial system. The judicial system is not there to promote justice. It is there to keep order. This is exactly why my husband is in prison. Prison is somewhere to put people whom society is afraid to have walking around the streets. True, there are some good people working in the system who try to do good things. Anytime there is a good judge, I am happy because of him; and anytime there is a lawyer who fights for someone deprived, I am happy. But the system operates primarily to prevent resistance.

What my husband David is saying when he talks about draft resistance is, "Claim your life." Say an absolute "No" to that system and then try to build a different basis for action.

What I am most aware of is people's concept of power. Power is something everyone has, and yet few people in this society truly believe they have power. If the people (not the politicians) could feel in themselves a genuine sense of power, they could behave in a very different way. They would not have to throw rocks. A lot of radicals are really into violence, and, so far as I am concerned, violence is reactionary. In fact, there is a contradiction in terms when we say "violent revolutionary," because revolution means change, and violence is a reversion to a former pattern.

When one raises his fist and shouts "Power," it appears to me he does this because he thinks somebody else has power and he wants to take it for himself. But if he assumes that he is born with power, he doesn't feel the need to grasp it away from someone else. There is enough to go around when we recognize our own power.

To me, what is worth building and organizing is the power of love.

I don't think our alternative can be found within the present educational system. I think the educational system we have now should be replaced. In the context of this society, education would always end up being the same—it would wind up being nationalism.

The basic issues in all of life are never met in the existing educational system. How do you relate to God, no God, sex, drugs, truth, openness, honesty, fear, parents, etc.? And finally, how are you going to treat other people? Are you going to kill people or are you not going to kill people? You cannot discuss that in school because it is taken for granted that you will kill people. They call it defending your country, but it means killing people. Most of us do not see ourselves involved in the process of murder, but we very much are.

Revolution to me would mean people recognizing the sanctity of human life, and that's the revolution that has never happened. There have been lots of revolutions—people throwing over the government and taking other people's property. But all the good that comes out of a violent revolution comes in spite of the violence.

If we could learn to fight in a different way—get different weapons—then we could really have a chance to win. But for the first time since time began, men would have to recognize that there is only one thing that is really sacred, and that thing is life.

BACK TO BACHIMBA

By Enrique Hank López

I am a *pocho* from Bachimba, a rather small Mexican village in the state of Chihuahua, where my father fought with the army of Pancho Villa. He was, in fact, the only private in Villa's army.

Pocho is ordinarily a derogatory term in Mexico (to define it succinctly, a *pocho* is a Mexican slob who has pretensions of being a gringo sonofabitch), but I use it in a very special sense. To me that word has come to mean "uprooted Mexican," and that's what I have been all my life. Though my entire upbringing and education took place in the United States, I have never felt completely American, and when I am in Mexico, I sometimes feel like a displaced gringo with a curiously Mexican name—Enrique Preciliano López y Martinez de Sepulveda de Sapien de Quien-sabe-quien. One might conclude that I'm either a schizo-cultural Mexican or a cultured schizoid American.

In any event, the schizo-ing began a long time ago, when my father and many of Pancho Villa's troops fled across the border to escape the oncoming *federales* who eventually defeated Villa. My mother and I, traveling across the hot desert plains in a buckboard wagon, joined my father in El Paso, Texas, a few days after his hurried departure. With more and more Villistas swarming into El Paso every day, it was quickly apparent that jobs would be exceedingly scarce and insecure; so my parents packed our few belongings and we took the first available bus to Denver. My father had hoped to move to Chicago because the name sounded so Mexican, but my mother's meager savings were hardly enough to buy tickets for Colorado.

There we moved into a ghetto of Spanish-speaking residents who chose to call themselves Spanish Americans and resented the sudden migration of their brethren from Mexico, whom they sneeringly called *surumatos* (slang for "southerners").

These so-called Spanish Americans claimed direct descent from the original *conquistadores* of Spain. They also insisted that they had *never* been Mexicans, since their region of New Spain (later annexed to the United States) was never a part of Mexico. But what they claimed most vociferously—and erroneously—was an absence of Indian ancestry. It made no difference that any objective observer could see by merely looking at them the results of considerable fraternization between the conquering Spaniards and the Comanche and Navaho women who crossed their paths. Still, these *manitos*, as they were snidely labeled by the *surumatos*, stubbornly refused to be identified with Mexico, and would actually fight anyone who called them Mexican. So intense was this intergroup rivalry that the bitterest "race riots" I have ever witnessed—and engaged in—were between the look-alike, talk-alike *surumatos* and *manitos* who lived near Denver's Curtis Park. In retrospect the harsh conflicts between us were all the more silly and self-defeating when one recalls that we were all lumped together as "spiks" and "greasers" by the Anglo-Saxon community.

Predictably enough, we *surumatos* began huddling together in a subneighborhood within the larger ghetto, and it was there that I became painfully aware that my father had been the only private in Pancho Villa's army. Most of my friends were the sons of captains, colonels, majors, and even generals, though a few fathers were admittedly mere sergeants and corporals. My father alone had been a lowly private in that famous Division del Norte. Naturally, I developed a most painful complex, which led me to all sorts of compensatory fibs. During one brief spell I fancied my father as a member of the dreaded *los dorados*, the "golden ones," who were Villa's favorite henchmen. (Later I was to learn that my father's cousin, Martin López, was a genuine and quite notorious *dorado*). But all my inventions were quickly un-invented by my very own father, who seemed to take a perverse delight in being Pancho's only private.

No doubt my chagrin was accentuated by the fact that Pancho Villa's exploits were a constant topic of conversation in our household. My entire childhood seems to be shadowed by his presence. At our dinner table, almost every night, we would listen to endlessly repeated accounts of this battle, that stratagem, or some great act of Robin Hood kindness by *el centauro del norte*. I remember how angry my parents were when they saw Wallace Beery in *Viva Villa!* "Garbage by stupid gringos," they called it. They were particularly offended by the sweaty, unshaven sloppiness of Beery's portrayal. "Pancho Villa was clean and orderly, no matter how much he chased after women. This man's a dirty swine."

As if to deepen our sense of *Villismo*, my parents also taught us "Adelita" and "*Se llevaron el cañon para Bachimba*" ("They took the cannons to Bachimba"), the two most famous songs of the Mexican revolution. Some twenty years later (during my stint at Harvard Law School), while strolling along the Charles River, I would find myself softly singing "*Se llevaron el cañon para Bachimba, para Bachimba, para Bachimba*" over and over again. That's all I could remember of that poignant rebel song. Though I had been born there, I had always regarded "Bachimba" as a fictitious, made-up, Lewis Carroll kind of word. So that eight years ago, when I first returned to Mexico, I was literally stunned when I came to a crossroad south of Chihuahua and saw an old road marker: "Bachimba 18 km." Then it really exists—I shouted inwardly—Bachimba is a real town! Swinging onto the narrow, poorly paved road, I gunned the motor and sped toward the town I'd been singing about since infancy. It turned out to be a quiet, dusty village with a bleak worn-down plaza that was surrounded by nondescript buildings of uncertain vintage.

Aside from the songs about Bachimba and Adelita and all the folk tales about Villa's guerrilla fighters, my early years were strongly influenced by our neighborhood celebrations of Mexico's two most important patriotic events: Mexican Independence Day on September 16 and the anniversary of the battle of Puebla on May 5. On those two dates Mexicans all over the world are likely to become extremely chauvinistic. In Denver we would stage annual parades that included three or four floats skimpily decorated with crepe paper streamers, a small band, several adults in threadbare battle dress, and hundreds of kids marching in wild disorder. It was during one of these parades—I was ten years old then—that I was seized with acute appendicitis and had to be rushed to a hospital. The doctor subsequently told my mother that I had made a long, impassioned speech about the early revolutionist Miguel Hidalgo while the anesthetic was taking hold, and she explained with pardonable pride that it was the speech I was to make at Turner Hall that evening. Mine was one of the twenty-three *discursos* scheduled on the postparade program, a copy of which my mother still retains. My only regret was missing the annual *discurso* of Don Miguel Gómez, my godfather, a deep-throated orator who would always climax his speech by falling to his knees and dramatically kissing the floor, almost weeping as he loudly proclaimed: *"Ay, Mexico! Beso tu tierra, tu mero corazon"* ("Ah, Mexico! I kiss your sacred soil, the very heart of you"). He gave the same oration for seventeen years, word for word and gesture for gesture, and it never failed to bring tears to his eyes. But not once did he return to Chihuahua, even for a brief visit.

My personal Mexican-ness eventually produced serious problems for me. Upon entering grade school I learned English rapidly, and rather well, always ranking either first or second in my class; yet the hard core of me remained stubbornly Mexican. This chauvinism may have been a reaction to the constant racial prejudice we encountered on all sides. The neighborhood cops were always running us off the streets and calling us "dirty greasers," and most of our teachers frankly regarded us as totally inferior. I still remember the galling disdain of my sixth-grade teacher, whose constant mimicking of our heavily accented speech drove me to a desperate study of *Webster's Dictionary* in the hope of acquiring a vocabulary larger than hers. Sadly enough, I succeeded only too well, and for the next few years I spoke the most ridiculous high-flown rhetoric in the Denver public schools. One of my favorite words was "indubitably," and it must have driven everyone mad. I finally got rid of my accent by constantly reciting "Peter Piper picked a peck of pickled peppers" with little round pebbles in my mouth. Somewhere I had read about Demosthenes.

During this phase of my childhood the cultural tug of war known as "Americanization" almost pulled me apart. There were moments when I would identify completely with the gringo world (what could have been more American than my earnest high-voiced portrayal of George Washington, however ridiculous the cotton wig my mother had fashioned for me?); then quite suddenly I would feel so acutely Mexican that I would stammer over the simplest English phrase. I was so ready to take offense at the slightest slur against Mexicans that I would imagine prejudice where none existed. But on other occasions, in full confidence of my belonging, I would venture forth into social areas that I should have realized were clearly forbidden to little chicanos from Curtis Park. The inevitable rebuffs would leave me floundering in self-pity; it was small comfort to know that other minority groups suffered even worse rebuffs than we did.

The only non-Mexican boy on our street was a Negro named Leroy Logan, who was probably my closest childhood friend. Leroy was the best athlete, the best whistler, the best liar, the best horseshoe player, the best marble shooter, the best mumblety-pegger, and the best shoplifter in our neighborhood. He was also my "partner," and I thus entitled myself to a fifty-fifty share of all his large triumphs and petty thefts. Because he considered "Mexican" a derogatory word bordering on obscenity, Leroy would pronounce it "Mesican" so as to soften its harshness. But once in a while, when he'd get angry with me, he would call me a "lousy Mesican greasy spik" with the most extraordinarily effective hissing one can imagine. And I'm embarrassed to admit that I would retaliate by calling him "alligator bait." As a matter of fact, just after I had returned from the hospital, he came to visit me, and I thoughtlessly greeted him with a flippant, "Hi, alligator ba—" I never finished the phrase because Leroy whacked me on the stomach with a Ping-Pong paddle and rushed out of my house with great, sobbing anger.

Weeks later, when we had re-established a rather cool rapport, I tried to make up for my stupid insult by helping him steal cabbages from the vegetable trucks that rumbled through our neighborhood on their way to the produce markets. They would come down Larimer Street in the early dawn, and Leroy and I would sneak up behind them at the 27th Street stop sign, where they were forced to pause for cross traffic. Then Leroy, with a hooked pole he had invented, would stab the top cabbages and roll them off the truck. I would be waiting below to catch them with an open gunny sack. Our system was fabulously successful for a while, and we found a ready market for the stolen goods; but one morning, as I started to unfurl my sack, a fairly large cabbage conked me on the head. Screaming with pain, I lunged at Leroy and tried to bite him. He, laughing all the while—it was obviously a funny scene—glided out of my reach, and finally ran into a nearby alley. We never engaged in commercial affairs thereafter.

Still and all, I remember him with great affection and a touch of sadness. I say sadness because eventually Leroy was to suffer the misery of being an outsider in an already outside ghetto. As he grew older, it was apparent that he longed to be a Mexican, that he felt terribly dark and alone. "Sometimes," he would tell me, "I feel like my damn skin's too tight, like I'm gonna bust out of it." One cold February night I found him in the coal shed behind Pacheco's store, desperately scraping his forearm with sandpaper, the hurt tears streaming down his face. "I got to get this off, man. I can't stand all this blackness." We stood there quietly staring at the floor for a long, anguished moment, both of us miserable beyond word or gesture. Finally he drew a deep breath, blew his nose loudly, and mumbled half audibly, "Man, you sure lucky to be a Mesican."

Not long after this incident Leroy moved out of Denver to live with relatives in Georgia. When I saw him off at the bus station, he grabbed my shoulder and whispered huskily, "You gonna miss me, man. You watch what I tellya." "Indubitably," I said. "Aw, man, cut that stuff. You the most fancy-pants Mesican I know." Those were his last words to me, and they caused a considerable dent in my ego. Not enough, however, to diminish my penchant for fancy language. The dictionary continued to be my comic book well into high school.

Speaking of language, I am reminded of a most peculiar circumstance: almost every Mexican American lawyer that I've ever met speaks English with a noticeable Spanish accent, this despite the fact that they have all been born, reared, and educated exclusively in America. Of the forty-eight lawyers I have in mind, only three of us are free of any accent. Needless to say, our "cultural drag" has been weighty and persistent. And one must presume that our ethnic hyphens shall be with us for many years to come.

My own Mexican-ness, after years of decline at Harvard University, suddenly burst forth again when I returned to Chihuahua and stumbled on the town of Bachimba. I had long conversations with an uncle I'd never met before, my father's younger brother, Ramón. It was Tio Ramón who chilled my spine with eyewitness stories about Pancho Villa's legendary *dorados*, one of whom was Martin López. "He was your second cousin. The bravest young buck in Villa's army. And he became a *dorado* when he was scarcely seventeen years old because he dared to defy Pancho Villa himself. As your papa may have told you, Villa had a bad habit of burying treasure up in the mountains and also burying the man he took with him to dig the hole for it. Well, one day he chose Martin López to go with him. Deep in the mountains they went, near Parral. And when they got to a suitably lonely place, Pancho Villa told him to dig a hole with pick and shovel. Then, when Martin had dug down to his waist, Villa leveled a gun at the boy. "Say your prayers, *muchacho*. You shall stay here with the gold—forever." But Martin had come prepared. In his large right boot he had a gun, and when he rose from his bent position, he was pointing that gun at Villa. They stood there, both ready to fire, for several seconds, and finally Don Pancho started to laugh in that wonderful way of his. "*Bravo, bravo, muchacho!* You've got more guts than a man. Get out of that hole, boy. I need you for my *dorados*."

Tio Ramón's eyes were wet with pride. "But what is more important, he died with great valor. Two years later, after he had terrorized the *federales* and Pershing's gringo soldiers, he was finally wounded and captured here in Bachimba. It was a bad wound in his leg, finally turning to gangrene. Then one Sunday morning they hauled Martin López and three other prisoners to the plaza. One by one they executed the three lesser prisoners against that wall. I was up on the church tower watching it all. Finally it was your uncle's turn. They dragged him off the buckboard wagon and handed him his crutches. Slowly, painfully, he hobbled to the wall and stood there. Very straight he stood. 'Do you have any last words?' asked the captain of the firing squad. With great pride Martin tossed his crutches aside and stood very tall on his one good leg. 'Give me, you yellow bastards, give me a gun—and I'll show you who is the man among . . .' Eight bullets crashed into his chest and face, and I never heard that final word. That was your second cousin. You would have been proud to know him."

As I listened to Tio Ramón's soft nostalgic voice that evening, there in the sputtering light of the kerosene lamp on his back patio, I felt as intensely Mexican as I shall ever feel.

But not for long. Within six weeks I was destined to feel *less* Mexican than I had ever felt. The scene of my trauma was the Centro Mexicano de Escritores, where the finest young writers of Mexico met regularly to discuss works in progress and to engage in erudite literary and philosophical discussions. Week after week I sat among them, dumbstruck by my inadequacy in Spanish and my total ignorance of their whole frame of reference. How could I have possibly imagined that I was Mexican? Those conversations were a dense tangle of local and private allusions, and the few threads I could grasp only magnified my ignorance. The novelist Juan Rulfo was then reading the initial drafts of his *Pedro Páramo*, later to be acclaimed the best avant-garde fiction in Mexican literature. Now that I have soaked myself in the *ambiance* of Mexico, Rulfo's novel intrigues me beyond measure; but when he first read it at the Centro, he might just as well have been reading "Jabberwocky" in Swahili for all I understood of it. And because all of the other Mexican writers knew and greatly appreciated *Páramo*, I could only assume that I was really "too gringo" to comprehend it. For this reason, I, a person with no great talent for reticence, never opened my mouth at the Centro. In fact, I was so shell-shocked by those sessions that I even found it difficult to converse with my housekeeper about such simple matters as dirty laundry or the loose doorknob in the bathroom.

Can any of us really go home again? I, for one, am convinced that I have no true home, that I must reconcile myself to a schizo-cultural limbo, with a mere hyphen to provide some slight cohesion between my split selves. This inevitable splitting is a plague and a pleasure. Some mornings as I glide down the Paseo de la Reforma, perhaps the most beautiful boulevard in the world, I am suddenly angered by the *machismo*, or aggressive maleness, of Mexican drivers who crowd and bully their screeching machines through dense traffic. What terrible insecurity, what awful dread of emasculation, produces such assertive bully-boy conduct behind a steering wheel? Whatever the reasons, there is a part of me that can never accept this much-celebrated *machismo*. Nor can I accept the exaggerated nationalism one so frequently encounters in the press, on movie screens, over the radio, in daily conversations—that shrill barrage of slogans proclaiming that "there is only one Mexico."

Recently, when I expressed these views to an old friend, he smiled quite knowingly: "Let's face it, Hank, you're not really a Mexican—despite that long, comical name of yours. You're an American through and through." But that, of course, is a minority view and almost totally devoid of realism. One could just as well say that Martin Luther King was not a Negro, that he was merely an American. But the plain truth is that neither I nor the Martin Luther Kings of our land can escape the fact that we are Mexican and Negro with roots planted so deeply in the United States that we have grown those strong little hyphens that make us Mexican-American and Negro-

American. This assertion may not please some idealists who would prefer to blind themselves to our obvious ethnic and racial differences, who are unwittingly patronizing when they insist that we are all alike and indistinguishable. But the politicians, undoubtedly the most pragmatic creatures in America, are completely aware that ethnic groups *do* exist and that they seem to huddle together, bitch together, and sometimes vote together.

When all is said and done, we hyphenated Americans are here to stay, bubbling happily or unhappily in the great non-melting pot. Much has been gained and will be gained from the multiethnic aspects of the United States, and there is no useful purpose in attempting to wish it away or to homogenize it out of existence. In spite of the race riots in Watts and ethnic unrest elsewhere, there would appear to be a kind of modus vivendi developing on almost every level of American life.

And if there are those of us who may never feel completely at home, we can always make that brief visit to Bachimba.

BIOGRAPHIES

MANUEL ARAGON (*THEIR HERITAGE—POVERTY*) was graduated from San Francisco State College in 1962 and has written a number of articles on the problems of the Chicano, as well as of students in Latin America.

He served as Executive Director of the Economic and Youth Opportunities Agency in Los Angeles and in a number of capacities for the Economic Development Administration and other agencies.

A specialist in urban planning and development, he is now general manager of an investment company providing management capital and assistance to minority-group businessmen.

ROBERTO and JOSÉ ARAGON (*A CHICANO VOTING RIGHTS ACT*) are second-generation Mexican Americans; Roberto was born in Los Angeles in 1935, José in Douglas, Arizona, in 1943.

José Aragon has worked with the UCLA Student Counseling Office and is now completing work for a degree in law at the University of Southern California. He lives in Los Angeles with his wife and two children, and his main interests are politics, law, and music.

Roberto Aragon has been an executive director of the Los Angeles Urban Coalition and is presently working in a special Mexican American program of the Harvard Business School.

RONALD ARIAS (*WE'RE SUPPOSED TO BELIEVE WE'RE INFERIOR* and *THE BARRIO*), born in Los Angeles in 1941, is a graduate of the University of California at Los Angeles with a degree in Spanish and Journalism. He served in the Peace Corps in Peru and on newspapers in Buenos Aires, Argentina, and Caracas, Venezuela, and has been published widely as a free-lance writer.

This article was written in connection with his work as a research assistant for the UCLA Mexican American Study

Project, as was THEIR HERITAGE—POVERTY, by Manuel Aragon, also included in this anthology.

Mr. Arias now lives in Washington, D. C., where he is a writer and editor for the Inter-American Development Bank.

JESÚS ASCENSION ARREOLA, JR. (*MY NAME IS JESÚS*) was born in Seguin, Texas, in 1944. He served three years in the army and attended Arlington State College at Arlington, Texas, where he majored in the liberal arts. His poetry has appeared in *The Texas Observer*.

RAYMOND BARRIO (*THE PLUM PLUM PICKERS*) lives and works in Santa Clara County, California—the setting for this chapter of his novel, *The Plum Plum Pickers*—with his Mexican-born wife Yolanda and their four little Chicanos.

A World War II veteran of the European theater, he attended the City College of New York, Yale University, the University of California at Berkeley, and the Art Center College of Los Angeles.

He has taught at Ventura College and at the University of California at Santa Barbara, and has recently been teaching adult education art classes in the San Francisco Bay area.

He has published numerous articles in art magazines and was art critic for the Palo Alto *Times*. He is the author of *Experiments in Modern Art* and his fiction has been published in *Trace, Dust, December, Midwestern University Quarterly, Laurel Review*, and other literary journals.

ELIU CARRANZA (*THE GORKASE MIRROR*) is an Associate Professor in the Departments of Speech-Communication and Mexican American Graduate Studies at San Jose State College. He is the former chairman of the Mexican American Studies Department, the only graduate department in Mexican American Studies in the United States.

Professor Carranza received his B. A. in Philosophy from San José State College, did graduate work in Philosophy at Stanford University and as a University Fellow at Washington University in St. Louis, from which he received his M. A. He is presently an Urban Fellow at the University of California, Berkeley, completing graduate work toward a Ph. D. in Education. Professor Carranza is author and co-author of several books in the fields of philosophy and Mexican American Studies.

"The Gorkase Mirror" in this anthology is one of several essays from a forthcoming book entitled *Ensayos on Los Chicanos*.

RICHARD DOKEY (*SÁNCHEZ*) was born in Stockton, California, the locale of his story, "Sánchez." His descriptions of the Flotill Cannery, of Stockton's recent skid row and Center Street, and even of the steel ball of a redevelopment wrecking crew are taken from today's reality.

Mr. Dokey has worked for the railroad, in a shipyard, in a soda pop bottling company, and in an ink manufacturing company, all in a labor capacity.

He graduated from the University of California at Berkeley and is a teacher in humanities. He lives in Lodi, California, with his wife and two children.

His poetry has appeared in a number of publications, and his stories have been published in *Southwest Review, Descant, Quartet, Literary Artpress*, and *Story*, among others. He is currently working on a novel, but "Sánchez" is his favorite story for, as he says, "In a very real sense, Sánchez and I are the same man."

DANIEL GARZA (*SATURDAY BELONGS TO THE PALOMÍA* and *STRIPPER WHIRLWIND: THE PIZCADORES AND THE MACHINES*), whose parents came from Mexico, was born in Hillsboro, Texas, received his B. A. from Texas Christian in 1961, and served as a lieutenant in the U. S. Army.

The two articles by Garza in this anthology appeared in different magazines at different times: SATURDAY BELONGS TO THE PALOMÍA, winner of the *Harper's Magazine Southwest Literature Award*, in *Harper's* (July, 1962) and STRIPPER WHIRLWIND: THE PIZCADORES AND THE MACHINES in *Southwest Review* (Autumn,

1966). But, as Margaret L. Hartley of *Southwest Review* points out, the two, with their sad contrast, both describing the lives of the *pizcadores*, seem to complement each other.

Garza writes, "You'll probably notice the two articles are written in different styles. I wrote "Palomía" in Spanish and then translated it into English, trying to keep the flavor of the language. The other was written in straight English."

MRS. DAVID HARRIS—Joan Baez—(*THOUGHTS ON A SUNDAY AFTERNOON*) is well known as a top professional folk singer and entertainer and, perhaps of greater importance, as a sensitive and perceptive human being. We suspect that she would rather be known as a co-founder, with Ira Sandperl, of the Institute for the Study of Nonviolence— or more simply, as Mrs. David Harris.

The *Joan Baez Songbook* is a classic in the field of folk music. Her autobiography, *Daybreak*, and David's book, *Goliath*, are both best sellers.

It has been said that there are mainly two kinds of people in the world: those who feel deeply and those who do not feel deeply. Joan's depth of feeling puts her into the first category, and in this instance her depth is coupled with a searching and independent intelligence.

ALBERT HERRERA (*THE NATIONAL CHICANO MORA-TORIUM* and *THE MEXICAN AMERICAN IN TWO CULTURES*) is a first-generation Mexican American who was born in Mazátlan, Sinaloa, Mexico, and who entered the United States with his parents as a small boy.

He has worked at many jobs over the years—fruit picker, baker's helper, telegrapher, postmaster, freight agent, and finally labor representative. Much of his time has been occupied with Chicano and labor movements, and he is author of the *Union Member's Handbook*, published by Public Affairs Press.

He is married, has one daughter, and lives in Los Angeles, California.

ENRIQUE HANK LÓPEZ (*BACK TO BACHIMBA*) was born in Chihuahua, Mexico, and came to the United States as a child, with his parents.

He attended public schools in Denver, received his B. A. from the University of Denver and his L. L. B. from Harvard Law School. Among his many activities and assignments, he has practiced law in Los Angeles and New York and specialized in international law in Mexico City. He has acted in 94 half-hour television shows, "The Verdict is Yours."

He is the author of a novel, *Afro-6*, published in 1969; of *My Brother Lyndon*, by Sam Houston Johnson, as told to Enrique Hank López; of *Memoirs of a Rebel Daughter*, an autobiography by Katherine Anne Porter, as told to Enrique Hank López; and co-editor, with Ramon Xiran, of *Diologos*, an anthology of Latin American literature.

His shorter work has been published in *Harper's Magazine, The Atlantic Monthly, Life, Horizon, American Heritage, Contenido, El Universal, Journal of American Bar Association, Frontier*, and many others.

He was a founding member of MAPA (Mexican American Political Association), and vice-president, 1959–60; National Coordinator, VIVA KENNEDY CLUBS, in the 1960 presidential campaign headquarters in Washington, D. C.; and Democratic candidate for Secretary of State of California in 1958, receiving 2,500,000 votes but losing by less than one percent of the total.

DURANGO MENDOZA (three stories) was born in 1945 near Dustin, Oklahoma. His father was Mexican American and his mother American Indian (Creek).

He writes, "I was not accepted as being either Chicano or Indian, and of course certainly not as white. My situation was as an observer, not a joiner."

He attended the University of Missouri from 1963 to 1967, receiving a B. A. in English. His story "Summer Water and Shirley" won 1st prize in the 1965 Annual Mahan Fiction Contest; "The Passing" won 2nd prize in the same contest in

1966; and "The Woman in the Green House" won 3rd prize in 1967.

He adds, "As you may gather from my stories, they are not slanted about my being a Chicano, but about human beings who happen to be brown, and being brown in a white culture, or Chicano in an Indian culture, gives a certain flavor to being a man that is unique.

"Propaganda and race- or culture-selling is not my bag. But being brown and springing from brown roots is my reality—a reality that has shaped my life and given me a great concern for all people, a concern that I might not otherwise have known as strongly."

SISTER MARY PRUDENCE MOYLAN, B. V. M. (*THE NUN'S TALE*) is one of several Sisters who participated with Cesar Chavez and his workers on their march to the California State Capitol at Sacramento during *La Huelga*. At the time of writing her poem, she was at the Guadalupe Convent near Los Gatos, California; later, in 1966, she returned to Mundelein College in Chicago, where she taught European history until 1969.

She writes, "At present I am on leave from Mundelein for the purpose of earning a Ph. D. in history at the University of Illinois at Urbana. Though my teaching duties have prevented me from taking a very active part in the continuing struggle of the farmworkers, I was able to help in the grape boycott by picketing food stores and arranging speaking engagements for the Union representatives in Chicago."

AMADO MURO (two stories) is a first-generation Mexican American who was born in Parral, Chihuahua, Mexico, and came to El Paso, Texas, with his parents, at the age of nine.

He has lived most of his life in El Paso, where he has worked at a number of jobs, one of the more recent being that of laborer on the Pacific Fruit Express ice docks.

His avocation is writing stories and sketches, mostly of old Mexico, where he recalls his grandfather's making a living by playing his Ramirez guitar and singing revolutionary ballads such as "The Wet Buzzard" and "The Three Bald-Headed Women."

His work has appeared in *Arizona Quarterly*, *New Mexico Review*, and others.

PHILIP D. ORTEGO (*THE EDUCATION OF MEXICAN AMERICANS*), the son of a migrant worker, was born in Chicago. "However," he writes, "my formative years were spent in Pittsburgh, where, frustrated and alienated, I dropped out of school while in the 10th grade—like the typical Chicano I describe in 'The Education of Mexican Americans'—to work at a variety of jobs from shining shoes to racking pool balls."

During World War II, Mr. Ortego served in the Pacific and China. Upon discharge he returned to Pittsburgh as a laborer in the steel mills. Under the GI bill of rights he managed to study at the University of Pittsburgh, where he specialized in comparative literature and linguistics.

He served in the Air Force during the Korean conflict and exited as a captain. He then taught high school until he earned a Master's degree in English language and literature at the University of Texas, El Paso. He has since taught at New Mexico State University and he is now teaching at the University of New Mexico.

His work has been published in leading national, scholarly, and literary magazines, journals, and newspapers, including *El Grito: A Journal of Contemporary Mexican-American Thought; The Denver Post; The Nation; Books Abroad; The New Mexican Review; International Language Reporter*, and *The Texas Observer*.

REIES LÓPEZ TIJERINA (*FROM PRISON*), although a forceful and dynamic speaker, has never written for publication, with the exception of the piece "From Prison," in this anthology. This was written in the New Mexico State Penitentiary before he was transferred to the U. S. Federal Prison at Springfield, Missouri, where he was at the time of the publication of this book.

His communication consenting to the publication of the material in *The Chicanos* indicates that despite his imprisonment he is happy and content because of the cause he is serving.

FELICIANO RIVERA (*THE TEACHING OF CHICANO HISTORY*), born in Morley, Colorado, in 1932, attended primary schools in Mexico and later graduated from the Rocky Ford High School in Colorado.

He received an M. A. in Latin American History from the University of Colorado in 1963, an M. A. in Spanish Language and Literature from the University of Denver in 1964, and a Ph. D. in Latin American Studies from the University of Southern California in 1970.

He has been an instructor in Spanish Language and Latin American Culture with the Peace Corps Training Center, University of Denver, and was associated with the United States Air Force, Intelligence Division, from 1950 to 1960.

His published work includes *A Guide to the Study of the Mexican American* (Fearon Publishers, 1969) and *A Mexican American Source Book* (Educational Consulting Associates, 1970).

At present he is the Director of the Bilingual Institute in Social Studies, Associate Professor of History, and Coordinator of Mexican American Graduate Studies, all at San José State College, San Jose, California. He also acts as Manuscript Consultant for a number of publishers and for the Department of Health, Education and Welfare, Washington, D. C.

He lives in San Jose with his wife and two children, Feliciano Luis and Felipe Alberto.

LUIS VALDEZ (*THE TALE OF LA RAZA* and *EL TEATRO CAMPESINO*) was born in Delano, the son of migrant workers, and was himself a *campesino* until he was eighteen. He worked his way through San Jose State College and was one of the earliest supporters of Cesar Chavez in *La Huelga*.

He spent a period of time with the San Francisco Mime Troupe and is founder and director of El Teatro Campesino (The Farmworker's Theater), which began as an open-air entertainment for the striking farmworkers at Delano and went on to win an Obie (Off-Broadway) award in 1968 which cited the Teatro "for creating a workers' theater to demonstrate the politics of survival."

The Teatro is now a part of the Mexican American Centro Campesino Cultural at Fresno, California.

RICHARD VÁSQUEZ (*CHICANO STUDIES: SENSITIVITY FOR TWO CULTURES*) has been a newspaperman, publicist, and screenwriter and a frequent contributor to the Los Angeles Chicano publication, *La Raza*. His latest occupation is that of correspondent for The Los Angeles *Times*, covering Mexican American activities.

He is probably best known at this time for his novel *Chicano*, published in 1970, a story of family migration from Mexico and of their struggle in the East Los Angeles barrio. It is the only recent novel of significance written about Chicanos and by a Chicano to be released by a major publisher. Budd Schulberg says, "The Chicanos have found their novelist as black people found their voice in Richard Wright and Ralph Ellison a generation ago."

With his wife, Lucy, Mr. Vásquez lives in Altadena, California, where he is at work on a new novel.

SELECTED BIBLIOGRAPHY

This bibliography of books relating to the Mexican American does not attempt to include the many published articles, reports, and dissertations on the subject. Neither does it include books which, at the time of this writing and to our knowledge, are no longer in print. In the case of new or small publishers whose addresses may not be easily obtainable, those addresses are given.

A *Bibliography of Bibliographies Relating to Mexican American Studies* appeared in the Summer, 1970 issue of *El Grito*: *A Journal of Contemporary Mexican-American Thought*.

ALBA, Victor: *The Mexicans*, New York: Pegasus, 1970.

ALLEN, Steve: *The Ground Is Our Table*, New York: Doubleday & Co., 1966.

ATWATER, James D., and RUIZ, Ramón E.: *Out From Under*, New York: Doubleday & Co. (Zenith), 1969.

AZUELA, Mariano: *Two Novels of Mexico*, Berkeley and Los Angeles: UC Press, 1970.

————: *The Underdogs*, New York: Signet, 1963.

BALLIS, George, and FARM WORKER PRESS: *Basta!*, Delano: Farm Worker Press, Box 1060, Delano, California; 1966.

BARRIO, Raymond: *The Plum Plum Pickers*, Sunnyvale: Ventura Press, Box 2268, Sunnyvale, California; 1969.

BRENNER, Anita: *Idols Behind Altars*, Boston: Beacon Press, 1970.

BURMA, John H: *Spanish-Speaking Groups in the United States*, Durham: Duke University Press, 1954.

BUSTAMANTE, Charles J. and Patricia L.: *The Mexican-American and The United States*, Mountain View: Patty-Lar Publications, P. O. Box 4177, Mountain View, California 94040; 1969.

CABRERA, Arturo: *Emerging Faces—the Mexican Americans*, Dubuque: William C. Brown, Publ., 1971.

CHANDLER, David: *Huelga!*, New York: Simon & Schuster, 1970.

CHEVALIER, François: *Land and Society in Colonial Mexico*,
Berkeley and Los Angeles: UC Press, 1963.

CLARK, Margaret: *Health in the Mexican American Culture*, Berkeley and Los Angeles: UC Press, 1970.

CLINE, Howard F.: *Mexico: From Revolution to Evolution*,
New York: Oxford University Press, 1963.

COCKCROFT, James D.: *Intellectual Precursors of the
American Revolution*, Austin and London: University of
Texas Press, 1968.

CUMBERLAND, Charles C.: *Mexico*, New York: Oxford
University Press, 1968.

DAY, A. Grove: *Coronado's Quest*, Berkeley and Los Angeles:
UC Press, 1964.

del CASTILLO, Bernal Diaz: *The Discovery and Conquest of
Mexico*, New York: Farrar, Straus & Giroux, 1956.

DIAZ, Bernal: *Conquest of New Spain*, Baltimore: Penguin
Books, 1963.

DUFOUR, Charles L.: *The Mexican War, a Compact History, 1846–1848*, New York: Hawthorn, 1968.

DUNNE, John Gregory: *Delano*, New York: Farrar (Noonday), 1967.

FUENTES, Carlos: *The Good Conscience*, New York: Farrar
(Noonday), 1970.

GALARZA, Ernesto: *Merchants of Labor*, Charlotte and
Santa Barbara: McNally and Loftin, 1964.

———: *Spiders in the House and Workers in the Field*, Notre
Dame and London: University of Notre Dame Press,
1970.

———: *Barrio Boy*, Notre Dame and London: University of
Notre Dame Press, 1971.

GONZALES, Rodolfo: *I Am Joaquin*, Denver: El Gallo,
1967.

GONZÁLEZ, Nancie L.: *The Spanish-Americans of New
Mexico*, Albuquerque: University of New Mexico Press,
1969.

HELLER, Celia S.: *Mexican American Youth: Forgotten
Youth at the Crossroads*, New York: Random House
(Vintage), 1966.

LEONARD, Irving A.: *Baroque Times in Old Mexico*, Ann Arbor: University of Michigan Press, 1966.

LEON-PORTILLA, Miguel: *The Broken Spears*, Boston: Beacon Press, 1966.

LEWIS, Oscar: *The Children of Sanchez: Autobiography of a Mexican Family*, New York: Random House (Vintage), 1963.

————: *A Death in the Sanchez Family*, New York: Random House (Vintage), 1970.

————: *Five Families*, New York and Toronto: New American Library (Mentor), 1959.

————: *La Vida*, New York: Random House (Vintage), 1965.

————: *Life in a Mexican Village*, Urbana: University of Illinois Press, 1963.

————: *Pedro Martinez: A Mexican Peasant and His Family*, New York: Random House (Vintage), 1964.

McWILLIAMS, Carey: *Brothers Under the Skin*, Boston: Little, Brown, 1964.

————: *The Mexicans in America—A Students' Guide to Localized History*, New York: Teachers College Press, Columbia University, 1968.

————: *North from Mexico*, New York: Greenwood Press, Publishers, Inc., 1968.

MADSEN, William: *The Mexican-Americans of South Texas*, New York: Holt, Rinehart and Winston, 1964.

MANUEL, Hershel T.: *Spanish-Speaking Children of the Southwest: Their Education and Public Welfare*, Austin: University of Texas Press, 1965.

MARQUEZ, Gabriel Garcia: *One Hundred Years of Solitude*, New York and Evanston: Harper and Row, 1970.

MATTHIESSEN, Peter: *Sal Si Puedes: Cesar Chavez and the New American Revolution*, New York: Random House, 1969.

MOORE, Truman: *The Slaves We Rent*, New York: Random House, 1965.

MOQUIN, Wayne, Ed.: *A Documentary History of the Mexican Americans*, New York and London: Praeger Publishers, 1971.

MORIN, Raul: *Among the Valiant: Mexican Americans in World War II and Korea*, Alhambra: Borden Publishing Co., 1966.

NABOKOV, Peter: *Tijerina and the Courthouse Raid*, Albuquerque: University of New Mexico Press, 1969. Revised edition by Ramparts Press, distributed by Simon and Schuster, 1971.

NANCE, Joséph Milton: *After San Jacinto*, Austin: University of Texas Press, 1963.

NELSON, Eugene: *Huelga*, Delano: Farm Worker Press, Box 1060, Delano, California; 1966.

PARADES, Américo: *With His Pistol in His Hand*, Austin: University of Texas Press, 1958.

PAZ, Octavio: *The Labyrinth of Solitude: Life and Thought in Mexico*, New York: Grove Press (Evergreen), 1961.

———: *An Anthology of Mexican Poetry*, Bloomington: University of Indiana Press, 1965.

———: *New Poetry of Mexico*, New York: Dutton, 1970.

PICON-SALAS, Mariano: *A Cultural History of Spanish America*, Berkeley and Los Angeles: UC Press, 1968.

PITT, Leonard: *The Decline of the Californios—a Social History of the Spanish-Speaking Californians, 1846–1890*, Berkeley and Los Angeles: UC Press, 1966.

PRESCOTT, William: *The Conquest of Mexico*, ed. by Roger Howell, New York: Washington Square, 1966.

RAMOS, Samuel: *Profile of Man and Culture in Mexico*, Trans. by Peter C. Earle, Austin: University of Texas Press, 1962.

REED, John: *Insurgent Mexico*, New York: Simon and Schuster, 1969.

RIVERA, Feliciano: *A Mexican American Source Book with Study Guideline*, Menlo Park: Educational Consulting Associates, 1970.

ROBINSON, Cecil: *With the Ears of Strangers*, Tucson: University of Arizona Press, 1963.

ROMANELL, Patrick: *Making of the Mexican Mind*, Notre Dame and London: University of Notre Dame Press, 1967.

ROMANO, Octavio I.-V.: *El Espejo*, Berkeley: Quinto Sol
    Publications, 1969.
RUBEL, Arthur: *Across the Tracks*, Austin: University of
    Texas Press, 1966.
RULFO, Juan: *Pedro Paramo*, New York: Grove Press, 1959.
SAMORA, Julian, ed.: *La Raza: Forgotten Americans*, Notre
    Dame and London: University of Notre Dame Press,
    1963.
SIMPSON, Leslie Byrd: *Many Mexicos* (4th edition), Berke-
    ley and Los Angeles: UC Press, 1941–1967.
SOMMERS, Joseph: *After the Storm*, Albuquerque: Univer-
    sity of New Mexico Press, 1968.
STEINBECK, John: *Tortilla Flat*, New York: Bantam, 1935–
    1965.
STEINER, Stan: *La Raza*, New York and Evanston: Harper
    and Row, 1970.
TEBBEL, John, and RUIZ, Ramón E.: *South by Southwest*,
    New York: Doubleday & Co. (Zenith), 1969.
THOMAS, Piri: *Down These Mean Streets*, New York: New
    American Library (Signet), 1967.
TORRES-RIOSECO, Arturo: *The Epic of Latin American
    Literature*, Berkeley and Los Angeles: UC Press, 1961.
VAILLANT, G. C.: *Aztecs of Mexico*, Baltimore: Penguin
    Books, 1966.
VÁSQUEZ, Richard: *Chicano*, New York: Doubleday & Co.,
    1970.
WRIGHT, Dale: *They Harvest Despair*, Boston: Beacon
    Press, 1965.

MAGAZINES

CON SAFOS: P. O. Box 31085, Los Angeles, California
    90031.
EL GRITO: Quinto Sol Publications, P. O. Box 9275, Berke-
    ley, California.
REGENERACIÓN: P. O. Box 54624, Los Angeles, Cali-
    fornia 90054.

NEWSPAPERS

BASTA YA!: P. O. Box 12217, San Francisco, California.

CARTA EDITORIAL: P. O. Box 54624, Terminal Annex, Los Angeles, California 90054.

COMPASS: 1209 Egypt St., Houston, Texas 77009.

EL GALLO: 1567 Downing Street, Denver, Colorado (distributor of *I Am Joaquin*).

EL GRITO DEL NORTE: Rte. 2, Box 5, Espanola, New Mexico 87532.

EL MALCRIADO: P. O. Box 130, Delano, California 93215 (The Voice of the Farmworker).

EL PAPEL: P. O. Box 7167, Albuquerque, New Mexico 87104.

INFERNO: 321 Frio City Road, San Antonio, Texas 78207.

INSIDE EASTSIDE: P. O. Box 63273, Los Angeles, California 90063.

LA RAZA: 2808 Altura, Los Angeles, California 90031·

Some other books published by Penguin
are described on the following pages.

THE AMERICAN INDIAN TODAY

Edited by Nancy O. Lurie and Stuart Levine

Thirteen articles by Indian and white anthropologists and educators probe the present condition of the American Indian. The history of the Indian's relationship to the United States government is surveyed, and the contributors explore recent tendencies to establish an Indian "identity" transcending tribal loyalties. Case histories demonstrate specific problems confronting Indians in various parts of the country today. Winner of an Anisfield-Wolf Award as an outstanding book in the field of race relations.

THE SACRED PIPE

Black Elk's Account of the
Seven Rites of the Oglala Sioux

Recorded and edited by Joseph Epes Brown

A unique account of the ancient religion of the Sioux Indians. Black Elk was the only qualified priest still alive when he gave the material in this book to Joseph Epes Brown during the latter's stay at Pine Ridge Reservation in South Dakota. Beginning with White Buffalo Cow Woman's first visit to the Sioux to give them the sacred pipe, he discusses the seven rites, which were disclosed to the Sioux through visions. He takes the reader through the sun dance, the purification rite, the "keeping of the soul," and the other ceremonies, showing how the Sioux have come to terms with God, nature, and their fellow men.

SURVIVING THE 70'S

Benjamin DeMott

A survival manual for the 1970's by one of America's top social critics. In these pages Benjamin DeMott considers the liberated woman, the college dropout, the "ecological summons," the new sexuality, and various other patterns of thought and action that characterize the contemporary scene. He asks: "How can a human being cope with the tilts of assumption and belief now occurring regularly in all corners of the culture? . . . What kinds of order can a mind work out for itself?" In answering such questions, *Surviving the 70's* looks not only at the mixed nature of experience today but also at the opportunities that lie beyond.